CHILD MAINTENANCE –

THE NEW LAW

CHILD MAINTENANCE – THE NEW LAW

Roger Bird LLB

District Judge, Bristol County Court and
District Registry

Family Law
2000

Published by
Family Law, a publishing
imprint of Jordan Publishing Limited
21 St Thomas Street
Bristol BS1 6JS

British Library Cataloguing-in-Publication Data

A catalogue record for this book is available from the British Library.

ISBN 0 85308 691 5

Photoset by Mendip Communications Ltd, Frome, Somerset
Printed in Great Britain by MPG Books Ltd, Bodmin, Cornwall

PREFACE

In some ways, this has been a difficult book to write. Previous editions of *Child Maintenance* have sought to explain the law of child support as it was at the date of publication. This book does not attempt that task; the law as it now is (save for intervening statutory amendments such as the Social Security Act 1998) will be found in the third edition of *Child Maintenance*, and this will remain the case until mid-2002 when it is intended that the changes effected by the Child Support, Pensions and Social Security Act 2000 will come into force. The purpose of this book is to explain the changes effected by the 2000 Act and to alert readers to what is to come.

It will not escape the reader's attention that the present author is less than impressed by the contents of the 2000 Act. It seemed almost impossible that the 1991 Act (as amended in 1995) could be made worse, but readers may think that that remarkable feat has been achieved. If the various criticisms of the Act had to be summarised, the burden of them would have to be that its philosophy runs counter to not only the strongly held convictions of family lawyers but even the law as it is in the family law context. Those with long memories will recall that this was precisely the criticism made of the 1991 Act.

It is immensely depressing to see a government which acknowledges that the 1991 Act was a disastrous failure making the same mistakes as its predecessors and refusing to accept that the advice of those who are actively involved in the practice of family law might usefully be heeded.

ROGER BIRD
November 2000

CONTENTS

TABLE OF CASES

References are to paragraph numbers.

TABLE OF STATUTES

References are to paragraph numbers.

TABLE OF STATUTORY INSTRUMENTS

References are to paragraph numbers.

TABLE OF ABBREVIATIONS

CA 1989	Children Act 1989
CSA	Child Support Agency
CSA 1991	Child Support Act 1991
CSA 1995	Child Support Act 1995
CSAT(P)Regs 1992	Child Support Appeal Tribunals (Procedure) Regulations 1992
CS(CE)Regs 1992	Child Support (Collection and Enforcement) Regulations 1992
CS(CEOFM)Regs 1992	Child Support (Collection and Enforcement of other Forms of Maintenance) Regulations 1992
CSC(P)Regs 1992	Child Support Commissioners (Procedure) Regulations 1992
CS(IED)Regs 1992	Child Support (Information, Evidence and Disclosure) Regulations 1992
CSA(JOC) Order 1993	Child Support Appeals (Jurisdiction of Courts) Order 1993
CS(MAJ)Regs 1992	Child Support (Maintenance Arrangements and Jurisdiction) Regulations 1992
CS(MAP)Regs 1992	Child Support (Maintenance Assessment Procedure) Regulations 1992
CS(MASC)Regs 1992	Child Support (Maintenance Assessments and Special Cases) Regulations 1992
CSPSSA 2000	Child Support, Pensions and Social Security Act 2000
DOE	Department of Education and Employment
DPMCA 1978	Domestic Proceedings and Magistrates' Courts Act 1978
DSS	Department of Social Security
FPR 1991	Family Proceedings Rules 1991
HFEA 1990	Human Fertilisation and Embryology Act 1990
LEA	Local Education Authority
MCA 1973	Matrimonial Causes Act 1973
MCA 1980	Magistrates' Courts Act 1980

MOD	Ministry of Defence
NFCA	National Foster Care Association
PRFD	Principal Registry of the Family Division
RSC 1965	Rules of the Supreme Court 1965
SSAC	Social Security Advisory Committee
SSAT	Social Security Appeal Tribunals

CHAPTER ONE

The Background to and General Principles of the Act

1. Introduction

1.1 The Child Support, Pensions and Social Security Act 2000 (CSPSSA 2000) received Royal Assent on 28 July 2000. Part I of the Act represents the Government's attempt to reform the law relating to child support and will come into force in 2002. The purpose of this book is to explain the law as it will be when the amendments made to the Child Support Act 1991 (CSA 1991) by the CSPSSA 2000 come into force.

Although the CSPSSA 2000 makes extensive changes to the law of child support, the CSA 1991 remains the source of law, with many sections being amended and some entirely replaced. Accordingly, the Act as it will be is examined in detail and the implications of any changes are set out.

Much of the detailed law relating to child support is contained in regulations made under the CSA 1991; and previous editions of *Child Maintenance* (Jordans) have considered this delegated legislation at some length. The author and publishers now face a dilemma because completely new regulations will clearly be needed for some aspects of the law whereas it may well be that some of the areas which are unamended will retain the same form of regulations. At this stage, it is impossible to know what will happen. Accordingly, the following formula has been adopted.

When it is clear, as, for example, with the rules as to variation (formerly called departures), that a completely new set of regulations will be required, the previous regulations are ignored except where it is thought that they might contain some guidance for the future. Where it seems that the present law remains unchanged, as, for example, with special cases, the existing regulations are summarised, although not in the detail contained in previous editions of *Child Maintenance*. In any event, the regulations themselves are not contained in the Appendices; they appear in previous editions of *Child Maintenance* and the primary purpose of this book is to consider the new law.

It must be emphasised that the present law contained in the unamended CSA 1991 will remain in force until the amended Act comes into force in 2002 and will continue in force on a transitional basis for some existing cases for some time thereafter.

1.2 Before 1990, the idea that the courts were not the appropriate forum for decisions as to child maintenance when the parents could not agree would have seemed foreign to most lawyers and members of the public in this country. Maintenance of children was regarded as a branch of family law which fell naturally within the jurisdiction of the courts, and there were few who thought that it should be removed into some free-standing system. Nevertheless, this is what the CSA 1991 attempted to achieve. As will be seen, a complete assumption of the role of the court has not yet been accomplished, although the Act has been in force for seven years.

1.3 It is unnecessary in this book to set out a detailed account of the genesis and passage into law of this measure. Previous editions dealt in detail with the Antipodean origins of the concept, the White Paper 'Children Come First', the lively parliamentary debates, and the eventual enactment of the Bill; to dwell on these matters now might be of some academic interest, but would not help the reader who seeks a reliable guide to the workings of the Act and regulations. Accordingly, a more severely practical approach will be adopted here.

Having said that, it may be of interest briefly to bring up to date the historical section of the previous editions, before embarking on a more detailed analysis of the changes effected by the CSPSSA 2000.

1.4 In legal circles, the CSA 1991 was always a controversial measure. Nevertheless, at the outset, it enjoyed a generally favourable reception from the media and other opinion formers. Typical of such reactions was that of the then Bishop of Gloucester, speaking on behalf of the Church of England in one of the parliamentary debates. He said that he believed:

> 'that the creation of a single, powerful, and well-publicised Child Support Agency could be significant of the nation's will to grapple with the problem of the children who are at risk and suffering as a result of family breakdown.' (House of Lords, Official Report, 25 February 1991 col 808)

What was remarkable was the speed with which this goodwill evaporated. The press were not slow to publicise stories of men who had, allegedly, committed suicide because of what were regarded as extortionate assessments. More significantly, a series of both official and independent reports began to highlight serious deficiencies in the performance of the Child Support Agency (CSA), and hardships which resulted from the rigid application of the formula. A pattern emerged of critical Select Committee reports every autumn, followed by amended regulations the following spring. The CSA failed to meet its performance targets for 1993/94; the Select Committee report published in November 1994[1] was highly critical; the Ombudsman's Report[2] revealed serious maladministration.

The conclusions of one typical independent report[3] were similar. The authors' conclusions were that the Act had done nothing to improve the well-being of children in lone parent families on benefits; on the contrary, the emotional distress and material losses which had been experienced by a number of children were clearly damaging rather than beneficial to their welfare. As a consequence of the Act, some of the very poorest children in the UK had already experienced a net reduction in the material quality of their lives, and others were facing such reductions in the near future, as fathers became unable to pay for the treats, shoes, clothes and outings which afforded a temporary escape from the

1 The Operation of the Child Support Act; Proposals for Change (HC 470 1994–95, HMSO).

2 Investigation of Complaints against the Child Support Agency (HC 135 1994–95, HMSO).

3 Glendinning, Clarke and Craig 'The impact of the Child Support Act on lone mothers and their children' *Journal of Child Law* vol 7 no 1 p 18.

deprivations of life on the poverty line. Children witnessed renewed tension and arguments between parents; the Act threatened to undermine both the frequency and the quality of relationships between children and their fathers.

1.5 The government of the day attempted to improve the operation of the CSA 1991 Act and set out its proposals in a White Paper 'Improving Child Support' (Cm 2745, 1995). These proposals were translated into law by the Child Support Act 1995 and the various sets of regulations flowing therefrom. One of the features of these enactments seemed to be that it was recognised that the CSA 1991 had been unduly rigid and prescriptive and provision was made for the amelioration of the formula approach by means of, inter alia, Departure Directions. However, this did not stem the flow of criticism.

In 1998 in their book *Child Support in Action*,[4] three eminent academic authors succinctly recorded the drawbacks of the system.

> 'The media picture of the misery visited upon absent fathers is borne out in part, but even more striking is the evidence of a catastrophic administrative failure leading to the abandonment of many of the basic tenets of administrative justice. The reasons for this do not lie primarily in the perceived unfairness of the formula but rather in the failure of those drafting the Child Support Act 1991 to appreciate the impact of such change upon the rest of our hugely complex benefit structure and their failure also to grasp that the problems of inadequate disclosure and ineffective enforcement – with which courts had grappled for decades – could not be tackled successfully by a distant bureaucracy.'[5]

The book concluded with some suggestions which seem to have been accepted, in principle at least, by those responsible for the current legislative changes.

> 'One option worthy of serious consideration is a move closer to the Australian model. In the first place, this would involve simplifying the formula by abandoning the current shadowing of income support rates. Instead, the central principle would be the deduction of a specified percentage of income according to the number of children involved. The introduction of a disregard of maintenance payments when calculating Income Support entitlement would also provide a real incentive for mothers to co-operate and fathers to pay.'[6]

1.6 As will be seen, the recommendations of Davis et al have been incorporated in the new legislation (although it is only fair to them to point out that they also recommended[7] the abandonment of the element of discretion represented by departures, which has in fact been retained under the name of 'variation'). In the event, the Government's proposals were contained in a White Paper 'Children First' (Cm 3992, 1998). In the introduction the Prime Minister said 'the system of child support we inherited is a mess', and 'the system needs urgent reform'. He continued: 'we will replace the highly complicated formula for assessing maintenance by a radically simpler calculation. It will be transparent so that fathers [*sic*] will know in advance exactly how much they must pay.' The White

---

4 Gwynn Davis, Nick Whiteley and Richard Young (Hart Publishing, 1998).
5 Op cit, p v.
6 Ibid, p 232.
7 Ibid, p 223.

Paper invited comments but, unsurprisingly perhaps, the draft legislation when published showed little sign of second thoughts.

The purpose of this book is to put the new provisions into context, that context being the CSA 1991. Part I of the CSPSSA 2000 does no more than amend the CSA 1991 by inserting large amounts of new material in substitution for the original material. Accordingly, this book will consist of an examination of the provisions of the CSA 1991 as amended. References will be made to delegated legislation where appropriate, but not in the detail contained in earlier editions of this book.

2. The General Principles and Characteristics of the Act

1.7 The long title of the CSA 1991 is 'An Act to make provision for the assessment, collection and enforcement of periodical maintenance payable by certain parents with respect to children of theirs who are not in their care; for the collection and enforcement of certain other kinds of maintenance; and for connected purposes'. The CSPSSA 2000 amends that Act.

In later chapters, the detail of the Act as amended and the way in which it is intended to work will be examined. Here, it is intended to set out in outline the general scheme of the Act, to consider its basic principles and to examine some of its key terms and concepts. It will be seen that some terms (eg 'parent') have a different meaning under this Act from that adopted in other legislation, even legislation as close in time and subject matter as the Children Act 1989 (CA 1989).

3. The Duty to Maintain

1.8 Section 1 of the CSA 1991 sets out the basic principle underlying the whole Act, namely that parents have an obligation to maintain their children, and then deals with how that obligation may be discharged. By s 1(1):

> '. . . each parent of a qualifying child is responsible for maintaining him.'

This defines the obligation in general terms. Section 1(2) then goes on to provide that for the purposes of the Act:

> '. . . a non-resident parent shall be taken to have met his responsibility to maintain any qualifying child of his by making periodical payments of maintenance with respect to the child of such amount, and at such intervals, as may be determined in accordance with the provisions of this Act.'

In other words, once the obligations imposed by the Act have been discharged, no further liability under the Act, or otherwise, exists.

Section 1(3) introduces the concept of the 'maintenance calculation'; and provides that:

> 'Where a maintenance calculation made under this Act requires the making of periodical payments, it shall be the duty of the non-resident parent with respect to whom the assessment was made to make those payments.'

In s 1, therefore, are found the statutory obligations to maintain (s 1(1)), and to pay the maintenance calculation (s 1(3)) and, in s 1(2), a statement of the sufficiency of making payments under the Act.

1.9 Section 1 introduces the terms 'qualifying child', 'non-resident parent' and 'maintenance calculation'. These are all terms new to English law, as are 'person with care', and 'child support maintenance', which appear in s 3. These terms are central to the philosophy of the Act and their meaning must be considered in detail. It should be noted that the CSPSSA 2000 has changed some of the terminology, so that 'non-resident parent' replaces 'absent parent' and 'maintenance calculation' replaces 'maintenance assessment'. This is dealt with in detail in Chapter Two.

For the present purposes, however, the general principle of the Act may be stated as follows: the Act imposes obligations upon the parents of children where:

(a) the parents are or are presumed to be the natural or adoptive parents of the child;
(b) one or both parents do not live in the same household as the child;
(c) the child lives with a person with care who provides for the child.

Section 1(3) above refers to a 'maintenance calculation', which, by s 54, is defined as 'a calculation of maintenance made under this Act'. There is no further definition in the Act but the meaning is clear in the context of the Act, since, as will be seen, a maintenance calculation can be made by only the Secretary of State or an officer under his authority. Section 3(6) provides that 'periodical payments which are required to be paid in accordance with a maintenance calculation are referred to in this Act as "child support maintenance"'.

4. The Welfare of the Children

1.10 The marginal note to s 2 of the CSA 1991 describes that section as 'welfare of the children: the general principle'. Section 2 itself provides that:

> 'Where, in any case which falls to be dealt with under this Act, the Secretary of State is considering the exercise of any discretionary power conferred by this Act, he shall have regard to the welfare of any child likely to be affected by his decision.'

Section 2 was not included in the original Bill and so represents the result of further thought on the part of the Government. In considering what this provision will mean it may be useful to begin with a comparison with two other statutory provisions in related fields.

Section 1(1) of the CA 1989 repeats a principle contained in earlier statutes, namely that in proceedings concerned with the upbringing of a child or the administration of a child's property or the application of any income arising from it:

> 'the child's welfare shall be the court's paramount consideration.'

Section 25(1) of the Matrimonial Causes Act 1973 (MCA 1973) was amended in 1984 to include the provision that, when considering any application for financial relief, whether for the parties to a marriage or their child, it is the duty of the court to have regard to all the circumstances of the case:

'first consideration being given to the welfare while a minor of any child of the family who has not attained the age of eighteen.'

Section 2 of the CSA 1991 differs from its predecessors in three important respects. First, it imposes obligations on the Secretary of State, reflecting the fact that it is officers acting under his authority rather than the courts who will be making decisions affecting children. This will be significant when the question of remedies for breach of the statutory obligations is considered.

Secondly, it does not make the welfare of children the first or paramount consideration; it merely says that regard is to be had to such welfare. It therefore carries less force than the other provisions.

Thirdly, s 2 has a wider ambit than the other provisions in that it directs attention to the welfare of any child likely to be affected by the decision. The other statutes require regard to be had to the welfare of a child who is directly involved in the litigation; the reference to 'any child' goes very much further than this.

1.11 There are many occasions on which the Secretary of State will have to have regard to the welfare of the children. A complete list is set out in the section on judicial review in Chapter Eight part 7. When making any of these decisions the Secretary of State (or officer under his authority) must 'have regard to' the welfare of any child. What does this mean? As has been seen, the welfare of children is not the first or paramount consideration. Would the production of a completed checklist showing that the officer concerned had gone through a prescribed procedure and applied his mind to the welfare of children be sufficient?

Only a tentative answer can be given to such questions. It is suggested that, where it could be shown that the consequences of any decision would be detrimental to the welfare of any child in question, it could then fairly be argued that the officer concerned had not had regard to the welfare of that child. It might be thought that the areas which are most likely to produce a challenge to the discretionary powers of the Secretary of State are reduced benefit directions, liability orders and distress.

The requirement to have regard to the welfare of any child likely to be affected by the decision is a wide one. It clearly includes not only the children in respect of whom maintenance calculations are being made or enforced but also the children in the home of the non-resident parent for whom that parent provides. The possibility might then arise of a conflict of interest between the child whose maintenance calculation was not being paid, and whose needs were therefore not being provided for, and the child of the non-resident parent who would suffer deprivation if the non-resident parent were forced to pay money which he could not afford or were committed to prison.

1.12 What is the remedy of a person who considers that the Secretary of State has failed to observe the statutory duty imposed by s 2? In principle, the answer is an application for judicial review. This is considered further in Chapter Eight and will not be discussed in detail here, save to say that judicial review is concerned with the propriety of the decision-making process rather than the merits of the decision itself, and that judicial review would not be appropriate where the structure of the Act itself contained a right of appeal.

5. The Child Support Agency

1.13 Moving the second reading of the Child Support Bill on 25 February 1991 the Lord Chancellor said:

> '. . . a Child Support Agency will be established as a next steps agency under the authority of . . . the Secretary of State for Social Security. The agency will trace absent parents, investigate the parents' means and assess, collect and enforce payments of child maintenance . . . [A]s a next steps agency, the agency will have no independent existence in statute. The powers that it will need to do its work are, therefore, expressed as powers of . . . the Secretary of State for Social Security.'

Although in reality the CSA looms large in any consideration of the new law and procedure it is nowhere mentioned in the Act, for the reason given above by the Lord Chancellor. Instead, the Act confers all the powers to be exercised by the Agency on the Secretary of State.

Section 13 is now repealed by the Social Security Act 1998. The functions of the child support officer are now transferred to the Secretary of State. All decisions, determinations and calculations previously falling to the child support officer are now to be made by the Secretary of State or an officer of the Secretary of State acting under his authority.

When procedure is considered in Chapter Two, it will be seen that, under s 4(1), applications for child support maintenance ('a maintenance calculation') must be made to the Secretary of State, on whom s 4 imposes certain obligations. It is the function of an officer under the authority of the Secretary of State to consider the application, to obtain such information as he requires, to make the calculation and, if necessary, to take steps to enforce it.

1.14 The other significant personnel to feature in the Agency's work will be the inspectors. By s 15(1), the Secretary of State may appoint 'on such terms as he thinks fit, persons to act as inspectors'. Section 15(2) provides that:

> 'The function of inspectors is to acquire information which the Secretary of State needs for any of the purposes of this Act.'

Their powers will be considered further in Chapter Two, but here it may be noted that they have wide powers of investigation and entry.

6. The Formula

1.15 We must now consider how maintenance calculations are to be made and what principles are to be employed.

Section 11(6) provides that:

> 'The amount of child support maintenance to be fixed by a maintenance calculation shall be determined in accordance with Part I of Schedule 1 unless an application for a variation has been made and agreed.'

Variation is then dealt with in s 11(7) which provides that:

> 'If the Secretary of State has agreed to a variation, the amount of child support maintenance to be fixed shall be determined on the basis he determines under section 28F(4).'

Finally, s 11(8) provides that Part II of Schedule 1 makes further provision with respect to maintenance calculations.

Schedule 1 will be considered in detail in Chapter Three. Here, it is only necessary to note the vital fact that it contains a formula for the determination of maintenance calculations. The formula which now exists as a result of the CSPSSA 2000 is a completely different formula from that which hitherto applied. The previous formula was based on a 'maintenance requirement' for the children of any family and the apportionment of that requirement between the parents on the basis of their respective incomes and allowable outgoings. The new formula is based entirely on a percentage of the non-resident parent's income, although, as will be seen, the calculation is not as simple as might have been hoped. However, provision is made for variation of the formula in certain cases, and this is at the discretion of the Secretary of State. Variation is considered in Chapter Five. Subject to variation, however, the intention of the CSA 1991 remains: by reference to the formula a 'correct' decision should be arrived at in every case.

1.16 The belief that the proper application of the formula would give an unchallengeable answer was given as the reason why the role of the courts had been rendered unnecessary and explains the thinking behind the system of revision and appeal. A child support officer originally applied the formula to the facts of a particular case as if he were calculating a benefit such as income support. This has now changed only in the sense that the formula is, ostensibly, easier to calculate since it requires only a pocket calculator. In the original 1991 formula, no element of discretion was possible. When the Act was amended in 1995 an element of discretion was introduced in the shape of departure directions. That element of discretion has been carried into the new law under the name of variation.

The purity of the original doctrine has therefore been sullied and made more unpredictable by the introduction of a discretionary element. However, in most cases the basic principle remains and the proponents of the Act envisage that the formula will reign undisturbed.

7. The Exclusion of the Court

1.17 One of the novel features of the new child support law introduced in 1991 was the virtual total exclusion of the jurisdiction of the courts.

Section 8 applies where the Secretary of State would have jurisdiction to make a maintenance calculation with respect to a qualifying child and a non-resident parent of his on an application duly made by a person entitled to apply (s 8(1)). The section applies, and the jurisdiction of the court is excluded, even where the circumstances of the case are such that the Secretary of State would not make a calculation if it were applied for (s 8(2)); this means that, for example, if the result of the formula is that no calculation should be made, there is no alternative remedy available to the person with care.

Therefore, where a person entitled to apply for a maintenance calculation in respect of a qualifying child and a non-resident parent wishes to apply for maintenance, it must be done by means of an application to the Secretary of State and not to the courts. The jurisdiction of the courts is completely excluded. Some of the possible reasons for this have already been discussed. Whatever the reason may be, the intention of the legislation is clear. Child maintenance is assessed by means of the formula which is certain and unchallengeable. To permit the courts to become involved, whether in making or reviewing calculations, would be to introduce an element of discretion which might result in departures from the formula. This could not be contemplated; hence the exclusion of the role of the courts. This is all discussed in more detail in Chapter Ten.

1.18 In the context of breakdown of marriage, there are certain implications. For example, a court dealing with an application for a property adjustment order pursuant to s 23 of the MCA 1973 cannot make an order in respect of the children of the marriage as part of its overall disposition except by consent; moreover, a parent with care who is, or will at any time in the future be, in receipt of benefit cannot contract out of the right to receive or the duty to pay child maintenance as part of a larger 'package deal'. Insofar as they can, the parties and the court have to predict what the liability of the non-resident parent is likely to be and bear that in mind when negotiating or ordering that part of the financial and other obligations and liabilities with which the court can deal.

The courts retain jurisdiction in respect of non-qualifying children such as stepchildren. In respect of qualifying children, the role of the court is limited. This is discussed in more detail in Chapter Ten.

8. The Link with State Benefits

1.19 The fact that the child support system introduced by the CSA 1991 is the creature of the Department of Social Security has never been concealed. The Secretary of State responsible is the Secretary of State for Social Security. The original system of child support officers, Chief Child Support Officer, inspectors, and tribunals was modelled on the social security system and the amounts of maintenance calculations were originally based on social security rates of payment. However, there are further provisions in the Act which impose particular obligations on a person with care of a qualifying child who is in receipt of benefit.

Section 6 provides that where income support, an income-based jobseeker's allowance, or any other benefit of a prescribed kind, is claimed by or paid to the parent with care of a qualifying child, the Secretary of State may treat that parent as having applied for a maintenance calculation and take action to recover from the non-resident parent on the parent with care's behalf the child support maintenance so determined.

The remainder of the section will be considered in detail in Chapter Two but the extract given above sets out the basic principle.

1.20 The principle is therefore clear: a parent (normally a mother) who is in receipt of benefit must apply for a maintenance calculation. The specific benefits cited are of a non-contributory nature and so the Department of Social Security

(DSS) would gain from the making of a maintenance calculation by an appropriate reduction in the maintenance recovered. The other benefits which the Secretary of State has prescribed are of the same nature and do not include contributory benefits such as unemployment benefit or sickness benefit.

The duty to give information means that the mother has to name the father and give all necessary information to enable him to be traced.

The system is tailor-made for the parent on benefit; the whole organisation of calculation and enforcement makes it easier and more effective for such a parent (or, more accurately, the DSS, to which in fact the financial gain will accrue) to recoup money from a non-resident parent. However, a distinctive feature of the system is that the parent who is not in receipt of benefit has to go through exactly the same procedure, if maintenance is to be recovered other than by voluntary agreement.

9. The Role of Delegated Legislation

1.21 During the parliamentary debates on the Bill, one criticism frequently made was that so much remained to be determined by statutory instrument. On dozens of occasions, power is conferred on the Secretary of State to make regulations to govern a particular implementation of the Act. The result was that it was sometimes difficult to predict exactly how the Act was going to work, although it must be said that some of the regulation-making powers are quite specific about what the regulations may provide (eg the regulations as to protected income provided for under Sch 1, para 6).

Whatever the reasons or justification for this state of affairs, it is a fact that the complete picture of how the Act works emerged only when all the regulations were made and published, and this is a process which continues from year to year.

10. General Summary

1.22 The CSA and the apparatus of law and regulations which it operates has been a part of British law for nearly 10 years. In that time, the whole system of calculation and recovery of financial support for children has very radically changed. The Government admits that it has been a dismal failure and so concedes that, up to now, the changes have not been for the better; however, it remains convinced that the amended version now enacted will solve the previous problems. Only time will tell. However, the basic philosophy of the CSA 1991 remains.

The system of child maintenance under which parents pursue their remedies through the courts is, in principle, almost completely abolished. Subject to limited exceptions and transitional provisions, the only way to recover maintenance is to apply to an organ of the State which will calculate maintenance according to a predetermined formula with only limited scope for discretion. This State agency also has powers of investigation for the purposes of obtaining information for the calculation and is charged with the task of enforcing and recovering the money due under its calculation. Parents in receipt of State benefits are compelled to apply for calculations and, subject to statutory obligations, to provide information to the agency.

The CSA 1991 therefore clearly represented a major centralisation and extension of the role and powers of the State into what had hitherto been regarded as an area of private law.

CHAPTER TWO

Procedure for Obtaining Maintenance Calculations

1. Introduction

2.1 A person with care of a qualifying child who decides to apply for a calculation will probably do so for one of three reasons. First, she may have no choice; if she is in receipt of State benefits, the CSA 1991 imposes an obligation on her to do so (see para **2.11**). Secondly, the non-resident parent may be paying nothing, or not enough, for the support of the child. Thirdly, the parents may have agreed a figure but the person with care wishes to have the protection of a formal arrangement (although once a calculation is applied for the result will be determined by the formula rather than by any agreement which has been made; the relevance of agreements will be considered below at para **2.25** when those who may not apply are considered).

2.2 As was seen in Chapter One, the CSA 1991 establishes separate provisions for those persons with care who are in receipt of State benefits and those who are not; in effect, a two-tier system is established. This distinction will have to be borne in mind throughout this chapter.

As will be seen, the first two questions to be considered will be the jurisdiction of the Secretary of State, including whether the child is a qualifying child. Once those hurdles are crossed, the questions of who may, must, or may not apply will arise. The procedure, properly so called, is then introduced, with particulars of forms for application and reply, time-limits, the duty to co-operate, interim and default calculations, and so on. Then some of the other features in the system such as inspectors and, finally, termination of calculations, will be dealt with.

2. Jurisdiction

2.3 The first point to be established in any case is whether the Secretary of State has jurisdiction to make a calculation. Section 44(1) of the CSA 1991 provides that he has jurisdiction only with respect to a person who is:

(a) a person with care;
(b) a non-resident parent; or
(c) a qualifying child,

if that person is habitually resident in the United Kingdom, except in the case of a non-resident parent who falls within subsection (2A).

Section 44(2A) applies to a non-resident parent if he is not habitually resident within the United Kingdom but is:

(a) employed in the civil service of the Crown, including Her Majesty's Diplomatic Service and Her Majesty's Overseas Civil Service;
(b) a member of the naval, military or air forces of the Crown, including any person employed by an association established for the purposes of Part XI of the Reserve Forces Act 1996;
(c) employed by a company of a prescribed description registered under the Companies Act 1985 in England and Wales or in Scotland, or under the Companies (Northern Ireland) Order 1986, SI 1986/1032; or
(d) employed by a body of a prescribed description.

Subject to the exception in subsection (2A), which is designed to 'catch' British public servants working overseas, therefore, it is necessary for all three persons (the essential players in the drama) to be habitually resident; if any of them is not habitually resident, the Secretary of State will not have jurisdiction. The term 'habitually resident' is not defined in the Act, probably because it appears in other legislation, for example the Domicile and Matrimonial Proceedings Act 1973, s 5(2)(b), and its meaning has been judicially considered and defined in many cases under that legislation. Habitual residence does not require continuous presence in a country but involves the establishment of a sufficient degree of settled residence in a country to justify the court, or, in this case, the Secretary of State, assuming jurisdiction. Each case has to be decided on its merits, and the overall picture will have to be considered.

The United Kingdom means Great Britain (England, Wales and Scotland) and Northern Ireland. It does not include, for example, the Channel Islands or the Isle of Man.

Where the person with care is not an individual, it is not necessary for that person to show habitual residence. Where both parents are absent, at least one of them must be habitually resident.

2.4 By s 44(3), the Secretary of State may make regulations to provide for the cancellation of any calculation where any of the three persons mentioned above ceases to be habitually resident. The existing regulations are contained in reg 7(1) and (2) of the Child Support (Maintenance Arrangements and Jurisdiction) Regulations 1992 (CS(MAJ)Regs 1992), SI 1992/2645.

3. Is the Child a Qualifying Child?

2.5 The question of whether the child is a qualifying child is, of course, part of the whole issue of the jurisdiction of the Secretary of State. If the child is not a qualifying child, that is an end of the matter as far as the Secertary of State is concerned, and the person with care will have to apply to the courts.

By s 3(1), a child is a 'qualifying child' if:

'(a) one of his parents is, in relation to him, a non-resident parent; or
(b) both of his parents are, in relation to him, non-resident parents.'

Section 3(2) defines a 'non-resident parent' as follows:

'The parent of any child is a "non-resident parent", in relation to him, if –
(a) that parent is not living in the same household with the child; and
(b) the child has his home with a person who is, in relation to him, a person with care.'

This definition leads on to the definition of 'person with care'; by s 3(3), this is a person:

'(a) with whom the child has his home;
(b) who usually provides day to day care for the child (whether exclusively or in conjunction with any other person); and
(c) who does not fall within a prescribed category of person.'

Section 3(3)(c) requires clarification. By reg 51(1) of the Child Support (Maintenance Assessment Procedure) Regulations 1992 (CS(MAP)Regs 1992), SI 1992/1813, the prescribed persons who may *not* be persons with care are:

'(a) a local authority;
(b) a person with whom a child who is looked after by a local authority is placed by that authority under the provisions of the Children Act 1989, . . .
(c) in Scotland, a person with whom a child is boarded out by a local authority under the provisions of section 21 of the Social Work (Scotland) Act 1968.'

The Act also sets out a list of persons whom the Secretary of State may *not* prescribe as a category under s 3(4). They are:

'(a) parents;
(b) guardians;
(c) persons in whose favour residence orders under section 8 of the Children Act 1989 are in force;
(d) in Scotland, persons having the right to custody of a child.'

The result of this combination of double negatives is, therefore, that these persons are always capable of being persons with care.

2.6 This somewhat exhaustive examination has been necessary to establish what the CSA 1991 means by 'qualifying child'; at the same time, the meanings of 'non-resident parent' and 'person with care' have been established. However, two further terms remain to be defined, namely 'child' and 'parent'. Clearly, a person cannot be a qualifying child unless he is a child, or what the Act recognises as a child, and 'parent' needs some clarification.

Section 55(2) states clearly who is *not* a child for the purposes of the Act; this is a person who:

'(a) is or has been married;
(b) has celebrated a marriage which is void; or
(c) has celebrated a marriage in respect of which a decree of nullity has been granted.'

The essential excluding factor is, therefore, the participation in a ceremony of marriage whether or not this was a valid ceremony; a person under 16 who had taken part in a ceremony of marriage (which would be void *ab initio*) would be excluded from the provisions of the Act. 'Marriage' is not defined by the Act but, presumably, it means a ceremony which was intended to comply with the provisions of the Marriage Acts.

2.7 By s 55(1), a person *is* a child if he falls within any of the following:

'(a) he is under the age of 16;
(b) he is under the age of 19 and receiving full-time education (which is not advanced education) –
  (i) by attendance at a recognised educational establishment; or
  (ii) elsewhere, if the education is recognised by the Secretary of State; or
(c) he does not fall within paragraph (a) or (b) but –
  (i) he is under the age of 18, and
  (ii) prescribed conditions are satisfied with respect to him.'

Section 55(4) provides that the Secretary of State may recognise education provided otherwise than at a recognised educational establishment only if he is satisfied that education was being provided for the child immediately before the age of 16. Section 55(6) provides that, in determining whether a person falls within s 55(1)(b), no account shall be taken of such interruptions in his education as may be prescribed.

2.8 With the aid of the above, and of the regulations, the following framework emerges (it is assumed that the other requirements, eg as to non-resident parent etc, are satisfied).

Person under 16

A person under 16 must be a qualifying child unless he has gone through a ceremony of marriage.

Person over 16 but under 19

A person over 16 but under 19:

(a) is *not* a qualifying child if in advanced education (ie a course in preparation for a degree, diploma of higher education, HND or HNC, teaching qualification, or any course of a standard above ordinary diploma, national diploma, etc (see para 2 of Sch 1 to the CS(MAP)Regs 1992));
(b) *is* a qualifying child if in non-advanced education recognised by the Secretary of State;
(c) otherwise, *is not* a qualifying child *unless*:
  (i) he is under 18; and
  (ii) registered to work or for training under youth training with the Department of Education and Employment (DOE) or Ministry of Defence (MOD) or a local education authority (LEA) in England and Wales, or an education authority in Scotland, or a corresponding body in an EU country, but not receiving a youth training allowance or income support; and
  (iii) he is not engaged in remunerative work, other than work of a temporary nature that is due to cease before the end of the extension period which applies to him, for more than 24 hours per week; and
  (iv) the extension period has not expired; and
  (v) immediately before the extension period, he is a child for the purpose of the Act without regard to this paragraph.

(See, generally, CS(MAP)Regs 1992, Sch 1.)

Interruptions in education of up to six months may be ignored, provided there is a reasonable excuse, for example sickness or holidays.

2.9 The other term to be defined is 'parent'. Section 54 defines parent, in relation to any child, as any person who is in law the mother or father of the child. To be a parent, therefore, it is necessary to be the biological mother or father of a child, or to have adopted the child (an adoption order in respect of a child of which a person is a parent will mean that that person ceases to be a parent).

However, because of advances in medical science, the matter does not end there. The position is governed both by common law and by ss 27 and 28 of the Human Fertilisation and Embryology Act 1990 (HFEA 1990), the combined effect of which is as follows:

(a) a woman who bears a child will, at the child's birth, always be regarded as the child's mother (HFEA 1990, s 27(1));
(b) in principle, the father of a child is the person who provides the sperm which leads to conception. However, this is subject to the following exceptions:
    (i) the husband of a woman who is artificially inseminated is treated as the father of the child unless it is proved that he did not consent to the treatment (HFEA 1990, s 28(2));
    (ii) where a woman has been artificially inseminated in the course of treatment provided for her and a man under the licensing procedure established by the HFEA 1990, then the man is treated as the father (HFEA 1990, s 28(3));
(c) a donor of sperm for the purposes of 'treatment services' provided under the HFEA 1990 is not to be treated as the child's father;
(d) at common law, a number of presumptions arise, all of which are capable of being rebutted, for example the husband of a married woman is the father of the child, and a man whose name is entered as father in the Register of Births is the father.

4. Who may Apply?

2.10 In order to reach this stage, it will have been established that there is:

- a qualifying child;
- a non-resident parent;
- a person with care.

The next question to be decided is whether a person intending to apply for a calculation is entitled to do so. Therefore, a distinction must be made between those who *may* apply and those who will be treated as having applied and, in effect therefore, *must* apply; this is the difference between applications under s 4 and s 6; or those where the applicant is not in receipt of State benefits and those where she is.

Section 4(1) of the CSA 1991 provides that either the person with care or the non-resident parent may apply to the Secretary of State for a calculation. However, s 4(9) provides that no application may be made under s 4 if there is in force a calculation made in response to an application made under s 6.

At this stage, therefore, matters relating to applications have to be subdivided as follows:

- Section 6 applications (see part 5 of this chapter).

- Section 4 applications (see part 6 of this chapter).

In addition, further subdivisions arise, as follows:

- The effect of court orders or agreements (part 7 of this chapter).
- Multiple applications (part 8 of this chapter).

5. Applications by Parents Receiving Benefit

2.11 The CSA 1991 distinguishes between those persons with care who are in receipt of benefit and those who are not; since, it may be argued, the Act is designed for the benefit of the former, it seems logical to deal with them first.

Section 6 applies where 'income support, an income-based jobseeker's allowance or any other benefit of a prescribed kind is claimed by or in respect of, or paid to or in respect of, the parent of a qualifying child who is also a person with care of the child.' In this section, that parent (ie the parent who is the person with care) is referred to as 'the parent'.

When the above conditions apply, s 6(3) applies. This provides that:

> 'The Secretary of State may –
> (a) treat the parent as having applied for a maintenance calculation with respect to the qualifying child and all other children of the non-resident parent in relation to whom the parent is also a person with care; and
> (b) take action under this Act to recover from the non-resident parent, on the parent's behalf, the child support maintenance so determined.'

The following initial points should be noted. First, s 6(6) provides that subsection (1) has effect regardless of whether any of the benefits mentioned is payable with respect to any qualifying child. Accordingly, the payment of benefit of a prescribed kind of any amount or nature empowers the Secretary of State to impose this requirement.

Secondly, although s 6(3) refers to the Secretary of State taking action, it is clear that when he does so he takes action on behalf of the parent with care; he is not entitled to make an application on his behalf and, if the parent with care refuses to make any application, there is nothing the Secretary of State can do except penalise the parent with care (see 'The requirement to co-operate', at para **2.13**). This is emphasised by s 6(4) which provides that, before taking action, the Secretary of State must notify the parent in writing of the effects of subsections (3) and (5) and of section 46. Subsection (5) provides that the Secretary of State may not act under subsection (3) if the parent asks him not to (a request which need not be in writing).

Section 6 refers to a 'parent' while s 4 refers to a 'person' with care. The distinction is important. Only a person with care who is a parent may be compelled to take action under s 6.

2.12 Under the present regulations, the Secretary of State notifies his requirement under s 6(1) by supplying the parent with care with a Maintenance Application Form; this is a form which covers applications under s 6 and s 4. Where it is known that the parent with care is in receipt of benefit, a shorter version of this form, which omits much of the detail about the applicant's means, will normally be supplied. The Secretary of State is obliged to supply forms free of charge (CS(MAP)Regs 1992, reg 2(2)).

The Maintenance Application Form must contain the form of authority for the Secretary of State to take action on behalf of the parent with care, and must indicate in general terms the effect of completing and returning it (s 6(6) and (7)). In fact, with the application form, the parent with care receives a 'Child Support maintenance application pack'; this document is 35 pages long and explains the child support system, including the obligation to authorise the Secretary of State to proceed.

The requirement to co-operate

2.13 By s 6(5), the parent with care must, unless she has made a request under subsection (5), comply with the regulations made by the Secretary of State 'so far as she reasonably can'. The regulations in question are those which are made with a view to the Secretary of State's being provided with the information which is required to enable:

> '(a) the non-resident parent to be identified or traced;
> (b) the amount of child support maintenance payable by him to be calculated; and
> (c) that amount to be recovered from him.'

The information to be supplied under the present regulations is prescribed by reg 3(2) of the Child Support (Information, Evidence and Disclosure) Regulations 1992 (CS(IED)Regs 1992), SI 1992/1812; it includes the following:

(a) the habitual residence and name and address of the non-resident parent;
(b) the name and address of any current or recent employer of a non-resident parent;
(c) persons living in the same household as the non-resident parent.

It is also provided that the obligation to provide information which is required by subsection (7) does not apply in such circumstances as may be prescribed and may, in prescribed circumstances, be waived by the Secretary of State.

2.14 This raises few problems in the context of marriage breakdown where there is normally little doubt as to the identity of the absent parent. However, difficulties may arise in the case of a single mother and the CSA 1991 contains sanctions to 'encourage' a parent with care to give the prescribed information. These provisions gave rise to controversy during the parliamentary passage of the Act, which was mentioned in previous editions of this book; this is now history and there seems little point in repeating it here.

The final sanction which the Secretary of State may apply is a reduced benefit direction. This is considered at para **2.19**, but there is a procedure which must be exhausted before that stage can be reached.

The procedure is contained in s 46. This comes into effect under s 46(1) where any person (referred to as 'the parent'):

'(a) has made a request under section 6(5);
(b) fails to comply with any regulation made under section 6(7); or
(c) having been treated as having applied for a maintenance calculation under section 6, refuses to take a scientific test (within the meaning of section 27A).'

It is made clear, therefore, that the section applies only to parents who come within s 6(1) and have either requested the Secretary of State to take no action, failed to supply the information required, or failed to co-operate when tests are required to ascertain paternity (as to which, see Chapter Six).

2.15 What follows is laid down in s 46(2). The Secretary of State may serve written notice on the parent requiring her, before the end of a specified period:

(a) where she has made a request under s 6(5), 'to give him her reasons for making the request';
(b) where she has failed to comply with the regulations, 'to give him her reasons for failing to do so'; or
(c) where she refuses to take a scientific test, 'to give him her reasons for her refusal'.

2.16 When the period specified in the notice has expired, the Secretary of State must consider whether, if:

(a) he 'were to do what is mentioned in section 6(3)', ie to treat her as having applied for a maintenance calculation and take action to recover the sums so determined; or
(b) the parent 'were to be required to comply' with her obligations under s 6(7); or
(c) the parent took the scientific test,

'there would be a risk of her, or of any children living with her, suffering harm or undue distress as a result of his taking such action or her complying or taking the test'.

2.17 If the Secretary of State decides that there are no such reasonable grounds, he may, except in prescribed circumstances, make a reduced benefit decision with respect to the parent. Where the circumstances which have triggered this position are the parent's request to the Secretary of State not to take action on her behalf (under s 6(5)), the Secretary of State under s 46(6):

> 'may, from time to time, serve written notice on the parent requiring her, before the end of a specified period –
> (a) to state whether her request under section 6(5) still stands; and
> (b) if so, to give him her reasons for maintaining her request.'

This seems to be an effort by the Secretary of State to give the parent an opportunity to reflect on the error of her ways.

As to 'prescribed circumstances' mentioned in s 46(5), there was a similar wording in the version of s 46 contained in the unamended Act, but no such circumstances were in fact prescribed.

2.18 Neither the CSA 1991 nor the present regulations give any guidance as to what may, or may not, constitute 'harm or undue distress'. It will be for the

Secretary of State to make a value judgement, in the light of the ordinary meanings of those words.

The following cases would justify the Secretary of State in deciding not to proceed:

- the parent has been the victim of rape;
- the absent parent has sexually assaulted a child living in the household of the parent with care;
- the child was conceived as a result of incest;
- the absent parent is a 'celebrity' and unwelcome publicity might result which would be adverse to the welfare of parent and child.

In the following cases, the Secretary of State should proceed:

- the absent parent is seeking contact;
- the parent with care wants to sever all links with the absent parent;
- the absent parent is, or was at the time of conception of the child, under 16;
- the absent parent is married to someone else;
- a voluntary agreement exists.

2.19 If the Secretary of State is not satisfied that reasonable grounds are shown, a reduced benefit direction may be given. Section 46(10)(b) defines a reduced benefit direction as 'a decision that the amount payable by way of any relevant benefit to, or in respect of, the parent concerned be reduced by such amount, and for such period, as may be prescribed'. By section 46(10)(c) 'relevant benefit' means 'income support or an income-based jobseeker's allowance or any other benefit of a kind prescribed for the purposes of section 6'.

By s 46(7), the Secretary of State must send a copy of the reduced benefit direction to the parent concerned.

Revisions and appeals generally are dealt with in Chapter Seven.

2.20 The present detail about reduced benefit directions is to be found in reg 36 of the CS(MAP)Regs 1992. There is a two-stage reduction. The first, which lasts for 26 weeks, is equal to 20% of the single adult income support allowance, and the second, which lasts for 52 weeks, is equal to 10% of such allowance. Under the new proposals, it is intended that the reduction will be 40%.

2.21 Under the existing regulations, there are certain provisions designed to mitigate the harshness of the reduced benefit procedure. These were set out in detail in the third edition of *Child Maintenance* (Jordans, 1996). Given that the CSPSSA 2000 sets out a new statutory framework, there seems little point in repeating further here what was in the previous regulations.

6. Applications by Persons Not Receiving Benefits

2.22 A person with care who is not receiving benefits is in a different position from one who is receiving benefits in that there is no compulsion on her to take or authorise action, nor is there any sanction, other than the abandoning of the claim, if she fails to supply the necessary information. Nevertheless, the procedure for applying for an assessment is broadly similar and the result will be calculated in the same way.

Either the person with care or the non-resident parent may apply to the Secretary of State for a maintenance calculation. There is a series of regional offices for the CSA, and application should be made to the office nearest to the applicant. Fees are payable (see para **2.43**).

2.23 Section 4(4) and (7) contain provisions identical to those in s 6 which require the parent with care to supply the Secretary of State with information about the non-resident parent, to enable the non-resident parent to be traced and a calculation made. On the face of it, there seems little point in this, since the parent concerned cannot be compelled to make the application. However, this confirms the information which the Secretary of State needs, and, if he does not have it, he will not be able to make a calculation.

2.24 Under the present regulations, an application is an effective application provided it is made on the Maintenance Application Form and is completed in accordance with the Secretary of State's instructions (CS(MAP)Regs 1992, reg 2(4)). When the Secretary of State considers that the application is not effective, he may either return it to the applicant with, if he thinks fit, a new Maintenance Application Form and request that the application be resubmitted, or request the applicant to provide such additional information or evidence as he may specify (reg 2(5)).

An effective application may be amended by notice in writing to the Secretary of State at any time before an assessment is made, but no amendment may relate to any change of circumstances arising after the effective date of an assessment resulting from an effective application (reg 2(6) and (7)).

A person who has applied for a calculation may at any time request the Secretary of State to cease acting (CSA 1991, s 4(5)), and it shall be the duty of the Secretary of State to comply with that request (s 4(6)).

7. The Effect of Court Orders or Agreements

2.25 The existence of a court order or agreement is relevant to be considered at this stage since it may have the effect of preventing a person from making an application for a calculation. The ability of the parties to make an agreement, and the jurisdiction of the courts, are considered in Chapter Ten.

The only purpose in mentioning the subject here, therefore, is to alert the reader to the fact that the existence of an order or agreement must be borne in mind when deciding whether or not an application may be made. The effect of the amendments to s 4 of the CSA 1991 made by the CSPSSA 2000 is that, if a court order is made after a prescribed date, it will not be possible to apply for a maintenance calculation under s 4 for one year. At present, the existence of a court order prevents the Secretary of State from assuming jurisdiction under s 4 at all. It is the Government's intention that, from the date which it will in due course prescribe, this will last for only one year, after which the parent with care will be able to apply for a maintenance calculation.

8. Multiple Applications

2.26 More than one person may be a person with care in relation to a qualifying child (s 3(5)). The CSA 1991 provides that where more than one application for a calculation is made, regulations may provide for two or more applications to be treated as a single application, and for the replacement of a maintenance calculation made on the application of one person by a later calculation made on the application of that or any other person (Sch 1, Part II, para 14).

The existing regulations are contained in reg 4 of and Sch 2 to the CS(MAP)Regs 1992, and Sch 2 sets out the permutations which may apply. They appear complicated, but may be summarised as follows.

(a) The basic position is that only one application for a maintenance calculation should be proceeded with (s 5(2)).
(b) Where a person with care or a non-resident parent makes an effective application for a maintenance calculation (or in Scotland the child makes such an application) and, before the calculation is made, makes another application in respect of the same non-resident parent or person with care, as the case may be, the applications will be treated as a single application (Sch 2, paras 1 and 2).
(c) Applications by different persons are dealt with in Sch 2, para 3.

The table below shows how multiple applications are at present dealt with. It should be noted that in all these cases, where the applications are not in respect of identical qualifying children, the application with which the Secretary of State proceeds will be treated as a single application in respect of ALL the qualifying children with respect to whom applications have been made (para 3(13)). However, where the Secretary of State is satisfied that the same person with care does not provide the principal day-to-day care for all such qualifying children, he must make separate calculations in relation to each person with care providing such principal day-to-day care (para 3(14)).

	Applications made by	Applications to be proceeded with
1.	Person with care and non-resident parent	Person with care (para 3(2))
2.	(In Scotland only)	
	The child and either parent	The parent (para 3(31))
	The child and both parents	The parent with care (para 3(4))
	The child and the parents, and a person with parental responsibility	The parent with care (para 3(4))
	More than one qualifying child	The eldest child (para 3(5))
3.	Two persons, both treated as non-resident parents	To be dealt with as one application (para 3(7))
4.	The person with care and a person having parental responsibility	The parent with care (para 3(8))

	Applications made by	Applications to be proceeded with
5.	More than one person with care, both having parental responsibility, one of whom falls to be treated as a non-resident parent	The one who is not to be treated as a non-resident parent (para 3(9))
6.	As 5, but where there is more than one person who does not fall to be dealt with as a non-resident parent	As in 7
7.	More than one person with care, neither having parental responsibility	The application of the principal provider of day-to-day care, as determined in accordance with para 3(12)

Note

Schedule 2, para 3(12) may be summarised as follows. Where the Secretary of State can establish with which person the child spends the greater part of its time (or, in the case of more than one child, the greatest proportion of their time, taking account of the time each child spends with each person with care), the application of that person will proceed. Where he cannot so determine, and child benefit is paid to one person with care but not both, the application of the person receiving child benefit will proceed. Where all else fails, the application of the applicant 'who in the opinion of the Secretary of State is the principal provider of day-to-day care . . .' will proceed.

Where there is more than one person with care of a qualifying child and one or more, but not all, of them have parental responsibility for (in Scotland, parental rights over) the child, only those persons with parental responsibility (rights) may apply (s 5(1)). 'Parental responsibility' is defined by s 3(1) of the Children Act 1989 as 'all the rights, duties, powers, responsibilities and authority which by law a parent has in relation to the child and his property'.

9. Information Required from Non-Resident Parent

2.27 By s 11(1) of the CSA 1991, any application for a maintenance calculation (whether or not the person with care is receiving benefit) received by the Secretary of State shall be dealt with by him in accordance with the Act. In order to make a calculation, he needs information from the person with care and the non-resident parent. The obligation of the former to supply information has already been considered above.

Section 14(1) empowers the Secretary of State to make regulations requiring any information or evidence needed for the determination of any application under the Act, or any question arising in connection with such an application, to be furnished by such person as may be prescribed by regulations and in accordance with the regulations. A person who is required to comply with any regulations as to the supply of information who fails to comply with such a request is guilty of an offence. It is also an offence for such a person to make a statement or representation which he knows to be false, or to provide or knowingly cause or knowingly allow to be provided a document which he knows to be false in a material particular. It is a defence to prove that there was reasonable excuse for failure to comply with a request for information. The maximum penalty is a fine not exceeding level 3 on the standard scale.

2.28 Some guidance as to the future regulations may be derived from the existing regulations. Regulation 5(1) of the CS(MAP)Regs 1992 provides that, when an effective application for a maintenance calculation has been made, the Secretary of State shall, as soon as is reasonably practicable, give notice in writing of that application to the relevant persons other than the applicant. 'Relevant persons', for this purpose, includes the non-resident parent (reg 1(2)).

Any person to whom notice is given must also be given a Maintenance Enquiry Form and a written request that the form be completed and returned (reg 5(2)). A notice to the non-resident parent must also specify the effective date of the maintenance calculation, if one is to be made, and set out in general terms the provisions relating to interim maintenance calculations (as they stand under the present law) (reg 5(3)). The clear intention of this is to warn the non-resident parent of the consequences of delay.

Regulation 6(1) of the CS(MAP)Regs 1992 provides that a person who has received a Maintenance Enquiry Form must complete the form in accordance with the Secretary of State's instructions and return it within 14 days of its having been sent or given. The information given may be amended in writing at any time before a maintenance calculation is made. However, no amendment may relate to any change of circumstances arising after the effective date of any maintenance calculation (reg 6(3)).

2.29 The CS(IED)Regs 1992 contain provisions which overlap with the CS(MAP)Regs 1992 to some extent, relating to the information which the Secretary of State may require to be given. The general duty to give information is set out in CS(IED)Regs 1992, reg 2(1). It covers many possibilities, and may be summarised as providing that where an application for a maintenance calculation has been received, a 'relevant person' (in this context, the non-resident parent or a person who is alleged to be the father of the qualifying child) shall furnish such information or evidence as is required by the Secretary of State, and which is needed to enable a determination to be made in relation to one or more of the matters listed in reg 3(1).

By reg 3(2), the information or evidence to be furnished may, in particular, include information as to (inter alia) the following:

(a) the name and address of any current or recent employer of a non-resident parent;
(b) the address from which a non-resident parent who is self-employed carries on his trade or business, the trading name, and the gross receipts and expenses and other outgoings of the trade or business;
(c) any other income of a non-resident parent;
(d) income of persons living in the same household as the non-resident parent;
(e) housing costs;

(f) the identifying details of any bank, building society or similar account held in the name of the non-resident parent and statements relating to any such account.

The maintenance enquiry form contains questions designed to elicit all this information.

2.30 In addition to the information which he obtains from the person with care and the non-resident parent, the Secretary of State may also obtain information from other persons. Not surprisingly, such other persons include government departments and other public bodies.

Section 14(2) provides that the Secretary of State may make use of any information in his possession which was acquired by him in connection with his functions under any of the benefit Acts. He may therefore inspect files relating to any other benefit application made by any person.

2.31 However, the clearest departure from what used to be regarded as the principle of confidentiality in government records occurs in Sch 2 to the Act. This provides for the provision of information to the Secretary of State from Inland Revenue records and local authority records.

Paragraph 1 of Sch 2 applies where the Secretary of State requires information for the purpose of tracing the current address of a non-resident parent or the current employer of a non-resident parent. Paragraph 1(2) states:

> 'In such a case, no obligation as to secrecy imposed by statute or otherwise on a person employed in relation to the Inland Revenue shall prevent any information obtained or held in connection with the assessment or collection of income tax from being disclosed to –
> (a) the Secretary of State;
> (b) the Department of Health and Social Services for Northern Ireland; or
> (c) an officer of either of them authorised to receive such information in connection with the operation of this Act or of any corresponding Northern Ireland legislation.'

It will be seen that the obligation as to secrecy may be waived only if the current address or current employer of a non-resident parent is not known. Where such information is already known, no application to the Inland Revenue may be made. However, Sch 2 imposes no limit on the information which may be disclosed once it is established that information may be given; para 1(2) refers to 'any information obtained in connection with the assessment or collection of income tax'. This obviously includes details of the non-resident parent's earnings and entitlement to allowances, and it would seem that all this may be revealed once the obligation as to secrecy has been removed.

2.32 Paragraph 2 of Sch 2 deals with local authority records and applies, in effect, where the Secretary of State requires relevant information for the discharge of his functions under the Act; this is clearly a broad mandate, and means that the power can be invoked at will.

The Secretary of State may give a direction to the appropriate authority requiring it to give him such relevant information in connection with housing benefit or community charge benefit to which a non-resident parent or person with care is entitled as the Secretary of State considers necessary in connection with his determination of that person's income of any kind, housing costs or protected income. Under para 2(4), 'appropriate authority' means, in relation to housing benefit, the housing or local authority concerned, and, in relation to community charge benefit, the charging authority or, in Scotland, the levying authority. The community charge has been replaced by the council tax, to which similar principles apply.

As a kind of quid pro quo, reg 9 of the CS(IED)Regs 1992 permits the Secretary of State to disclose to the authorities mentioned above any information held for the purposes of the Act.

Finally, it should be noted that the parents or parties to the application do not have the right to obtain information from the Secretary of State. In *Re C (A Minor) (Child Support Agency: Disclosure)* [1995] 1 FLR 201, Ewbank J held that there was no power vested in the Secretary of State to disclose information about the address of a parent.

2.33 Given the very wide powers to collect information from a variety of sources, it is not surprising that the CSA 1991 contains sanctions against the unauthorised disclosure of information. Section 50 of the Act and reg 11 of the CS(IED)Regs 1992 contain a list of persons affected; this includes any CSO or any other civil servant involved in functions under the Act, Tribunal staff, and others ranging from the Comptroller and Auditor-General to anyone employed by the DSS.

Any such person is guilty of an offence if, without lawful authority, he discloses any information which was acquired by him in the course of his employment and relates to a particular person. A person guilty of an offence under s 50 is liable on conviction on indictment to imprisonment for up to two years or a fine or both, and on summary conviction to imprisonment for up to six months or a fine or both.

It is not an offence to disclose information in the form of a summary or collection of information in general terms (s 50(2)). Section 50(3) also provides a statutory defence to a prosecution under the section for an officer who believed that he was making the disclosure in question with lawful authority and had no reasonable cause to believe otherwise, or who believed that the information had been previously disclosed with lawful authority. Section 50(6) defines what is lawful authority, and should be referred to where the question arises.

2.34 Having dealt with the Secretary of State's powers to obtain information from other public authorities, his powers as to other persons, in particular members of the public, must now be considered. The Secretary of State has wide powers to require different classes of persons to furnish information or evidence. However, this can only be for a lawful purpose; reg 3(1) of the CS(IED)Regs 1992 provides that the information or evidence may only be required if needed to enable certain decisions to be made or purposes to be fulfilled. These purposes are set out in full in the regulation but may be summarised as decisions as to whether to proceed or whether there is jurisdiction on which application should proceed, identification and tracing of non-resident parents, calculating and enforcing child support maintenance, and identifying related proceedings.

2.35 The persons who may be required to furnish information are listed in reg 2(2). It will be noted that different classes of person may be required to give the information or evidence only if it is required for certain specific purposes; not all the matters listed in reg 3(1) apply to such persons.

The first class of person is 'the relevant person', defined as a person with care, a non-resident parent and a child who applies under s 7; such a person is liable in respect of all the purposes set out in reg 3(1).

A person who is alleged to be the parent of a child but who denies parentage is required to give information or evidence for the purpose of reg 3(1)(b), viz a decision to be made as to whether the Secretary of State has jurisdiction, and reg 3(1)(d), viz a non-resident parent to be identified.

A current or recent employer of either parent is so required for the purposes of identifying or tracing a non-resident parent, assessing and recovering child support maintenance, and enforcing court orders.

A local authority in whose area either parent lives is so required for the purpose of making a decision as to whether there exists a qualifying child, a non-resident parent and a person with care.

Finally, in any case where, in relation to the qualifying child or children, or the non-resident parent, there is or has been a relevant court order, or there have been or are pending related proceedings before a court, certain information or evidence may be required. The persons liable to supply such information include the senior district judge, the district judge of a district registry, the proper officer of a county court, a clerk to the justices, and (in Scotland), the deputy principal clerk of session or the sheriff clerk, as the case may be. The requirement is limited to cases where the information or evidence is required for the purpose of ascertaining that the amount payable under a relevant court order, recovering the same from a non-resident parent, or identifying any related proceedings. By reg 1(2), 'related proceedings' are defined as proceedings in which a relevant court order was being sought, this in turn being defined as orders as to periodical or capital provision or variation of property rights made under one of the enactments set out in s 8(11) of the CSA 1991 (eg MCA 1973, DPMCA 1978, CA 1989) in relation to a qualifying child or a relevant person. Similar provisions exist for Scotland.

2.36 As to the nature of the information or evidence to be supplied, reg 3(2) sets out a very detailed list of particular matters; when considering any particular case, it should be borne in mind that the information can be required only for the specified purposes contained in reg 3(1) and (2), as set out above.

The information or evidence listed in reg 3(2) includes such matters as the habitual residence of the parents or child, their marital status, where the child spends its time, matters relevant to disputes as to parentage, names and addresses of employers, gross and net earnings of parents, amounts payable under court orders, persons living in the same household as parents and details of their incomes, benefits payable, housing costs, details of bank or building society accounts.

10. Inspectors

2.37 The final weapon in the armoury of the Secretary of State is the use of inspectors; this is a familiar feature in the field of social security. The function of inspectors is stated to be 'to acquire information which the Secretary of State needs for any of the purposes of this Act'.

Under section 15(4):

> 'an inspector has power, at any reasonable time and either alone or accompanied by such other persons as he thinks fit, to enter any premises which –
> (a) are liable to inspection under this section; and
> (b) are premises to which it is reasonable for him to require entry in order that he may exercise his functions under this section,
> and there may make such examination and enquiry as he considers appropriate.'

Under the previous law, the premises had to be specified in the certificate of appointment. This has now been changed, and s 15(4A) defines the premises which are liable to inspection under this section. They are

> 'those which are not used wholly as a dwelling house and which the inspector has reasonable grounds for suspecting are –
> (a) premises at which a non-resident parent is or has been employed;
> (b) premises at which a non-resident parent carries out, or has carried out, a trade, profession, vocation or business;
> (c) premises at which there is information held by a person ("A") whom the inspector has reasonable grounds for suspecting has information about a non-resident parent acquired in the course of A's own trade, profession, vocation or business.'

'Premises' includes moveable structures and vehicles, vessels, aircraft, offshore installations and 'places of all descriptions whether or not occupied as land or otherwise'. It is difficult to think of anywhere an inspector could not go. Subsection (4A)(a) and (b) are clear and need no elaboration. By (c), it seems that an inspector would be entitled to enter the offices of, say, a doctor or solicitor and require the production of files, records, etc which might contain details of the work record of a patient or client.

2.38 The inspector may, therefore, require entry to certain premises. Once there, he is empowered to question any person aged 18 or over whom he finds on the premises (s 15(5)).

Section 15(6) provides that, if required to do so by an inspector exercising his powers, any person who is within the definition above shall furnish to the inspector all such information and documents as the inspector may reasonably require:

> 'If required to do so by an inspector exercising his powers, any such person shall furnish to the inspector all such information and documents as the inspector may reasonably require.'

2.39 Anyone who fails to co-operate with the inspector is liable to a penalty. Section 15(7) provides that no person shall be required under s 15 to answer any question or give any evidence tending to incriminate himself, or, in the case of a person who is married, his or her spouse; however, 'incriminate' means render himself liable to criminal proceedings, and this would not normally apply.

Subject to this, under s 15(9):

> 'If any person –
> (a) intentionally delays or obstructs any inspector exercising his powers; or
> (b) without reasonable excuse, refuses or neglects to answer any question or furnish any information or to produce any document when required to do so under this section,
>
> he shall be guilty of an offence and liable on summary conviction to a fine not exceeding level 3 on the standard scale.'

11. The Calculation

2.40 Once the Secretary of State has sufficient information, he makes a calculation. This calculation must be made in accordance with Part I of Schedule 1; the detail of how calculations are made is contained in Chapter 3.

Regulations made under the previous legislation provided for such matters as the manner in which decisions were to be communicated to the parents, and the dates on which child maintenance would start to be payable. Since the amended legislation adopts a different form of words, it is inevitable that these regulations will be amended and there seems little point in summarising the existing regulations here.

12. Interim and Default Maintenance Decisions

2.41 Even with the wide powers available to him, the Secretary of State may find that he still has insufficient information to enable him to make an accurate calculation. Section 12 is designed to deal with this position. Under s 12, the Secretary of State has two distinct powers: the first is to make a default maintenance decision and the second is to make an interim decision. These must be considered separately.

The power to make a default maintenance decision arises where either the Secretary of State is required to make a maintenance calculation (ie where an application has been made under s 4 or is treated as having been made under s 6) or is proposing to make a decision under s 16 or s 17 (ie on a review) and 'it appears to him that he does not have sufficient information to enable him to do so'. In such circumstances, he may make a default decision and regulations will prescribe the procedure for doing so and the default rate.

The default rate replaces what used to be called an interim assessment under the old s 12. It was thought that the previous system of interim assessments was unduly harsh and resulted in very poor returns. The Government's intentions were explained in the following terms:

> 'we intend that default rates of maintenance will be put in place quickly and that they will be set according to whether there are one, two or three or more children to be

maintained. We envisage rates of £30, £40 and £50 for those children, which reflects the average net income of the non-resident parent. In other words, they are not punitive. They are simply an averaging – a default payment which someone will pay until the final determination has been made. This will prevent large amounts of arrears building up and, because default rates will be put into place quickly, they will be easier to enforce.'[1]

However, somewhat confusingly, interim assessments (now called interim decisions) have not been abolished altogether; they reappear in the context of applications for variation. Variations are dealt with in more detail in Chapter Five. Here, it is only necessary to note that s 12(2) provides that 'where an application for a variation has been made under section 28A(1) in connection with an application for a maintenance calculation (or in connection with such an application which is treated as having been made), the Secretary of State may make an interim maintenance decision'. Procedure will be prescribed by regulations but the amount of child support maintenance which may be fixed by an interim maintenance decision is determined by reference to Part I of Schedule 1.

Part I of Schedule 1 is the part of the Act which sets out the new formula; it is discussed in detail in Chapter Three. The provisions for variation are contained elsewhere in the Act. What this means, therefore, is that the interim decision would require payment of the 'standard rate', depending on the income of the non-resident parent but without regard to any of the matters which might permit a variation.

The significance of this is that the Secretary of State would be able to refuse to consider the application for a variation if the amount due under the interim decision were not paid. Since the application for variation would be based on the argument that the non-resident parent could not afford the 'going rate' this might seem harsh. However, this subject is examined in more detail in Chapter Five.

13. Termination of Calculations (Other Than Interim Calculations)

2.42 The CSA 1991 and the existing regulations provide for circumstances in which a maintenance calculation may terminate or cease to have effect.

Paragraph 16(1) of Sch 1 to the Act provides that a calculation shall cease to have effect:

'(a) on the death of the non-resident parent, or of the person with care, with respect to whom it was made;
(b) on there no longer being a qualifying child with respect to whom it might have effect;
(c) on the non-resident parent with respect to whom it was made ceasing to be a parent of –
  (i) the qualifying child with respect to whom it was made; or
  (ii) where it was made with respect to more than one qualifying child, all of the qualifying children with respect to whom it was made.'

---

1 Baroness Hollis, Official Report (HL) 8 May 2000 col 1327.

These provisions need little comment. A person would cease to be parent if an adoption order were made. A declaration of a court that an absent parent was not the father of the child would not, of itself, lead to termination, but would result in a review of the calculation.

14. Fees

2.43 By the Child Support Fees Regulations 1992, SI 1992/3094, the Secretary of State has power to charge fees for the use of the CSA. By reg 2, where a calculation is made following an application under ss 4, 6 or 7, fees shall be payable in accordance with regs 3 and 4.

Regulation 3 deals with the persons liable to pay the fees. These are the person with care and the non-resident parent with respect to whom the calculation was made. However, some people are exempt from paying fees. They are any person receiving income support, family credit or disability allowance, or who is under 16 or under 19 years of age and receiving full-time education which is not advanced education, or whose calculable income is nil, or is a non-resident parent whose protected income effects a reduction in any calculation.

The regulations do not specify which party is to pay the fee. However, the applicant must pay a fee to issue the application and the non-resident parent must pay a fee after a calculation is made, subject to exemption.

Regulation 1(2) defines 'collection fee' as a fee in respect of services provided by the Secretary of State for the collection of child support maintenance or for enforcing payment of such maintenance or for both collection and enforcement.

15. Repayment of Overpaid Maintenance

2.44 Section 41B of the CSA 1991 makes provision for repayment of child support maintenance which has been overpaid by a non-resident parent. This applies where:

(a) it would not be possible for the non-resident parent to recover the amount of the overpayment by way of an adjustment of the amount payable under a maintenance calculation; or

(b) it would be inappropriate to rely on an adjustment of the amount payable under a maintenance calculation as the means of enabling the non-resident parent to recover the amount of the overpayment.

Section 41B(2) provides that, in such circumstances, the Secretary of State may make such payment to the non-resident parent by way of reimbursement or partial reimbursement as he considers appropriate. When he does so, he may require 'the relevant person' to pay to him the whole, or a specified proportion, of the amount of the payment (s 41B(3)).

'Relevant person' is defined by s 41B(8) as the person with care to whom the overpayment was made. It also applies under s 41B(1A):

> 'where the non-resident parent has made a voluntary payment and it appears to the Secretary of State –

(a) that he is not liable to pay child support maintenance; or
(b) that he is liable, but some or all of the payments amount to an overpayment.'

Where (b) applies, the Secretary of State must also be satisfied that subsection (1)(a) and (b) above apply.

CHAPTER THREE

How Child Support is Calculated

1. Introduction

3.1 As was stated at para **1.1**, the changes effected by the CSPSSA 2000 are brought about by amendments of the CSA 1991. In order to ascertain the 'formula' or process by which child maintenance is calculated, therefore, it is still necessary to look to Part I of Sch 1 to the CSA 1991, but in its amended form.

Certain new terms have been introduced by the Act. The absent parent is no more; he is now described as the 'non-resident parent'.[1] However, the person with care continues to be so called. A maintenance assessment is now a maintenance 'calculation'.[2]

The legislation also still refers to the children with respect to whom the maintenance calculation falls to be made as 'qualifying children'; this definition is explained at para **2.5**.

3.2 The basic principle of the new formula is that child maintenance is based entirely on a calculation of the income of the non-resident parent. No account is taken of the income or other means of the person with care. No attempt is made to determine a 'maintenance requirement' based on the needs of the child. The only material which may be used to determine the amount of child maintenance in any case is the income of the non-resident parent. Comment on this change will be found at para **3.22**.

The stages through which any calculation of child maintenance must go, and the questions which must be asked in each case, are as follows.

(1) Which rate applies (ie basic, reduced, flat or nil rates)?
(2) When basic or reduced rate applies, what sum is payable?
(3) Should the result of (2) be apportioned?
(4) Is care shared? If so, how is the maintenance reduced?
(5) When the flat rate or nil rate applies, what sum is payable?

Each of these stages will be considered in this chapter. The chapter will conclude with a critical assessment of the new provisions and a model for assessing the maintenance liability in any case.

3.3 The usual rules for calculating child maintenance may be varied. Variation is a separate topic which will be considered in Chapter Five.

---

1 CSPSSA 2000, Sch 3, para 11(2).
2 Ibid, s 1(2).

2. Which Rate Applies?

3.4 The general rule is that the basic rate is applied,[3] and a fixed percentage of the non-resident parent's income is taken, as described in para **3.7**. However, this does not apply where that income falls below a certain level and in these cases a reduced rate, or even a flat or nil rate, may apply. The system is best described from the bottom upwards.

The nil rate

This applies (ie no child maintenance is payable) where the non-resident parent has a net income of below £5 or is of a prescribed description.[4] Regulations will prescribe what types of income fall within this category but it is thought that full-time students in advanced education and prisoners will be included.

The flat rate

This may be either a fixed amount of £5 or such sum as may be prescribed by regulations. The £5 fixed rate applies where the nil rate does not apply and either:

(a) the non-resident parent's net weekly income is £100 or less; or
(b) he receives any benefit, pension or allowance prescribed for this purpose; or
(c) he or his partner (if any) receives any benefit prescribed for this purpose.

The flat rate of a prescribed amount applies where the nil rate does not apply and:

(a) the non-resident parent has a partner who is also a non-resident parent; and
(b) the partner is a person with respect to whom a maintenance calculation is in force; and
(c) the non-resident parent or his partner receives any benefit prescribed for this purpose.[5]

3.5 A person's partner is defined as 'if they are a couple, the other member of that couple'. Where a person is a husband or wife by virtue of a marriage entered into under a law which permits polygamy, his partner may be 'another party to the marriage who is of the opposite sex and is a member of the same household'.[6]

'Couple' means a man and a woman who are either married to each other and are members of the same household or are not married to each other but are living together as husband and wife.[7]

3.6 The *reduced rate* is payable where:

(a) neither the nil rate nor a flat rate applies, and

---

3 CSA 1991, Sch 1, Part I, para 1(1).
4 Ibid, para 5.
5 Ibid, para 4.
6 Ibid, para 10C(4) and (5).
7 Ibid, para 10C(5).

(b) the non-resident parent's net weekly income is less than £200 but more than £100.[8]

At present, the percentage which will be taken under the reduced rate is not known. It is intended that regulations will provide for percentages to be applied to net income so that liability will increase in proportion to the amount by which net income exceeds £100; in effect, there will be a sliding scale.

3. Calculation of the Basic Rate

3.7 The general rule is that the basic rate is a percentage of the weekly net income of the non-resident parent. This percentage is:

15% where he has one qualifying child;
20% where he has two qualifying children;
25% where he has three or more qualifying children.[9]

The method of calculating net income is discussed at para **3.11**.

This is, therefore, a simple calculation. A non-resident parent earning £300 per week net will pay £45 for one child and £75 for three children, irrespective of their ages. The calculation ignores the income of the resident parent. There is a 'cap' or limit on the maintenance, as a result of a last-minute change of heart by the Government. The effect of this cap is that net income of over £2000 per week is ignored.[10]

It was originally the Government's firm intention that there should be no cap or limit on the income a percentage of which would be taken in child maintenance. The official view was that '... having an upper limit to the amount of maintenance payable would result in an inconsistency of treatment between non-resident parents with relatively high levels of income and those on more modest sums'.[11] It was also said that 'maintenance for all children will be based on what a father can afford, not what he or anyone else believes the children need'.[12] 'Placing an upper limit on the amount paid in respect of any one child is inconsistent with the Government's plan for a simple and transparent system of rates that protects the rights of all children to support from non-resident parents in keeping with their ability to provide.'[13]

Had this proposal been enacted, surprising results might have followed. It would probably have seemed curious to most people that a non-resident parent earning £10,000 per week would be required to pay £1500 per week for a child, whether that child is 15 months old or 15 years old. Such a sum would greatly exceed any conceivable needs of the child (and, of course, no account would be taken of the income of the person with care).

Whatever the merits of the proposal, a different view eventually prevailed. When the Lords amendments were finally considered (perhaps bearing in mind

---

8 CSA 1991, Sch 1, Part I, para 3.
9 Ibid, para 2.
10 Ibid, para 10(3).
11 Baroness Hollis at Official Report (HL) 8 May 2000, col 1251.
12 Ibid.
13 Ibid, col 1252.

the extreme lack of parliamentary time), the Government decided not to try to undo the amendment which imposed the £2000 limit. The official view adopted latterly was that 'we have been persuaded, however, that in the case of very high earners, the courts are better placed to unravel their financial affairs and to come to a sensible conclusion about the proper allocation of property, spousal maintenance, and child maintenance. Without a cap on child support liability, the courts might find it impossible to settle the family's financial affairs properly. With a cap, the courts will be able to work from a fixed maximum child support liability while settling other financial arrangements'.[14] The right to apply to the court for top-ups would be maintained (see Chapter Ten at para **10.8**).

3.8 However, the calculation contains a further complication. It is provided that allowance may be made for any 'relevant other children' of the non-resident parent.[15] 'Relevant other children' are defined as children other than qualifying children in respect of whom the non-resident parent or his partner receives child benefit, and such other children as may be prescribed.[16] These are therefore children living with the non-resident parent who are the children of either himself or his partner. No account is taken of any income of the partner nor of any income of the children.

The allowance which is made is by way of a percentage deduction from the net weekly income of the non-resident parent before the basic rate is calculated, and the percentages are:

15% where he has one relevant other child;
20% where he has two relevant other children;
25% where he has three or more relevant other children.[17]

3.9 If, therefore, the non-resident parent had a net weekly income of £300 and two relevant other children, 20% or £60 would first be notionally deducted from his net weekly income leaving £240. If there were two qualifying children he would have to pay 20% of the net figure of £240, namely £48 per week. Had he no relevant other children the sum payable would have been £60. The value which the scheme places on the support of the non-relevant children would therefore be £12 per week.

3.10 The results of these rules could be curious and their inflexibility makes them somewhat arbitrary. A non-resident parent earning £300 per week would pay the sums set out above whether the person with care was earning nothing, £500 per week or £10,000 per week. Many will consider this bizarre.

3.11 Net weekly income is to be determined in such manner as may be prescribed by regulations.[18] These regulations may in particular provide for the Secretary of State to estimate any income or make an assumption as to any fact

14 Angela Eagle MP in Official Report (HC) 24 July 2000, cols 793 and 794.
15 CSA 1991, Sch 1, para 2(2).
16 Ibid, para 10C(2).
17 Ibid, para 2(2).
18 Ibid, para 10(1).

where, in his view, the information at his disposal is unreliable, insufficient, or relates to an untypical period in the life of the non-resident parent.[19]

The exact nature of the regulations must be awaited, but it will be noted that the Secretary of State will have power to make his own judgement as to income if he does not accept the figures provided by the non-resident parent.

In addition, it is provided that the Secretary of State may by regulation provide that in such circumstances and to such extent as may be prescribed:

(a) where the Secretary of State is satisfied that a person has intentionally deprived himself of a source of income with a view to reducing the amount of his net weekly income, his net weekly income shall be taken to include income from that source of an amount estimated by the Secretary of State;
(b) a person is to be treated as possessing income which he does not possess;
(c) income which a person does possess is to be disregarded.[20]

4. Apportionment

3.12 Apportionment is applied where 'the non-resident parent has more than one qualifying child and in relation to them there is more than one person with care'.[21] In other words, the non-resident parent has two or more children who are living with different people. In such circumstances, the rate of maintenance liability is divided by the number of qualifying children and shared among the persons with care according to the number of qualifying children in relation to whom each is a person with care.[22]

3.13 For example, if a non-resident parent had a net income of £400 per week and three qualifying children, one of whom lived with A and two of whom lived with B, the starting point would be that his maintenance liability would be £100 (25% of £400). A would receive one-third of this sum (£33.33) and B would receive two-thirds (£66.66). The ages of the children would be irrelevant.

5. Shared Care

3.14 Under the previous legislation, an attempt was made to give some relief to non-resident parents (then called absent parents) who had a qualifying child living with them for longer than a certain period in each year. The formula which was applied was to treat one person as a non-resident parent where there were two or more persons not living in the same household who each provided day-to-day care for a child. Day-to-day care meant 104 nights or more in any 12-month period. In these circumstances, an algebraic formula was applied to apportion the maintenance liability between the two persons.[23]

---

19 CSA 1991, Sch 1, para 10(2).
20 Ibid, para 10B.
21 Ibid, para 6(1).
22 Ibid, para 6(2).
23 See CS(MASC)Regs 1992, reg 20.

3.15 These provisions were sometimes criticised as providing a spurious encouragement to non-resident parents to apply to the court for overnight contact. However, they applied only when the non-resident parent had the child or children for more than every weekend in one year. The new law goes further and provides even more of an encouragement to such disruption; the exact effect depends on whether the maintenance liability is based on the basic or reduced rate on the one hand or the flat rate on the other hand. These must be considered separately.

Basic and reduced rate

3.16 These provisions apply when the rate of child maintenance payable is the basic rate or the reduced rate and '... the care of a qualifying child is shared between the non-resident parent and the person with care, so that the non-resident parent from time to time has care of the child overnight'. In these circumstances, 'the amount of child support maintenance which he would otherwise have been liable to pay the person with care ... is to be decreased in accordance with this paragraph'.[24]

The first stage of the calculation is to calculate the decrease 'according to the number of such nights which the Secretary of State determines there to have been, or expects there to be, or both during a prescribed twelve-month period'.[25] The amount of decrease for one child is as follows.

Number of nights	*Fraction to subtract*
52 to 103	One-seventh
104 to 155	Two-sevenths
156 to 174	Three-sevenths
175 or more	One-half.[26]

3.17 It is then provided that, if the person with care is providing for more than one qualifying child of the non-resident parent, 'the applicable decrease is the sum of the appropriate fractions in the Table divided by the number of such qualifying children'.[27] There is then a further calculation to carry out in some cases. If the applicable fraction is one-half in relation to any qualifying child in the care of the person with care, the total amount payable to the person with care is then to be further decreased by £7 for each such child.[28]

Finally, if the application of these provisions would decrease the weekly amount of child support maintenance (or the aggregate of all such amounts) payable by the non-resident parent to the person with care (or all of them) to less than £5 per week, the non-resident parent is liable to pay only £5 per week.[29] In appropriate cases this would be apportioned as described in para **3.12**.

---

24 CSA 1991, Sch 1, para 7(1) and (2).
25 Ibid, para 7(3).
26 Ibid, para 7(4).
27 Ibid, para 7(5).
28 Ibid, para 7(6).
29 Ibid, para 7(7).

3.18 An example may assist. A and B have three children, C, D and E. The children live with A but have overnight contact with B in different proportions. C spends 70 nights per annum with B, D 140 nights and E 180.

The fractions to be aggregated are therefore one-seventh, two-sevenths and one-half. The result is thirteen-fourteenths. That fraction is then divided by three (the number of the children) so that the reduction is 4.33/14.

If the non-resident parent had a net income of £400 per week, the initial maintenance liability would have been £100. This would now be reduced by 4.33/14 resulting in a net figure of £69.08. Then that figure would be reduced by £7 because the fraction in respect of one of the children was one-half, so that the total sum payable would be £62.08.

Flat rate

3.19 Where the child maintenance payable is in accordance with the flat rate (except where this is so only because the non-resident parent's income is £100 or less), then if the care of a qualifying child is shared for at least 52 nights during a prescribed 12-month period, the amount of child support maintenance payable by the non-resident parent to the person with care of that child is nil.[30]

Miscellaneous matters

3.20 A few minor matters remain to be noted on the subject of shared care. First, the Secretary of State has to decide in any case what number of nights are to be regarded as shared: this can be on the basis of the past record, a prediction of the future, or a combination of the two. It is not clear how a dispute between the parties would be resolved, except by the Secretary of State accepting the word of one of them and then leaving the matter to the Appeal Tribunal.

Secondly, the Secretary of State may make regulations to provide for which nights are to count for the purposes of shared care or for how it is to be determined whether a night counts, and for the calculation to be based on a period other than 12 months.[31]

6. The Flat Rate and the Nil Rate

3.21 When the flat rate applies (as to which see para **3.4**), the sum payable will depend on which of the circumstances described apply. When the nil rate applies, nothing is payable.

7. Some Comments on the New Provisions

3.22 When the Bill was going through Parliament it was subjected to a number of criticisms. Some of those criticisms related to enforcement provisions (as to which see Chapter Nine). As far as the formula itself was concerned, the principal original criticisms were, first, that there was no limit on the liability of the non-resident parent and, secondly, that no account was taken of the means of

30 CSA 1991, Sch 1, para 7(8).
31 Ibid, para 9.

the parent with care. The Government purported to refute the first criticism by professing not to understand it; its view was that children were entitled as of right to share in the wealth of their parents, a view which most lawyers would think was unknown to English law and find somewhat alarming. In the event, disaster was avoided and a cap or limit was imposed, although as will be seen below, the Government's philosophy reappears in a different context.

As to the second criticism, it may seem to many that simple justice demands that some account be taken of the income of the person with care. The Government does not accept this view, and the proposal has been enacted. The proposal was justified on three principal grounds. First, it was said that the cost of maintaining a child is on average 30% of family income, which ought to be divided equally between the parents. The person with care already provides her share by housing costs, food, heat, etc; that is her contribution. The non-resident parent's contribution, because he is not living there, is in cash.[32]

The second ground was, again, that the child was entitled to a share of its parent's income: 'the child has the right to maintenance from his or her father [*sic*] irrespective of the income of the mother, exactly as if they were part of an intact family'.[33] Finally, it was said that the numbers of people who might be adversely affected by these proposals were so few that it was not really worth making special arrangements to cater for them.[34] This argument had originally been applied also to the cap on the non-resident parent's liability.

3.23 Whatever the merits of the arguments, this principle is now part of child support law. It may well have an effect on ancillary relief settlements. However, another factor which seems even more likely to affect ancillary relief is the fact that, in average income cases, maintenance calculations under the new provisions will be lower than under the old system. A likely consequence of this is that, whereas there has been a growing trend to agree clean break orders with no spousal maintenance on the basis that the non-resident parent would in reality never be able to pay more than the child support demanded by the old formula, this will no longer be an attractive option. It may well be that at least nominal spousal orders will be required, which, whatever the merits of the arguments, will reverse one of the important social developments of recent years.

8. A Possible Model for Use

3.24 It has been seen in this chapter that the new provisions do not result in as simple a calculation as might have been expected. The following model may serve as an aid to calculation (NRP = non-resident parent and PWC = person with care).

Stage 1 Calculate NRP's net income (described as A).

---

32 See Baroness Hollis at Official Report (HL) 8 May 2000, col 1254. The Baroness expressed herself 'baffled' that this argument was not understood (see col 1255).

33 Ibid at col 1260.

34 Ibid at col 1262.

Stage 2 Is A less than £5 per week or is he [of a prescribed description, eg a prisoner] ? If YES, stop here; nil rate applies.

Stage 3 Does NRP have a partner who is also an NRP in respect of whom a maintenance calculation is in force and do either of them receive [a prescribed benefit] ? If YES to all questions, flat rate of prescribed amount applies. If NO, proceed to Stage 4.

Stage 4 Is A less than £100 per week? If YES, flat rate of £5 per week applies.

Stage 5 Do NRP or partner (if any) receive [any benefit prescribed for this purpose]? If YES, flat rate of £5 per week applies. If NO, proceed to Stage 6.

Stage 6 Is A more than £100 per week but less than £200 per week? If NO, proceed to Stage 7. If YES, reduced rate applies. Sum payable = B. [More detail will be needed when the regulations are eventually published.]

Note: from this point, A is either the net income or £2000, whichever is the lower.

Stage 7 Does NRP have a 'relevant child' or children? If NO, A remains unchanged; proceed to Stage 8. If YES, deduct from A 15% for one such child, 20% for two and 25% for three or more such children. Now proceed to Stage 8 with the reduced A figure.

Stage 8 Multiply A by 15% for one child, 20% for two and 25% for three children. The result = C.

Stage 9 Is there more than one PWC in relation to the qualifying children? If NO, proceed to Stage 10. If YES, divide B or C by the number of children; result = D. How many children has each PWC? Multiply D by the number each PWC has.

Stage 10 Is the care of any qualifying child shared between PWC and NRP for more than 51 nights per year? If NO, B or C remain unchanged and are carried forward to Stage 11. If YES, in respect of EACH CHILD, reduce B or C as follows.

Number of nights	*Fraction to subtract*
52 to 103	One-seventh
104 to 155	Two-sevenths
156 to 174	Three-sevenths
175 or more	One-half

Now aggregate the total of the deductible fractions =
Divide this figure by the number of qualifying children of NRP with PWC =
Result = D
Now divide B or C (as the case may be) by D.
Carry forward result to Stage 11.

Stage 11 The figure brought forward from Stage 10 is the sum to be inserted in the maintenance calculation.

CHAPTER FOUR

Special Cases

1. Introduction

4.1 The rules for the making of maintenance calculations set out in Chapter Three were for the 'normal' case, or set of circumstances, in which liability for a calculation might arise. The CSA 1991 recognises that not all cases are normal, and, accordingly, provision is made for 'special cases', where the standard approach is not applicable.

Section 42(1) provides that the Secretary of State may by regulations provide that in prescribed circumstances a case is to be treated as a special case for the purposes of the Act. These regulations have been made, and are contained in the Child Support (Maintenance Assessments and Special Cases) Regulations 1992 (CS(MASC)Regs 1992), SI 1992/1815, Part III, regs 19–28. These regulations will be set out insofar as they may give some guidance as to the likely shape of future regulations. However, it must be remembered that the detailed formulae contained in the regulations are based on the 'old law' and the basic formula previously used.

The special cases contained in Part III will now be considered in turn.

2. Both Parents are Absent (now 'Non-Resident') (reg 19)

4.2 By s 3(2), a parent a is non-resident (previously called 'absent') parent where he is not living in the same household with the child and the child has his home with a person with care. It follows, therefore, that when neither parent lives in the same household with the child, and the child lives with a person who provides day-to-day care (as to which see below) and who is not incapable of being a person with care (as would be, for example, a local authority), both parents will be regarded as non-resident parents. This class of persons must be distinguished from those who are treated as non-resident parents under reg 20 (see below).

4.3 When both parents are non-resident, the CSO has to make two maintenance calculations, one for each parent, since they both have an obligation to pay for the child. However, the CSO may decide to proceed with an application against one of the non-resident parents only.

3. One of the Parents is Treated as an Absent (now 'Non-Resident') Parent (reg 20)

4.4 Regulation 20 applies when two or more persons who do not live in the same household each provide day-to-day care for the same qualifying child, and at least one of them is a parent of the child.

Day-to-day care is defined by reg 1(2) of the CS(MASC)Regs 1992. It means either 104 nights or more in the 12-month period ending with the relevant week, or in the same ratio of 104 nights per 12 months as the Secretary of State thinks more accurately reflects the current arrangements for the child.

4.5 The most common situation which may give rise to this position is where a child is being cared for by both parents, who do not live together. Another situation, which is not unusual, is where care of a child is shared between a parent and a grandparent. These are circumstances which may make it impossible for the usual approach to be adopted; the formula is dependent on there being a non-resident parent, and when there is no obvious candidate for that role a different approach has to be adopted.

The first decision the Secretary of State must make is, therefore, whether or not there is a non-resident parent. If not, he must decide who is to be treated as the non-resident parent.

Regulation 20(2)(a) provides that where both parents provide day-to-day care, the person to be treated as the non-resident parent will be:

> 'a parent who provides such care to a lesser extent than the other parent, person or persons who provide such care . . . '

This is, therefore, the case where the position is clear, and one parent provides less care than the other. Regulation 20(2)(b) deals with the position where the persons mentioned in reg 20(2)(a) include the parents of the child, and the circumstances are such that care is provided to the same extent by both, but each provides care to a greater or equal extent than any other person who provides such care. Here, the person to be treated as the non-resident parent will be:

(a) the parent who is not in receipt of child benefit for the child in question; or
(b) if neither parent is in receipt of child benefit for that child, the parent who, in the opinion of the Secretary of State, will not be the principal provider of day-to-day care for that child.

4.6 Having decided which parent is to be treated as absent, the Secretary of State can then make an assessment on the basis of reg 20(4). This introduces a new formula which, as explained at para **4.1**, is bound to be changed and will therefore not be considered here.

4. One Parent is Absent (now 'Non-Resident') and the Other is Treated as Absent (reg 21)

4.7 This special case arises where one parent is a non-resident parent and the other is treated as a non-resident parent by virtue of reg 20(2); reg 20(2) was considered at para **4.5**, and it will be remembered that it applies where a parent and another person (who may, or may not, be a parent) both provide day-to-day care for a child, the parent who provides the lesser amount of care being treated as a non-resident parent. Regulation 21 applies, therefore, where a parent and another person who is not a parent (eg a grandparent) are both providing day-to-day care, the parent is treated as a non-resident parent, and the other parent is a 'real' non-resident parent.

5. Multiple Applications Relating to an Absent (now 'Non-Resident') Parent (reg 22)

4.8 This applies where a non-resident parent has two or more children who are cared for by different persons with care. This is treated as a special case only when two or more applications for a maintenance calculation have been made. By reg 22(1), this is treated as a special case where an application for a maintenance calculation has been made in respect of a non-resident parent and:

> '(a) at least one other application for a maintenance assessment [calculation] has been made in relation to the same absent [non-resident parent] (or a person who is treated as an absent [non-resident] parent by regulation 20(2)) but to different children; or
>
> (b) at least one maintenance assessment [calculation] is in force in relation to the same absent [non-resident] parent or a person who is treated as an absent [non-resident] parent by regulation 20(2) but to different children.'

It will be seen, therefore, that this kind of situation will be treated as a special case only where two or more applications for a maintenance calculation are being or have been made. There seems little point in setting out the present detailed formula since it is bound to change.

6. Person Caring for Children of More Than One Absent (now 'Non-Resident') Parent (reg 23)

4.9 This applies where a person is a person with care in relation to two or more qualifying children, and in relation to those children there are different persons who are non-resident parents or persons treated as non-resident parents by reg 20(2). This would apply, for example, where a woman had living with her two children by different fathers; it would also apply where someone cared for two children all of whose parents lived elsewhere. The essential point is that there must be more than one child with different parents.

7. Persons With Part-Time Care – Not Including a Person Treated as an Absent (now 'Non-Resident') Parent (reg 24)

4.10 This applies where (reg 24(1)):

> '(a) two or more persons who do not live in the same household each provide day-to-day care for the same qualifying child; and

(b) those persons do not include any parent who is treated as an absent [non-resident] parent of that child by regulation 20(2).'

This situation would arise, for example, where two grandparents were each providing day-to-day care, while living apart from each other. The issues which the Secretary of State would have to address would be how much each natural parent should pay and how much each grandparent should receive.

4.11 This regulation is, in fact, concerned with method of payment rather than calculation. The starting point is reg 24(2)(a) which provides that a person whose application is being proceeded with shall be entitled to receive all of the child support maintenance payable for the child in question. The question of whose application should be proceeded with is a separate matter, the general principles of which are considered in Chapter Two at para **2.26**.

However, this right to receive all the maintenance payable is subject to reg 24(2)(b) which provides that, on a request being made to the Secretary of State by that person (ie the person whose application is being considered) or any other person who is providing day-to-day care for the child and intends to continue to provide that care:

> '. . . the Secretary of State may make arrangements for the payment of any child support maintenance payable under the Act to the persons who provide such care in the same ratio as that in which it appears to the Secretary of State, that each is to provide such care for the child in question.'

Before making such a decision the Secretary of State must, of course, consider all the circumstances and give all interested parties a chance to make representations.

4.12 The effect of all this is that the Secretary of State will first make a calculation at the request of one of the persons with care. In so doing, he may well have to treat the assessment as a special case under one of the other regulations, for example both parents being absent. It may then arise that this assessment has to be apportioned between two people who both care for the child or children and, in such a case, the Secretary of State will normally apportion on the basis of the number of days the child lives with each person.

8. Care Provided in Part by a Local Authority (reg 25)

4.13 This special case arises where a local authority and a person each provide day-to-day care for the same qualifying child. An example might be where a child was cared for by a local authority during the week and by a parent at weekends and during holidays. Different rules apply to cases where there is one child or there are children who spend the same amount of time in the care of the local authority, or, on the other hand, where there are children who spend different amounts of time in the care of the local authority.

In the first case, a maintenance calculation is made in an entirely conventional way, and is then divided by seven. The non-resident parent then has to pay to the person with care the result of that calculation multiplied by the number of nights the child spends with the person with care.

9. Cases where Child Support Maintenance is Not to be Payable (reg 26); Cases where an Absent (now 'Non-Resident') Parent is in Receipt of Income Support or Other Prescribed Benefit (reg 28)

4.14 These items are included here for the sake of completeness, but in fact have already been dealt with in Chapter Three. They relate to the position where the minimum amount would normally be payable, or a deduction equivalent to the minimum amount is made from income support, and to the position where no such deduction is made.

10. Child who is Boarder or In-patient (reg 27)

4.15 If a qualifying child is a boarder at a boarding school or is an in-patient in hospital, and, by reason thereof, the person who would otherwise provide day-to-day care is not doing so, the person who normally provides day-to-day care is treated as doing so while the child is away. A calculation is then made in the normal way.

CHAPTER FIVE

Variations

1. Introduction

5.1 The various attempts at establishing an administrative system for the calculation of child support maintenance since 1991 have all involved two elements. The first and principal element has been the creation of a rigid formula or system which will provide the answer to the amount of maintenance to be paid in any case and which can be operated and calculated by officials without any discretion. The second element recognises the fact that the application of a rigid formula may bring about injustice in some cases and seeks to provide a method of relief from such injustice. Accordingly, the original scheme had provision for 'special cases' to allow for unusual situations, although, even there, the amelioration was provided by means of another algebraic and equally unbending formula. In 1995 provision was made for 'departures', which allowed the child support officer to depart from the formula in certain defined classes of case and introduced some element of discretion.

The CSPSSA 2000 is no exception to the rule. The Government intends that the new method of calculating child support will provide a fair answer in most cases but recognises that there may be cases where the rates do not properly reflect a non-resident parent's ability to support his children. In such cases, which it is intended should be exceptional, there will be provision for the variation upwards and downwards of the standard rates. These exceptional cases are clearly defined and build on the provisions for departures introduced by the CSA 1995. Some of the cases in which variations may be allowed are remarkably similar to those in which a departure might previously have been permitted, but there are important differences.

5.2 The new rules as to variation will now be discussed. It should be noted that new procedures for applying for variations and dealing with the applications have been introduced; these are discussed at part 3 of this chapter. It should also be noted that the consideration of an application for variation may be subject to a regular payments condition; this is discussed at para **5.16**.

2. Cases where Variation may be Allowed

The basic rule

5.3 It is provided that the Secretary of State may agree to a variation if:

(a) he is satisfied that the case is one which falls within one or more of the cases set out in Part I of Schedule 4B of the CSA 1991 or in regulations made under that Part; and

(b) it is his opinion that, in all the circumstances of the case, it would be just and equitable to agree to a variation.[1]

This is, therefore, the basic statement of principle, and both parts of the principle must be satisfied. In deciding whether or not it would be just and equitable in any case to agree to a variation, the Secretary of State:

(a) must have regard, in particular, to the welfare of any child likely to be affected if he did agree to a variation; and
(b) must, or as the case may be, must not, take any prescribed factors into account, or must take them into account (or not) in prescribed circumstances.[2]

5.4 It will be noted that there is no provision for the Secretary of State to have regard to the welfare of any child likely to be affected if no variation is allowed. As to the prescribed factors, these will be contained in regulations which are not yet available. However, the 'just and equitable' formula is repeated from the previous provisions for departures, and the regulations made in connection with those provisions included the duty on the Secretary of State to consider whether the giving of a departure direction would result in a person ceasing paid employment and also a list of matters which must not be taken into account: these included whether the conception of a child was planned, the responsibility for the breakdown of the relationship, the existence of a new relationship and particular arrangements for contact. It may be that some or all of these provisions will be included in the new regulations.

The cases contained in Sch 4B will now be considered.

Special expenses

5.5 A variation applied for by a non-resident parent may be agreed by reference to his special expenses.[3] Special expenses is not a term to be interpreted according to the general dictionary meaning of the words. Instead, the term is defined as:

> 'the whole, or any amount above a prescribed amount, or any prescribed part, of expenses which fall within a prescribed description of expenses.'[4]

Regulations will, therefore, prescribe what expenses are and are not special. What is prescribed remains to be seen, but the Schedule itself[5] permits the Secretary of State to make particular provision for certain classes of expense. Experience of the earlier legislation shows that this is likely to be the complete list. These expenses are:

(a) costs incurred by a non-resident parent in maintaining contact with the child, or with any of the children, with respect to whom the application for a maintenance calculation has been made (or treated as made);
(b) costs attributable to a long-term illness or disability of a relevant other child;

---

1 CSA 1991, s 28F(1).
2 Ibid, s 28F(2).
3 Ibid, Sch 4B, para 2(1).
4 Ibid, para 2(2)
5 Ibid, para 2(3).

(c) debts of a prescribed nature incurred before the non-resident parent became a non-resident parent in relation to a child with respect to whom the maintenance calculation has been applied for (or treated as having been applied for):
   (i) for the joint benefit of both parents;
   (ii) for the benefit of any such child; or
   (iii) for the benefit of any other child falling within a prescribed category;
(d) boarding school fees for a child in relation to whom the application for a maintenance calculation has been made (or treated as made);
(e) the cost to the non-resident parent of making payments in relation to a mortgage on the home he and the parent with care shared, if he no longer has an interest in it, and she and a child in relation to whom the application for a maintenance calculation has been made (or treated as made) still live there.

5.6 This list therefore sets out what is likely to be an exhaustive list of what may be classed as special expenses. The Secretary of State will make regulations to prescribe the meanings of 'disability' and 'illness'[6] and how it is to be determined whether an illness is or is not 'long-term'. The Secretary of State will also make regulations to determine the meaning of 'boarding school fees'. It seems unlikely that the fees for, say, Eton or Ampleforth would qualify and it is more likely that these fees will be restricted to those of schools in the maintained sector where, for some reason, a child cannot remain at home.

The following comments may be made. First, it is noticeable that no account may be taken of the cost of travel to work. This was one of the most glaring omissions from the original formula in 1991 and was one of the first parts of that scheme to be amended. Eventually, there were two complementary methods of making allowance for these costs. It seems that under the new scheme, no account may be taken of such costs.

Secondly, while the allowance of the cost of making mortgage payments on the former home is understandable and welcome, the proviso that the non-resident parent may no longer have an interest in the home may cause problems. Clearly, it might be said that a person who retained an equal share of the proceeds of sale of a house should not be allowed a full deduction of mortgage payments since he would, in effect, be investing in his own future profits although, even here, it would be reasonable to make a distinction between payments of interest and capital. However, it may seem unjust to insist that the non-resident parent must divest himself of all interest in the property, no matter what its value, before he can qualify for this allowance. This may well have a detrimental effect on settlement negotiations in ancillary relief applications. It may be also that there is room to question whether a person who transfers all his interest in the property to the person with care in return for a charge redeemable at a later date still has an interest in the property.

Property or capital transfers

5.7 When what became the CSA 1991 was being debated, one of the pressing issues was the injustice that might be caused if a full maintenance calculation was levied on a person who, as part of a matrimonial settlement, had transferred his

6 Under CSA 1991, Sch 4B, para 2(4).

interest in a home or capital to his former spouse in return for some reduction in the periodical payments which he might have to pay for the person with care and any child. Such arrangements had been relatively common before that date. Various attempts were made to resolve this difficulty, culminating in a type of departure direction permissible after the 1995 changes. The present legislation is very similar to the previous position and, once again, restricts any relief to arrangements made before 5 April 1993.

5.8 It is provided that a variation may be agreed in certain circumstances if before 5 April 1993:

(a) a court order of a prescribed kind was in force with respect to the non-resident parent and either the person with care with respect to the application for the maintenance calculation or the child, or any of the children, with respect to whom that application was made; or
(b) an agreement of a prescribed kind between the non-resident parent and any of those persons was in force.[7]

The circumstances in which, given the above facts, a variation may be agreed (in other words, the essential conditions for their becoming relevant) are that in consequence of one or more transfers of property of a prescribed kind and exceeding (singly or in aggregate) a prescribed minimum value:

(a) the amount payable by the non-resident parent by way of maintenance was less than would have been the case had that transfer or those transfers not been made; or
(b) no amount was payable by the non-resident parent by way of maintenance.[8]

5.9 Regulations will prescribe the exact effect which may be given to these provisions. Given the similarity to the previous legislation, it may be predicted that a table will be produced which will attribute a weekly value to the property transferred and bring about a deduction in the maintenance calculation.

Additional cases

5.10 It is contemplated that there may be cases other than those contained in the previous provisions set out above which could justify a variation. Accordingly, it is provided that 'the Secretary of State may by regulations prescribe other cases in which a variation may be agreed'.[9] However, it should not be thought that this will confer carte blanche on the Secretary of State to do whatever is just; the provisions for departures in the earlier legislation contained a similar power and the regulations eventually made followed precisely the examples given in the statute of cases which might be provided for. Accordingly, it is likely that the regulations will deal with the following matters, the statute providing[10] that:

> 'regulations … may, for example, make provision with respect to cases where –
> (a) the non-resident parent has assets which exceed a prescribed value;

7 CSA 1991, Sch 4B, para 3.
8 Ibid, para 3(2).
9 Ibid, para 4(1).
10 Ibid, para 4(2).

(b) a person's life-style is inconsistent with his income for the purposes of a calculation made under Part I of Schedule 1;
(c) a person has income which is not taken into account in such a calculation;
(d) a person has unreasonably reduced the income which is taken into account in such a calculation.

5.11 It will be seen that, whereas the cases permitting variation under the previous headings are designed to assist a non-resident parent, these cases contemplate the opposite effect and are designed to prevent a non-resident parent from paying less than he should pay if his financial position is considered as a whole.

3. Procedure for Applying for Variation

5.12 Having considered the circumstances in which a variation might be permitted, it is now necessary to consider how an application for a variation is made and how the Secretary of State will or may deal with it.

Who may apply?
Whether an application for a maintenance calculation is made under s 4 or is treated as having been made under s 6, 'the person with care or the non-resident parent ... may apply to the Secretary of State for the rules by which the calculation is made to be varied in accordance with this Act'.[11]

When may application be made?
There are, in effect, two possibilities. First, it is provided[12] that an application for a variation may be made at any time before the Secretary of State has reached a decision under s 11 or s 12(2) on the application for a maintenance calculation (or the application having been treated as having been made under s 6). (Sections 11 and 12(2) are those which deal with the procedure for applying under s 4 of the CSA 1991.) In other words, if it is known that an application for a calculation has been made or is treated as having been made, either party may apply for a variation before the maintenance calculation is made. However, this need not be the end of the matter. It is also provided[13] that an application for a variation may be made when a maintenance calculation is in force, and when this happens the application will be treated as an application for a revision. The procedure for revision is considered in Chapter Four.

The principles which will be followed in either case are the same.

How is application made?
5.13 An application for a variation need not be in writing unless the Secretary of State directs that it must be.[14] In the first place, therefore, the application may be made orally (presumably, by telephone) and the Secretary of State will then decide whether or not written grounds are required. However, the application

11 CSA 1991, s 28A(1).
12 By ibid, s 28A(3).
13 By ibid, s 28A(1).
14 Ibid, s 28A(4)(a).

(whether oral or in writing) must say upon what grounds the application is made.[15] It is also provided that, in other respects, an application for a variation must be made in such manner as may be prescribed.[16]

Preliminary consideration

5.14 The first stage of any variation application is that the Secretary of State may give it a preliminary consideration.[17] This may lead to the rejection of the application *ad limine* with the Secretary of State proceeding to make his decision on the application for a maintenance calculation without any variation. The Secretary of State may do this only if it appears to him:

(a) that there are no grounds on which he could agree to a variation;
(b) that he has insufficient information to make a decision on the application for the maintenance calculation under s 11 (apart from any information needed in relation to the application for a variation) and therefore that his decision would be made under s 12(1); or
(c) that other prescribed circumstances apply.[18]

The first of these grounds is obvious enough and requires no comment. The third must await the regulations. As to the second ground, what is meant is that there is insufficient information in any event so that even where there is no application for a variation the Secretary of State would make a default maintenance decision under s 12(1) (as to which see Chapter Two at para **2.41**). This would, in effect, require the non-resident parent to pay £30 per week for one qualifying child, £40 for two children and £50 for three or more children.

Interim maintenance decision

5.15 A default maintenance decision is not to be confused with an interim maintenance decision. This is in effect a maintenance calculation made in accordance with the normal rules in Part I of Sch 1 to the CSA 1991[19] but without regard to the application for a variation; presumably, this would be done where there was sufficient information on which to base a maintenance calculation but not for the variation application. Regulations will prescribe the circumstances in which this may be done.

Regular payments condition

5.16 A regular payments condition may be imposed if two conditions are met. First, the non-resident parent must have applied for a variation. Secondly, the Secretary of State must have made an interim maintenance decision.[20] The regular payments condition may take one of two forms, namely that either:

(a) the non-resident parent must make the payments of child support maintenance specified in the interim decision; or

---

15 CSA 1991, s 28A(4)(b).
16 Ibid, s 28A(5).
17 Ibid, s 28B(1).
18 Ibid, s 28B(2).
19 Ibid, s 12(2) and (3).
20 Ibid, s 28C(1).

(b) the non-resident parent must make such lesser payments of child support maintenance as may be determined in accordance with regulations made by the Secretary of State.[21]

The effect of non-compliance with the regular payments condition is that the Secretary of State may, in prescribed circumstances, refuse to consider the application for a variation and instead reach his decision under s 11 (the application for a maintenance calculation) as if no application for a variation had been made.[22] This would, in effect, veto the variation application.

5.17 A regular payments condition will cease to have effect when the Secretary of State makes a decision on the application for a maintenance calculation, whether he agrees a variation or not, or when the application for a variation is withdrawn.[23] Provision is made for the written notification to all parties of any regular payments condition and of any determination of non-compliance with such a condition.

Determination of applications

5.18 If an application for a variation has not failed (in the sense of having been refused on preliminary consideration, or having lapsed or been withdrawn) the Secretary of State must determine it. He has three choices. He may agree the variation or not agree the variation. In either case, he will make a decision on the application for a maintenance calculation. Alternatively, he may refer the application to an appeal tribunal for the tribunal to determine what variation, if any, is to be made.[24] When the appeal tribunal deals with the application, it has the same powers as the Secretary of State would have had.

5.19 It is provided that in determining any application for a variation, the Secretary of State must have regard to certain general principles. These are:

(a) that parents should be responsible for maintaining their children whenever they can afford to do so; and
(b) where a parent has more than one child, his obligation to maintain any one of them should be no less of an obligation than his obligation to maintain any other of them.[25]

In addition, regard must be had to such other conditions as may be prescribed. This is exactly the same provision as was made in respect of departure directions but no additional conditions were ever prescribed.

5.20 The CSA 1991 contains provision for 'regulatory controls'. The basic principle is that 'no variations may be made other than those which are permitted under the regulations';[26] there is, therefore, no question of the Secretary of State

---

21 CSA 1991, s 28C(2).
22 Ibid, s 28C(5).
23 Ibid, s 28C(4).
24 Ibid, s 28D(1).
25 Ibid, s 28F(1).
26 Ibid, Sch 4B, para 5(2).

enjoying a discretion such as might be exercised by a court. Instead, regulations will govern what he can do.

The regulations may in particular make provision for a variation to result in:

(a) a person's being treated as having more, or less, income than would be taken into account without the variation in a calculation under Part I of Sch 1;
(b) a person's being treated as liable to pay a higher, or a lower, amount of child support maintenance than would result without the variation from a calculation under that Part.[27]

These provisions require little comment. The 'normal' payment may be adjusted upwards or downwards. There is also provision for the regulations to specify, in effect, an upper limit on any special expenses which may be taken into account and for different provisions for different levels of income.[28]

---

27 CSA 1991 Sch 4B, para 5(3).
28 Ibid, para 5(4).

CHAPTER SIX

Disputes as to Parentage

1. Introduction

6.1 This chapter is concerned with the manner in which a person alleged to be a non-resident parent may challenge the contention that he is a parent of the child concerned. Chapter Seven deals with the various other ways of challenging calculations etc; this chapter is limited to the issue of parentage.

Only a non-resident parent, or someone treated as such, can be required to pay a maintenance calculation under the provisions of the CSA 1991. 'Parent' is defined by s 54 as, in relation to any child, any person who is in law the mother or father of the child.

A person may become the mother or father of a child by virtue of an adoption order of the court. Apart from this, a woman is in law the mother of a child only if she has given birth to it, and a man is the father if he is the natural father in a biological sense; this statement may, to a limited extent, be qualified by the effect of the HFEA 1990, as to which see Chapter Two at para **2.9**, but this will apply in only a very limited number of cases.

Accordingly, in the vast majority of cases, only a 'natural' father or mother will be liable under the CSA 1991. A dispute as to parentage is, therefore, of greater importance in this field than in any other area of family financial relief. In matrimonial proceedings before the courts, a person may be liable for child maintenance, even though he or she is not a biological parent, if he or she has treated the child as a child of their family. This is not the case in relation to the Act, where the sole criterion is parentage.

6.2 In reality, this chapter is concerned almost entirely with the position of a man who denies that he is the father of a child. This is not because of any gender discrimination but because there is rarely any doubt as to whether a woman has given birth to a child. It is not impossible that a woman could deny being a non-resident parent, but that possibility will not be pursued further here.

2. The General Position

6.3 The general position is contained in s 26 of the CSA 1991. Section 26(1) provides that:

> 'Where a person who is alleged to be a parent of the child with respect to whom an application for a maintenance calculation has been made ("the alleged parent") denies that he is one of the child's parents, the Secretary of State shall not make a maintenance calculation on the assumption that the alleged parent is one of the child's parents unless the case falls within one of those set out in subsection (2).'

The effect of this is that where subsection (2) does not apply, the application for the calculation may not proceed until the issue of paternity has been determined. However, where subsection (2) does apply, the protests of the alleged parent will fall on deaf ears, and the calculation will be made.

In the event of a calculation being made, and the issue of parentage being raised thereafter for the first time, it would seem that the calculation would remain in force. However, this is dealt with at para **6.6**.

6.4 Section 26(2) sets out the cases in which a calculation may be made notwithstanding a denial of paternity. They are as follows.

'CASE A1

Where –
(a) the child is habitually resident in England and Wales;
(b) the Secretary of State is satisfied that the alleged parent was married to the child's mother at some time in the period beginning with the conception and ending with the birth of the child; and
(c) the child has not been adopted.'

This is a new case added by the CSPSSA 2000. Here, it is sufficient for the alleged father to have been married to the mother at some time during the nine months ending with the birth; presumably, given the difficulty of establishing an exact date for conception, nine months before birth will be taken to be the date of conception.

'CASE A2

Where –
(a) the child is habitually resident in England and Wales;
(b) the alleged parent has been registered as father of the child under section 10 or 10A of the Births and Deaths Registration Act 1953, or in any register kept under section 13 (register of births and still-births) or section 44 (Register of Corrections Etc) of the Registration of Births, Deaths and Marriages (Scotland) Act 1965, or under Article 14 or 18(1)(b)(ii) of the Births and Deaths Registration (Northern Ireland) Order 1976; and
(c) the child has not subsequently been adopted.'

Another addition in the CSPSSA 2000; little comment is needed here. Registration as father raises a presumption of paternity.

'CASE A3

Where the result of a scientific test (within the meaning of section 27A) taken by the alleged parent would be relevant to determining the child's parent's parentage, and the alleged parent –
(a) refuses to take such a test; or
(b) has submitted to such a test, and it shows that there is no reasonable doubt that the alleged parent is a parent of the child.'

This too is a new case added by the CSPSSA 2000. The Secretary of State may, therefore, ask an alleged parent to take a test; presumably this could be based entirely on information received from the mother. If he refused to take the test, a maintenance calculation could be made. Paragraph (b) quite reasonably entitles the Secretary of State to follow the results of a test.

The procedure for testing, and the law thereon, is considered in more detail below.

'Case A

> Where the alleged parent is a parent of the child in question by virtue of having adopted him.'

This requires little comment. The production of the adoption order would be conclusive. By s 26(3), 'adopted' means adopted within the meaning of Part IV of the Adoption Act 1976, or, in relation to Scotland, Part IV of the Adoption (Scotland) Act 1978.

'Case B

> Where the alleged parent is a parent of the child in question by virtue of an order under section 30 of the Human Fertilisation and Embryology Act 1990 (parental orders in favour of gamete donors).'

For the general effect of the HFEA 1990 see Chapter Two at para **2.9**. Section 30 enables a married couple who have provided the genetic material which has led to the conception of the child to apply to the court for a so-called 'parental order' which will provide for the child in question to be treated in law as their child. Production of the court's order would be a necessary prerequisite for this case to be applied.

'Case B1

> Where the Secretary of State is satisfied that the alleged parent is a parent of the child in question by virtue of section 27 or 28 of that Act (meaning of "mother" and of "father" respectively).'

This is another new case added by the CSPSSA 2000. Reference should be made to Chapter Two at para **2.9** for further explanation of this point.

'Case C

> Where –
> (a) either –
> (i) a declaration that the alleged parent is a parent of the child in question (or a declaration which has that effect) is in force under section 56 of the Family Law Act 1986 (declarations of parentage); or
> (ii) a declarator by a court in Scotland that the alleged parent is a parent of the child in question (or a declarator which has that effect) is in force; and
> (b) the child has not subsequently been adopted.'

Section 56 of the Family Law Act 1986 (substituted by s 22 of the Family Law Reform Act 1987) deals with the right of an individual to apply to the court for a declaration that a named person is or was his parent or that he is the legitimate child of his parents. No one other than the 'child' can make the application; a parent cannot apply for a declaration in respect of his child.

'CASE D

Where –
(a) a declaration to the effect that the alleged parent is one of the parents of the child in question has been made under section 27; and
(b) the child has not subsequently been adopted.'

This prevents a non-resident parent from raising the issue of parentage more than once. Once the court has adjudicated as to paternity under s 27 (as to which see below) the issue cannot be raised again.

'CASE E

Where –
(a) the child is habitually resident in Scotland;
(b) the Secretary of State is satisfied that one or other of the presumptions set out in section 5(1) of the Law Reform (Parent and Child) (Scotland) Act 1986 applies; and
(c) the child has not subsequently been adopted.'

'CASE F

Where –
(a) the alleged parent has been found, or adjudged, to be the father of the child in question –
(i) in proceedings before any court in England and Wales which are relevant proceedings for the purposes of section 12 of the Civil Evidence Act 1968 or in proceedings before any court in Northern Ireland which are relevant proceedings for the purposes of section 8 of the Civil Evidence Act (Northern Ireland) 1971; or
(ii) in affiliation proceedings before any court in the United Kingdom,
(whether or not he offered any defence to the allegation of paternity) and that finding or adjudication still subsists; and
(b) the child has not subsequently been adopted.'

This requires little comment; the 1968 Act has been extended by the Courts and Legal Services Act 1990, Sch 16, para 2. The effect is, again, that once parentage has been determined by a competent court, the issue may not be re-opened.

6.5 It will be seen, therefore, that the class in s 26(2) are all cases where, in one way or another, a court order exists which governs the position as to parentage. The remedy of the non-resident parent in any of those cases who wished to continue to deny parentage could only be to appeal or to make some other application in the proceedings in which the order had been made.

3. Procedure

6.6 The procedure to be followed in the event of a dispute as to parentage which does not fall within s 26(2) is dictated by s 27. It provides that the Secretary of State or the person with care may apply to the court for a declaration as to whether an alleged parent is one of a child's parents in certain circumstances (s 27(1A)).

These circumstances are set out in s 27(1), which provides that s 27(1A) applies in any case where:

'(a) an application for a maintenance calculation has been made, or a maintenance calculation is in force, with respect to a person ("the alleged parent") who denies that he is a parent of a child with respect to whom the application or calculation was made; and

(b) the Secretary of State is not satisfied that the case falls within one of those set out in section 26(2).'

It will be seen that the Secretary of State may apply to the court even where a calculation has been made; the implication here is that the non-resident parent may not have denied parentage at the outset and only raised the issue at a subsequent time. On the other hand, this may be designed to cover the position where a calculation has been made with no co-operation from the non-resident parent.

The application to the court is not mandatory. The Secretary of State may apply, or leave it to the person with care to apply, or not apply at all. If the calculation had not yet been made, the Secretary of State could not proceed unless the application to the court were made (s 26(1)). However, if the calculation had been made, and the denial of parentage was made at a later stage, and the Secretary of State decided to do nothing, it would seem that the assessment would remain in force; there is no provision in the Act for a non-resident parent to apply to the court.

The only remedy of the non-resident parent would be to apply to the courts under other provisions, or to apply for judicial review.

6.7 Similar provisions to those set out above exist in relation to Scotland.

6.8 The effect of s 27(4) of the CSA 1991, Sch 11 to the CA 1989, and the Children (Allocation of Proceedings) (Amendment) Order 1993, SI 1993/624 is that the court to which the Secretary of State or person with care must apply is, in England and Wales, a magistrates' court. This follows the usual Children Act procedure; the magistrates' court may refer a case 'upwards' if appropriate.

The function of the court dealing with the matter is dealt with in s 27(2), which provides that:

> 'If, on hearing any application under subsection (1A), the court is satisfied that the alleged parent is, or is not, a parent of the child in question it shall make a declaration to that effect.'

By s 27(3), a declaration under this section shall have effect only for the purposes of the Act and proceedings in which a court is considering whether to make a maintenance order in the circumstances mentioned in s 8(6), (7) or (8). The s 8 cases are where the Act permits applications to the court of a 'top-up' or supplementary nature (see Chapter Ten).

6.9 Section 27A deals with the position as to fees for scientific tests. It applies in any case where:

'(a) an application for a maintenance calculation has been made or treated as made or a maintenance calculation is in force;

(b) scientific tests have been carried out (otherwise than under a direction or in response to a request) in relation to bodily samples obtained from a person who is alleged to be a parent of a child with respect to whom the application or calculation is made or, as the case may be, treated as made;

(c) the results of the tests do not exclude the alleged parent from being one of the child's parents; and
(d) one of the conditions set out in subsection (2) is satisfied.'

The conditions in subsection (2) are as follows:

'(a) the alleged parent does not deny that he is one of the child's parents;
(b) in proceedings under section 27, a court has made a declaration that the alleged parent is a parent of the child in question; or
(c) (*applies to Scotland only*).'

When these conditions are met, s 27A(3) applies, the result of which is that the Secretary of State may recover any fees paid for the tests from the alleged parent as a debt due to the Crown.

Most of this is self-explanatory; s 27A(4) contains definitions of the various terms used in the section.

The broad thrust of the provision is that an alleged parent who is found to be, or admits to being, a parent of a child after tests have been carried out will be liable for the cost of the tests.

6.10 The question of blood tests was considered by the Court of Appeal in *Re A (A Minor) (Paternity: Refusal of Blood Test)* [1994] 2 FLR 463. Although this was not a case under the CSA 1991, it is worthy of consideration in this context since it deals with matters common to all cases of disputed paternity. The court has to consider the implications of a putative father's refusal to submit to blood tests which had been ordered by the court.

The court held that all issues of paternity now fell to be resolved within the framework of the CA 1989 by the courts, which have statutory freedom to deal with the evidence at large and to reach their own determination as to the significance to be attached to a person's refusal to consent to scientific tests directed by the court under the amended s 20 of the Family Law Reform Act 1990. A man who was unsure of his own paternity had it within his power to set all doubt at rest by submitting to a test. Against that background of law and scientific advance, it followed in justice and common sense that if someone chose to exercise his right not to be tested, the inference that he was the father should be virtually inescapable. He would have to advance very clear and cogent reasons for his refusal to be tested.

In *Re H (Paternity: Blood Test)* [1996] 2 FLR 65 CA, it was held that a mother's adamant refusal to undergo blood testing for herself and a child was not, of itself, determinative of the issue of paternity. Accordingly, the court made a direction for blood tests despite the mother's refusal; an inference adverse to the refusing party could be drawn irrespective of whether the refusal was before or after the court's direction. The welfare of the child was not the paramount consideration. Every child had a right to know the truth about its parentage, unless his welfare clearly justified a cover-up.

The law as to testing with a view to ascertaining parentage has now been changed by amendments made to the Family Law Reform Act 1969 by the CSPSSA 2000. These came about largely as a result of the decision of Wall J in *Re O and J (Paternity: Blood Tests)* [2000] 1 FLR 418, where it was held that the person having care and control of a child has an absolute right to refuse to allow a sample of blood to be taken from the child for the purpose of determining paternity. Section 82(3) of the CSPSSA 2000 amends s 21 of the 1969 Act (which deals with consents required for the taking of blood samples) to add to the words 'if the person who has the care and control of him consents' the words 'or, (b) where that person does not consent, if the court considers that it would be in his best interests for the sample to be taken'.

The intentions of the legislature were explained by the Minister Mr Jeff Rooker as follows:

> 'A child will have a right to know who its parents are, and that is why taking a sample may be necessary. However, a court – and obviously not the child – will judge whether that is in the child's interests. . . . The amendment therefore focuses on the best interests of the child. In deciding whether to give a direction for tests to establish paternity the court will have the flexibility to distinguish between cases where establishing paternity is in the child's best interests and those where it might not be. It will be up to the court to make the decision.'[1]

1 Official Report (HC) 29 March 2000, cols 414 and 415.

CHAPTER SEVEN

Revisions

1. Introduction

7.1 The CSA 1991 contained quite complicated provisions for reviews (as they were then called). Reviews were always carried out by a child support officer and might result in an assessment (as it was then called) or refusal to make an assessment being altered. It might be a periodic review, or the means of the child support officer correcting an error, or it might be the first stage of an attack on a decision of the child support officer which could lead to an appeal.

These provisions were contained in ss 16 to 19 of the CSA 1991. These sections have now been changed in two ways. First, they were replaced by new ss 16 and 17 by virtue of the Social Security Act 1998, s 41. This introduced the term 'revision' in place of 'review' and created a simplified procedure in line with other aspects of social security. Secondly, ss 8 and 9 of the CSPSSA 2000 amend those provisions. The position is now, therefore, entirely different from the pre-1998 position.

2. Revision of Decisions

7.2 The new s 16(1A) sets out the decisions to which s 16 applies. They include:

> '(a) a decision of the Secretary of State under section 11, 12 or 17',

which are any decisions relating to maintenance calculations or default and interim calculations, or any decision made which supersedes an earlier decision (as to which, see para **7.6**). There is one specific provision relating to default maintenance decisions under s 12(1)(b). When the Secretary of State revises such a decision pursuant to s 16, he may (if appropriate) do so as if he were revising a decision under s 11 (a 'full' maintenance calculation); if he does so, his decision as revised is to be treated as one under s 11 rather than s 12 (in particular, for purposes of appeal).[1]

> '(b) a reduced benefit decision under section 46;'.

This is self-explanatory.

> '(c) a decision of an appeal tribunal on a referral under section 28D(1)(b).'

As will be seen when appeals are considered in Chapter Eight, s 28D(1)(b) applies where an application for what used to be called a departure direction and is now called a variation is referred by the Secretary of State rather than it being dealt with by him.

---

1 CSA 1991, s 16(1B).

7.3 In effect, s 16 enables the Secretary of State to revise, that is to say, change or modify, any of the decisions which fall within the section. He may do so either within a prescribed period or in prescribed cases or circumstances.[2] He may do so either on an application made by anyone entitled to apply or of his own initiative.[3]

It is provided that regulations may prescribe the procedure by which a decision may be so revised; no doubt new regulations will be made to come into force at the same time as the CSPSSA 2000, but some guidance can be gained from the existing regulations[4] as they were after amendment in 1999 to take account of the 1998 statutory changes.

7.4 In the regulations, revision of decisions is governed by CS(MAP)Regs 1992, reg 17. Any decision may be revised where either application is made within one month of the date of notification of the decision (for late applications see below), the decision arose from official error, the original decision was erroneous due to misrepresentation, or where the Secretary of State commences action leading to revision within one month.[5] An interim (now to be called default) decision may be revised where the Secretary of State receives information which enables him to make a full maintenance assessment (now to be called a calculation) or where the Secretary of State is satisfied that there was unavoidable delay by the non-resident parent in returning the forms or supplying information.[6]

However, reg 17(1) shall not apply (ie there can be no revision under this regulation) where there has been or is likely to be a material change of circumstances since the decision, nor where an appeal against a decision, has been brought but not determined and a revision of the decision would be less to the advantage of the appellant than the original decision. [7]

7.5 Late applications are governed by reg 18. Any application for an extension of time must be made within 13 months from the notification of the decision, and must contain particulars of the grounds on which the extension is sought.[8] Extension shall not be granted unless the applicant satisfies the Secretary of State that it is reasonable to do so, the application has merit, and special circumstances are relevant to the application.[9] The greater the time between the expiration of one month from notification and the date of the application, the more compelling must be the special circumstances.[10] No account may be taken of any ignorance of law or procedure, nor of the fact that a Child Support Commissioner may have taken a different view of the law from that previously understood and applied.[11]

2 CSA 1991, s 16(1)(a).
3 Ibid, s 16(1)(b).
4 CS(MAP)Regs 1992, SI 1992/1813 (as amended).
5 Ibid, reg 17(1).
6 Ibid, reg 17(3).
7 Ibid, reg 17(6).
8 Ibid, reg 18(3).
9 Ibid, reg 18(4).
10 Ibid, reg 18(5).
11 Ibid, reg 18(6).

3. Decisions Superseding Earlier Decisions

7.6 Section 17 of the CSA 1991 makes provision for certain decisions to be superseded; the difference between revising and superseding would seem to be that the latter substitutes a completely new decision for the previous decision rather than merely changing it.

The decisions which may be superseded under s 17 are:

> '(a) any decision of the Secretary of State under section 11 or 12 or [s 17], whether as originally made or as revised under section 16;'[12]

This covers any decision involving a maintenance calculation or interim or default calculation or any decision made under s 17 superseding such a decision.

> '(b) any decision of an appeal tribunal under section 20;'[13]

The Secretary of State may, therefore, make a decision replacing the decision of an appeal tribunal.

> '(c) any reduced benefit direction under section 46;
> (d) any decision of an appeal tribunal on a referral under section 28D(1)(b);
> (e) any decision of a Child Support Commissioner on an appeal from such a decision as is mentioned in paragraph (b) or (d).'[14]

This is self-explanatory.

7.7 The Secretary of State may make a decision under any of the above either on an application made by any person entitled to apply or on his own initiative.[15] He need not consider any issue that is not raised by the application or, as the case may be, did not cause him to act on his own initiative.[16]

Regulations will prescribe the circumstances in which this jurisdiction may be exercised and the procedure to be adopted. Once again, it must be said that there will, no doubt, be new regulations in due course, but the present regulations probably give some guidance. It is provided[17] that a decision may be superseded by the Secretary of State on his own initiative where he is satisfied that there has been a material change of circumstances, or that the decision was made in ignorance of or was based on a mistake as to some material fact, or in consequence of a departure direction (now to be called a variation). A decision may also be superseded by the Secretary of State acting on his own initiative or on application where he is satisfied that the decision was erroneous in point of law.[18] The other cases where a decision may be superseded depend on an application by a person affected by the decision. A decision may be superseded on the ground that there has been or is likely to be a material change of circumstances

---

12 CSA 1991, s 17(1)(a).
13 Ibid, s 17(1)(b).
14 Ibid, s 17(1)(e).
15 Ibid, s 17(1).
16 Ibid, s 17(2).
17 By CS(MAP)Regs 1992, reg 20(2).
18 Ibid, reg 20(4) and (5).

since the decision was made and the Secretary of State is satisfied that the change of circumstances is or would be material.[19]

A decision may not be superseded where the monetary difference between the original decision and any superseding decision would be less than £10 per week. However, this does not apply where there is a protected income calculation and the amount fixed by the original decision is less than the amount that would be fixed by a superseding decision and the difference is less than £5 per week, nor where the non-resident parent has no assessable income.[20]

The question of the dates from which a decision is superseded is governed by reg 23.

19 CS(MAP)Regs 1992, reg 20(3).
20 Ibid, reg 21.

CHAPTER EIGHT

Appeals and Judicial Review

1. Introduction

8.1 As was seen in Chapter Seven, the normal first step for anyone aggrieved by a decision of the Secretary of State is an application for revision. Where the right to appeal exists, the first appellate tribunal is the appeal tribunal. From there, in certain cases, appeal lies to the Child Support Commissioner and thence, with permission, and on a point of law only, to the Court of Appeal.

Appeals as to disputed parentage are to the courts. Finally, although not an appeal as such, some decisions of the Secretary of State may be challenged by way of judicial review.

These possibilities will now be considered in turn. It should be noted that the system of appeals has changed quite radically since 1991, first as a result of changes in 1999 which affected all social security appeals, and now as a result of further changes effected by the CSPSSA 2000.

2. Appeal to an Appeal Tribunal

8.2 An appeal tribunal determining a misconceived appeal as a preliminary issue consists of one legally qualified panel member.[1] Otherwise, it must consist of one legally qualified member and one financially qualified member.[2] Each tribunal must have a clerk.

The right of appeal is restricted to 'a qualifying person',[3] defined[4] in different ways according to the type of appeal. The decisions in respect of which a right of appeal exists, and the persons who may appeal in each case, are as shown in the table below.

These provisions are clear enough. Sections 11 and 12 cover all maintenance calculations and this therefore provides a right of appeal against all such matters. Reduced benefit directions are dealt with in more detail in Chapter Two at para **2.14**. It should be noted, however, that no appeal will lie in respect of a reduced benefit direction unless the amount of the person's benefit is reduced in

1 Social Security and Child Support (Decisions and Appeals) Regulations 1999, SI 1999/991, reg 36(1).

2 Ibid, reg 36(3).

3 CSA 1991, s 20(1).

4 By ibid, s 20(2).

Type of appeal[5]	*Who may appeal*[6]
Decision under ss 11, 12, or 17 (whether as originally made or as revised under s 16)	The person with care or non-resident parent with respect to whom the decision was made
Decision not to make a maintenance calculation under s 11 or not to supersede a decision under s 17	Ditto
Reduced benefit decision	The person in respect of whom the benefits are payable
The imposition (under s 14A) of a requirement to make penalty payments, or their amount	The parent who has been required to make penalty payments
The imposition (under s 47) of a requirement to pay fees	The person required to pay fees

accordance with the reduced benefit direction.[7] This presumably covers the possibility that the Secretary of State might wish to make a reduced benefit direction but be prevented from doing so by one of the 'prescribed circumstances' under s 46(5). A person who was aggrieved by the principle, but who had suffered no loss, would not be able to appeal.

8.3 It is provided[8] that in deciding any appeal the tribunal need not consider any issue that is not raised by the appeal, and may not take into account any circumstances not obtaining at the time when the Secretary of State made the decision or imposed the requirement. The latter point means, clearly, that if the case is one where there might have been an application for revision, that is the remedy which should be sought rather than appeal.

If an appeal is allowed, the tribunal may either itself make such decision as it considers appropriate or remit the case to the Secretary of State with such directions (if any) as it considers appropriate.[9]

3. Procedural Matters

8.4 Procedure is now governed by the Social Security and Child Support (Decisions and Appeals) Regulations 1999, SI 1999/991, and the parts of those regulations which apply to child support appeals are regs 30 to 58. The most important parts are as follows.

5 See CSA 1991, s 20(1).
6 See ibid, s 20(2).
7 Ibid, s 20(6).
8 By ibid, s 20(7).
9 Ibid, s 20(8).

(a) The notice

An appeal, or an application for an extension of time, must be in writing either on a form approved for the purpose by the Secretary of State or in such other form as may be accepted as sufficient for the purpose by him. It must be signed by either the person who has the right of appeal or a person who has written authority to act as their representative, contain particulars of the grounds on which it is made, and contain sufficient particulars of the decision appealed against to enable it to be identified (reg 33(1)).

(b) Service of the notice

The notice must be sent to 'an appropriate office' (reg 33(1)), defined as an office of the CSA (reg 33(2)(d)).

(c) Time-limits

The appeal must be brought within one month of the date of notification of the decision against which the appeal is brought, or, where a written statement of reasons for that decision is requested, within 14 days of the expiry of one month from notification of the decision (reg 31(1)). Disputes as to whether an appeal was brought within time must be referred to a legally qualified panel member (reg 31(4)).

(d) Late appeals

The time for appeal may be extended but no appeal may be brought more than one year after the time has expired (reg 32(1)). The procedure for giving notice is that set out under reg 33 (see ***(a)*** above). Any such application is determined by a legally qualified panel member. The panel member must be satisfied that if the application is granted there are reasonable prospects of success that the appeal will be successful and that it is in the interests of justice for the application to be granted (reg 32(4)). However, it cannot be found that it is in the interests of justice for the application to be granted unless either certain defined special circumstances exist or some other special circumstances exist which are wholly exceptional and relevant to the application, and as a result of those special circumstances it was not practicable for the application to be made within the time-limits (reg 32(5)).

The defined special circumstances are that the applicant or a spouse or dependant of the applicant has died or suffered serious illness, or that the applicant is not resident in the United Kingdom, or that normal postal services were disrupted (reg 32(6)). In determining whether it is in the interests of justice to grant the application, the principle to be observed is, in effect, that the greater the delay the more compelling must be the special circumstances (reg 32(7)). No account may be taken of ignorance or misunderstanding of the law nor of the fact that a Commissioner or a court has taken a different view of the law from that previously understood or applied (reg 32(8)).

(e) Further information

Where an application or appeal is made by letter and not on a prescribed form, and does not contain sufficient information, the Secretary of State may request further particulars (reg 33(6)).

(f) Directions

A legally qualified panel member may give directions at any stage, either of his own motion or at the request of one of the parties (reg 38(2)).

(g) Dispensing with hearings

The clerk to an appeal tribunal will direct the appellant and any other party to notify him in writing whether he wishes to have an oral hearing or whether he is content to proceed without an oral hearing (reg 39(1)). If the appellant does respond within 14 days the appeal may be struck out (reg 39(2)). Where a party requests an oral hearing there must be an oral hearing (reg 39(4)).

(h) Summoning of witnesses

A chairman of an appeal tribunal may by summons require any person in Great Britain to attend as a witness at a hearing to answer any questions or produce any documents in his custody or under his control. Fourteen days' notice is required (except where the witness agrees) and conduct money must be paid (reg 43(1)). No person may be compelled to give evidence or produce documents which he could not be compelled to give or produce in court proceedings (reg 43(2)). The chairman must take into account the need to protect matter relating to intimate personal or financial circumstances, which is commercially sensitive, or concerns national security (reg 43(3)).

(i) Oral hearings

Oral hearings must be in public unless the appellant requests a private hearing or the chairman is satisfied that intimate personal or financial circumstances may have to be disclosed or considerations of national security are involved (reg 49(5)). A chairman may require evidence to be given on oath (reg 43(5)). Any party to the proceedings is entitled to be present and to be heard (reg 49(7)). He may also call evidence, address the tribunal and put questions to any party (reg 49(11)).

(j) Misconceived appeals

A misconceived appeal may be struck out by a legally qualified member but not before the appellant has been given notice (reg 46(4)). An appellant to whom such notice is given may, within 14 days thereafter, request an oral hearing (reg 48(1)).

4. Appeal to Child Support Commissioners

8.5 Any person who is aggrieved by a decision of an appeal tribunal, and the Secretary of State (who, presumably, does not have to feel aggrieved), may appeal to a Child Support Commissioner on a question of law.[10] No such appeal may be brought without the leave of the person who was the chairman of, or constituted, the appeal tribunal (or such other person as may be determined by regulations) or a Child Support Commissioner.[11]

---

10 CSA 1991, s 24(1).

11 Ibid, s 24(6).

Before the question of leave is considered, the new s 23A should be mentioned. This applies where an application is made for leave and the person who constituted or was the chairman of the appeal tribunal considers that the decision was erroneous in law. In such circumstances, he may set aside the decision and refer the case either for redetermination by the tribunal or for determination by a differently constituted tribunal.[12] An unnecessary appeal to the Commissioner may, therefore, be avoided.

However, the section goes further. Where 'each of the principal parties to the case' (defined[13] as the Secretary of State and those who are qualifying persons under s 20(2) in relation to the decision) expresses the view that the decision was erroneous in point of law, the person to whom the application for leave is made must set aside the decision and refer the case for determination by a differently constituted tribunal.[14]

8.6 The Commissioner must set aside the decision in question if he holds that it was wrong in law.[15] He may then either give the decision which should have been given, make such findings and give such decision as he considers appropriate, (on an appeal by the Secretary of State) refer the case to an appeal tribunal with directions for its redetermination, or (in other cases) refer to the Secretary of State or an appeal tribunal with directions for redetermination.[16]

8.7 Sections 28ZA to 28ZB contain provisions concerning appeals which involve issues arising on other appeals. They are complicated and of marginal interest to most family lawyers, but their existence should be noted.

8.8 The relevant regulations are contained in the Child Support Commissioners (Procedure) Regulations 1992 (CSC(P)Regs 1992), SI 1992/2640, the most important of which are as follows.

(a) Time-limits for application for leave

An application for leave to appeal must be made:

(i) in the case of application to a tribunal chairman, within three months of the date on which notice of the decision was sent to the applicant; or
(ii) in the case of application to a Commissioner, within 42 days of the date of sending notice of the chairman's refusal of leave (reg 2(1)).

(b) To whom is application for leave made?

Application must be made to the chairman of the tribunal which made the decision under appeal (s 24(6)(a) and reg 2(1)). Where it would cause undue delay, or be impracticable for the application to be made to that chairman, the application may be determined by any other chairman (reg 2(2)).

An application for leave to appeal may be made to a Commissioner only where the applicant has been refused leave to appeal by a tribunal chairman

12 CSA 1991, s 23A(2).
13 By ibid, s 23A(4).
14 Ibid, s 23A(3).
15 Ibid, s 24(2).
16 Ibid, s 24(3).

(reg 2(3)); however, where there has been failure to apply to the chairman in time or at all, an application may be made to a Commissioner who may accept and deal with it 'for special reasons' if he thinks fit (reg 2(4)); such an application may be made outside the period of 42 days, for special reasons (reg 2(5)).

(c) The notice

Application for leave must be by notice in writing to the clerk to the tribunal at the Central Office. It must contain:

(i) the name and address of the applicant;
(ii) the ground on which the applicant intends to rely;
(iii) the applicant's address for service;
(iv) when the applicant is to be represented by someone who is not a barrister or solicitor, the written authority of that person to represent him;
(v) the notice must have annexed to it a copy of the decision against which leave to appeal is sought. Where a chairman has refused leave, a copy of that decision must also be annexed, and the date on which notice of refusal was given must be stated. In the case of a late application, the reasons for delay must be stated (reg 3).

(d) Determination of application

A chairman will give a written determination which will be served on all parties (reg 4(1)). When a Commissioner grants leave, he may, with the consent of all parties, treat and determine any question arising as if it were a question arising on an appeal (reg 4(3)).

(e) Notice of appeal

Once leave to appeal has been granted, the appeal itself is by way of notice to a Commissioner, and the notice must contain:

(i) the name and address of the appellant;
(ii) the date on which leave to appeal was granted;
(iii) the ground on which the appellant intends to rely;
(iv) the appellant's address for service.

The notice must have annexed to it a copy of the determination granting leave to appeal and a copy of the decision appealed against (reg 5).

(f) Time-limit for appeal

The time-limit for appeal is 42 days from the date on which the applicant was given notice in writing that leave to appeal was granted (reg 6(2)). However, a Commissioner may accept a notice of appeal served after the expiry of 42 days if for special reasons he thinks fit (reg 6(2)).

(g) Directions

As soon as practicable after receipt of notice of appeal, a Commissioner must give such directions as appear necessary, specifying:

(i) the parties who are to be respondents to the appeal; and
(ii) the order in which and the time (not less than 30 days) within which any party is to be allowed to make written observations.

Where two or more parties appeal, the Commissioner will direct which of these is to be treated as appellant (reg 7). At any stage, a Commissioner of his own motion, or on application, may require any party to furnish such further particulars as may be reasonably required, or give such directions as may be necessary for the efficient and effective despatch of the proceedings. He may also direct any party to make such written representations as seem necessary. A party seeking a direction must do so in writing to the Commissioner (reg 10).

(h) Oral hearings

A Commissioner may determine any appeal, or application for leave to appeal, without an oral hearing (reg 11(1)). However, any party may request an oral hearing, and the Commissioner must grant such request unless he is satisfied that he can properly determine the appeal or application without a hearing. In that event, he must inform the party concerned, in writing, that the request for a hearing has been refused. He may then determine the matter. He may direct an oral hearing of his own motion (reg 11). Oral hearings are in public, unless otherwise directed, and all parties may attend and address the Commissioner. With the leave of the Commissioner, but not otherwise, they may give evidence, call witnesses, and question other witnesses (reg 13). A Commissioner may summon any person to attend or produce documents on not less than seven days' notice (reg 14).

(i) Decisions

Decisions of Commissioners are in writing. They may be set aside, under reg 20, on grounds similar to those in reg 15 of the Child Support Appeal Tribunals (Procedure) Regulations 1992 (CSAT(P)Regs 1992), SI 1992/2641.

8.9 Paragraph 4A of Sch 4 to the CSA 1991 permits authorised officers, who are not Commissioners, to determine any questions which are determinable by a Commissioner and which do not include the determination of any appeal, application for leave to appeal, or reference. The detail is contained in reg 23A of the CSC(P)Regs 1992, which, in effect, delegate to 'nominated officers' (ie an officer authorised by the Lord Chancellor or, in Scotland, the Secretary of State) functions which may be summarised as follows:

- giving directions on notice of appeal, or any other directions;
- granting leave to Secretary of State to intervene;
- making orders for oral hearings;
- summoning witnesses;
- ordering the postponement of oral hearings;
- giving leave to withdraw;
- extending or abridging time.

Any party may, within 10 days of receiving notice of such a decision, request a Commissioner to consider and confirm or replace the decision.

8.10 Child support law is, essentially, social security law, and the structure of review, appeal to tribunal and thence to Commissioners is the same as in social security appeals; indeed, the individuals who sit as Child Support Commissioners are normally also Social Security Commissioners. It may, therefore, be helpful to consider two decisions of Commissioners in the field of social security law which indicate the approach of Commissioners to their task.

In R(A)1/72 it was held that a decision was wrong in law if:

(a) it contained a false proposition of law on its face;
(b) it was supported by no evidence;
(c) the facts found were such that no person acting judicially and properly instructed as to the relevant law could have come to the determination in question.

Another decision, CSB29/81 cites R(I)14/75 as adding further grounds, namely breach of the requirements of natural justice and failure to state adequate reasons.

8.11 Section 24(2) provides that where, on an appeal under that section, a Child Support Commissioner holds that the decision appealed against was wrong in law he shall set it aside. If the decision is set aside, the Commissioner may adopt one of the four courses of action set out in s 24(3):

'(a) if he can do so without making fresh or further findings of fact, give the decision which he considers should have been given by the appeal tribunal;
(b) if he considers it expedient, make such findings and give such decision as he considers appropriate in the light of those findings; or
(c) on an appeal by the Secretary of State, refer the case to an appeal tribunal with directions for its determination; or
(d) on any other appeal, refer the case to the Secretary of State or, if he considers it appropriate, to an appeal tribunal with directions for its determination.'

When the Commissioner refers back to the Secretary of State, this must, subject to any direction of the Commissioner, be to one of his officers, or a person providing him with services, who has taken no part in the decision originally appealed against (s 24(4)), and when the matter is referred to an appeal tribunal, this must consist of persons who were not members of the tribunal which gave the decision which has been appealed against (s 24(5)).

5. Appeal from the Child Support Commissioner

8.12 The final stage of the appeal procedure provided by the CSA 1991 lies from the Child Support Commissioner, but only on a point of law.

Section 25(1) provides that an appeal on a question of law shall lie to the appropriate court from any decision of a Child Support Commissioner. 'Appropriate court' is defined by s 25(4) as either the Court of Appeal or the Court of Session depending on the circumstances of the case and, in particular, the convenience of the parties to the appeal.

8.13 By s 25(2), no appeal may be brought except:

'(a) with leave of the Child Support Commissioner who gave the decision or, where regulations made by the Lord Chancellor so provide, of a Child Support Commissioner selected in accordance with the regulations; or

(b) if the Child Support Commissioner refuses leave, with the leave of the appropriate court.'

The first application for leave must, therefore, always be to the Commissioner.

The parties who may apply for leave to appeal are specified in s 25(3); they are confined to:

'(a) a person who was a party to the proceedings in which the original decision, or appeal decision, was given;
(b) the Secretary of State; or
(c) any other person who is authorised to do so by regulations made by the Lord Chancellor.'

The reference to 'the original decision' means that a person cannot stand by and allow an appeal to reach this stage and then decide to join in. He must, at the very least, have been involved in the appeal procedure at the appeal tribunal stage.

8.14 The regulations governing these matters are contained in reg 25 of the CSC(P)Regs 1992. An application to a Commissioner under s 25 must be in writing and must be made within three months from the date on which the applicant was given notice of the decision. Where the Chief Child Support Commissioner decides that it is impracticable or would cause undue delay for the same Commissioner to determine the application for leave, a different Comissioner, or Tribunal of Commissioners, as the case may be, may determine the application.

8.15 The appeal to the Court of Appeal or Court of Session will follow the normal procedures for such appeals, which lie outside the scope of this book.

6. Appeals as to Parentage

8.16 As was seen in Chapter Seven, where a non-resident parent denies parentage at an early stage, the Secretary of State may not proceed to make an assessment except in certain specified cases; the issue of parentage has to be referred to a court for an adjudication.

It may be, however, that an assessment is made before the absent parent decides to raise the issue. In such a case, he would have to seek a revision under s 18. Normally, the next stage in the appeal process would be to the appeal tribunal, but there are special provisions for appeals as to parentage.

Section 45(1) of the CSA 1991 provides that the Lord Chancellor, or, in Scotland, the Lord Advocate, may by order make provision for certain appeals to be made to a court instead of an appeal tribunal. This provision is contained in the Child Support Appeals (Jurisdiction of Courts) Order 1993 (CSA(JOC) Order 1993), SI 1993/961, which provides for appeals under s 20 to go to a court instead of an appeal tribunal, where the issue involved is whether a particular person is a parent of the child. No such order has been made, so that there is at present no right of appeal from such a decision.

'Court' means a magistrates' court; the Children Act system applies, so that there can be a transfer to a higher court, where appropriate.

7. Judicial Review

8.17 Although judicial review is not available as a routine method of challenging decisions of the Secretary of State or an appeal tribunal, it should be considered in certain cases. Before such cases are examined, the nature of judicial review must be briefly explained, with the warning that, as this is not a textbook on administrative law, the explanation is of the most basic nature.

Before 1977, a challenge to the actions of public authorities was made by one of the prerogative writs of certiorari, prohibition or mandamus. In 1977 this was changed by means of a radical revision of procedure and the substitution of a new Ord 53 of the RSC 1965, SI 1965/1776. This created a new procedure called an 'application for judicial review', under which it is unnecessary to select any one of the prerogative remedies. This procedure is designed to enable the High Court to exercise its powers to supervise the proceedings and decisions of, inter alia, public bodies and tribunals in a flexible and uniform manner. The procedure for judicial review is now governed by the Civil Procedure Rules 1998, Part 54 and the accompanying Practice Direction.

Applications for judicial review must be made promptly and, in any event, within three months of the act or omission complained of. Application for leave is made to a single judge, normally without a hearing. If the application is renewed, it may be made to a single judge in open court.

8.18 It is important to note that judicial review is concerned with the decision-making process, not the decision itself (*Chief Constable of North Wales Police v Evans* [1982] 1 WLR 1155, HL). Provided the procedures have been properly employed, judicial review cannot be employed as a method of appeal against the substantive decision. Judicial review is therefore limited to ensuring that the person or body in question has acted within its powers and that the rules of natural justice have not been breached.

Furthermore, judicial review will not normally be granted where there is another avenue of appeal. Save in the most exceptional cases, the jurisdiction to grant judicial review will not be exercised where other remedies are available (*R v Epping and Harlow General Commissioners, ex parte Goldstraw* [1983] 3 All ER 257).

Until 1980, the only way to challenge the decision of a Social Security Commissioner was by way of judicial review. In 1980 this was changed, and the right of appeal to the Court of Appeal, or, in Scotland, the Court of Session, was introduced. As has been seen, this right exists in CSA 1991 cases.

An allegation that the rules of natural justice had not been observed would be an allegation that a particular decision was 'wrong in law', and would, therefore, justify an application for review and thence to the appeal tribunal.

It might seem, therefore, that the occasions on which there could be an application for judicial review are limited.

8.19 However, this must be seen in the light of the 'welfare principle'. As was seen in Chapter One, s 2 of the CSA 1991 provides that:

> 'Where, in any case which falls to be dealt with under this Act, the Secretary of State is considering the exercise of any discretionary power conferred by this Act, he shall have regard to the welfare of any child likely to be affected by his decision.'

This section was considered by Thorpe J in *R v Secretary of State for Social Security, ex parte Biggin* [1995] 1 FLR 851. In this case, a father appealed to the Family Division against the dismissal by magistrates of his appeal against a deduction from earnings order made under the CSA 1991. His principal ground of complaint had been that the justices had failed to consider the welfare principle in dealing with the case. The Secretary of State contended that any assertion that a duty under s 2 had not been observed was a public law question open to judicial review and confined to the High Court. Thorpe J agreed; it was quite clear that the remedy for a breach of duty under s 2 was to apply to the Divisional Court, and not to the justices.

8.20 This decision makes clear the type of case which may form the basis of an application for judicial review. There are many occasions on which the Secretary of State has to exercise discretion. The most important may be summarised as decisions whether to:

(a) arrange for the collection and enforcement of maintenance (s 4(2) and (3));
(b) require a person with care to give the authorisation to apply for a maintenance calculation (s 6(2));
(c) make a default calculation (s 12(1));
(d) make a fresh calculation (s 19);
(e) arrange for the collection of child support maintenance (s 29(1));
(f) collect and enforce other forms of maintenance, and how sums should be allocated (s 30(1) and (3)(c));
(g) make a deduction from earnings order (s 31(2));
(h) apply to magistrates for a liability order (s 32(2));
(i) enforce a liability order by distress (s 35(1));
(j) apply to magistrates for commitment to prison (s 40);
(k) give a reduced benefit direction (s 46(5)).

Not all these decisions are automatically susceptible to judicial review. It is only where the person aggrieved alleges a failure to observe the welfare principle that this will be the case. It will be noted that the section refers to 'any child likely to be affected'; it is not limited to qualifying children. It could apply, for example, to the children of a non-resident parent's cohabitant.

CHAPTER NINE

Collection and Enforcement

1. The Role of the Agency

9.1 The function of the CSA is to 'bring together in one organisation all matters to do with the assessment, collection and enforcement of child maintenance in the great majority of cases' (Mr Tony Newton, then Secretary of State for Social Services, *Hansard* vol 192, para 179). Assessment (now calculation) has already been considered in earlier chapters; the role of the Agency in collection and enforcement must now be considered.

As is often the case, the role of the CSA with respect to collection will depend on whether or not the person with care is in receipt of benefit. Under s 6(1) of the CSA 1991, a person receiving certain benefits must authorise the Secretary of State to recover child support maintenance from the non-resident parent; she has no choice. In the case of a non-benefit matter, under s 4(1), a person with care may apply to the Secretary of State for a maintenance calculation, and, by s 4(2), may request that the Secretary of State arrange for the collection of the child support maintenance in accordance with the calculation, and the enforcement of the obligation to pay. In the case of the person not receiving benefit, therefore, there is a choice as to whether the CSA deals with the collection, or whether a private arrangement is made. However, only the CSA may enforce a calculation.

Where a calculation has been made under s 4(1), the CSA will accept a request to collect in all cases.

9.2 The details as to collection are set out in part 2 below. Enforcement is dealt with in parts 3 et seq below, and it will be seen that the modes of enforcement available to the Secretary of State are as follows:

(a) deduction from earnings order;
(b) liability order;
(c) distress;
(d) county court enforcement;
(e) imprisonment and disqualification from driving.

It must be emphasised that the Secretary of State is limited to the methods of enforcement authorised by the Act. In *Department of Social Security v Butler* [1996] 1 FLR 65, CA, the Secretary of State applied to the court for a *Mareva* injunction to restrain a non-resident parent, who owed large arrears of child support maintenance, from disposing of the proceeds of sale of a former matrimonial home which he had received from his solicitors. The judge refused this application, and the Court of Appeal upheld that decision. The CSA 1991 provided a detailed code for the collection of payments due under maintenance calculations. The duty under s 1(3) is not expressed as a civil debt, and may not be enforced by any means in a civil court, save as provided by the Act. Even if the court had jurisdiction, an injunction should not be ordered except in unusual and compelling cases; the DSS had ample powers to prevent arrears from accruing.

The remedies available to the Secretary of State will be considered in turn.

2. Collection

9.3 By s 29(2) of the CSA 1991, the Secretary of State may make regulations to govern how payments should be made. These regulations are contained in Part II of the Child Support (Collection and Enforcement) Regulations 1992 (CS(CE) Regs 1992), SI 1992/1889, the effect of which may be summarised as follows:

(a) the Secretary of State may specify to whom payments are to be made, for example to the person with care, to himself or to another person (reg 2(1));
(b) payment must be made by whatever method the Secretary of State specifies as appropriate, for example standing order, direct debit, cheque or postal order or cash. He may direct a liable person to take all reasonable steps to open an account from which payments can be made (reg 3);
(c) the Secretary of State shall specify the day and the interval (ie weekly, monthly etc) of payment, and may from time to time vary such interval. In so doing he must have regard to the needs of the person entitled to receive payment, when the liable person's income is normally received and any period necessary for the clearance of cheques (reg 4);
(d) the Secretary of State must, so far as is reasonably practicable, provide the liable person and the person entitled to receive payments with an opportunity to make representations about all the above matters, and must have regard to such representations when exercising his powers (reg 6);
(e) the Secretary of State must send the liable person a notice stating the amount of child support maintenance, to whom it must be paid, the method of payment and the day and interval of payment as soon as is reasonably practicable after the making of a maintenance calculation or any change in requirements (reg 7).

All this shows that the CSA enjoys very wide powers to control how payments are to be made.

9.4 The CSA also has the power to collect payments of maintenance other than child support maintenance in certain circumstances. The power derives from s 30(1) of the CSA 1991, which provides that when the Secretary of State is arranging for the collection of any payments under a maintenance calculation he may also arrange for the collection of periodical payments and secured periodical payments of a prescribed kind, and s 30(2), which makes similar provision for cases in which the Secretary of State is not collecting payments under a maintenance calculation.

The current regulations made under s 30 are the Child Support (Collection and Enforcement of other Forms of Maintenance) Regulations 1992 (CS (CEOFM)Regs 1992); by reg 2, the periodical payments and categories of person prescribed are as follows:

(a) payments under a maintenance order made in relation to a child in accordance with the provisions of:
   - s 8(6) (top-up orders);
   - s 8(7) (expenses for instruction or training);
   - s 8(8) (expenses due to disability);

(b) any periodical payments under a maintenance order which are payable to or for the benefit of a spouse or former spouse who is the person with care of a qualifying child in respect of whom a maintenance calculation is in force and the Secretary of State has arranged for its collection under s 29;

(c) any periodical payments under a maintenance order payable to, or for the benefit of a former child of the family of the person against whom the order is made, that child having his home with the person with care.

9.5 The classes of orders set out in (a) are clear enough; they are part of the structure of the Act. In theory, it would be possible in the other two cases for the Secretary of State to collect maintenance due under a court order when there was no maintenance calculation. However, the Secretary of State has a discretion as to whether or not to collect, and he might choose not to do so where there was no calculation. Paragraph (b) relates to the collection of spousal maintenance where there is also a calculation. Paragraph (c) extends this to collection of maintenance due in respect of non-qualifying children where there is a calculation.

3. Enforcement by Deduction from Earnings Order

9.6 Attachment of earnings is a well-known and much used process for enforcing payment of judgments and orders in England and Wales. Such orders are obtained in county courts under the provisions of the Attachment of Earnings Act 1971. The order stipulates a 'normal deduction rate', ie the weekly or monthly sum to be deducted by the employer from the debtor's earnings, and a 'protected earnings rate', ie the sum, calculated by reference to income support rates, below which the debtor's income must not be allowed to fall.

It is important to note that deduction from earnings orders under the CSA 1991 are not the same as attachment of earnings orders made by the court. They are a discrete form of enforcement arising only under this Act. Moreover, the order is made by an administrative agency (the Secretary of State) and not a court.

9.7 The statutory power to make a deduction from earnings order derives from s 31(2) of the CSA 1991, which provides that the Secretary of State may make a deduction from earnings order to secure the payment of any amount due under the maintenance calculation in question. Section 31(3) provides that such an order may be made to secure the payment of arrears of child support maintenance and amounts which will become due under the calculation.

It is not necessary to wait for arrears to accrue. The Secretary of State would be entitled to use deduction from earnings as a routine method of enforcement if he so chose. However, the general policy, as revealed in the DSS handbook 'Notes to Advisers' is that this method of enforcement will be used only in limited circumstances where other forms of enforcement have failed.

9.8 The remainder of ss 31 and 32 deal with routine matters, the detail of which emerges in the regulations. These are currently contained in Part III of the CS(CE)Regs 1992, the most important parts of which are as follows.

(a) 'Earnings' are defined by reg 8(1), (3) and (4); the term includes wages, overtime and emoluments payable under a contract of service, private pensions, compensation for loss of office, and statutory sick pay. It does not include pay from HM Forces (although the Crown, generally, is not exempt), or pensions or benefits payable under any social security enactment.
(b) By reg 9, an order must specify, inter alia, a protected earnings rate and a normal deduction rate. These terms bear the same meanings as in the Attachment of Earnings Act 1971 (regs 11 and 19) with two exceptions: first, the protected earnings rate must be the same as the liable person's exempt income calculated at the time of the assessment; secondly, the requirement to specify a protected earnings rate is different when the order is in respect of an interim calculation. Here, the protected earnings rate is calculated in accordance with reg 11(3) and (4), which has to take account of the fact that not a lot may be known about the non-resident parent's means.
(c) By reg 12(6), an employer may deduct a sum not exceeding £1 in respect of his administrative costs. However, this sum is to be collected from the liable person, and not as a deduction from the sum due under the order. Payments deducted under the order must be paid to the Secretary of State by the 19th day of the month following the month in which the deduction is made (reg 14(1)).
(d) By reg 15(1), the Secretary of State may require a liable person to provide details of his employer, his current and anticipated earnings, and his place of work and pay number. Such details must be supplied within seven days of being given written notice to that effect. A liable person in respect of whom a deduction from earnings order is in effect must notify the Secretary of State in writing within seven days of every occasion on which he leaves employment or becomes employed or re-employed (reg 15(2)). Employers are under a similar duty (reg 16).
(e) The regulations also include detailed provisions as to the power to review (reg 17), vary (reg 18), or discharge orders (reg 20) and lapse of orders (reg 21).

9.9 Since the Secretary of State is able to make a deduction from earnings order without warning to the liable person, there has to be a means of challenging such an order. This is provided by s 32(5), the effect of which is that a liable person may appeal to a magistrates' court (or, in Scotland, the sheriff) if he is aggrieved by a deduction from earnings order, or by the terms of any such order, or if there is a dispute as to whether payments constitute earnings or as to any other prescribed matter. By s 32(6), it is made clear that the court cannot question the assessment by reference to which the deduction from earnings order was made.

The regulations are contained in reg 22 of the CS(CE)Regs 1992. Appeal is by way of complaint, and must be made within 28 days of the date on which the matter appealed against arose.

Regulation 22(3) specifies the grounds on which an appeal may be made, namely:

'(a) that the deduction from earnings order is defective;
(b) that the payments in question do not constitute earnings.'

These are very limited grounds. 'Defective' must mean some technical defect; for example, it might be argued that the order specified an incorrect protected earnings rate (as not being the same as exempt income), or that the figures contained some arithmetical error.

Any dispute as to earnings would normally be concerned with whether a person was employed or self-employed. Here, the court would be guided by reg 8(2) which provides that:

'. . . the relationship of employer and employee shall be treated as subsisting between two persons if one of them, as a principal and not as a servant or agent, pays to the other any sum defined as earnings . . . [under these regulations].'

What the court may definitely not do is to consider the reasonableness or even the accuracy of the assessment nor the reasonableness of the Secretary of State's decision to make a deduction from earnings order. Where there might be room for such a challenge, it must be made by way of judicial review (see Chapter Eight).

By reg 22(4), where the court is satisfied that the appeal should be allowed, its powers are limited to either quashing the deduction from earnings order or specifying which, if any, of the payments in question do not constitute earnings. In *DSS v Taylor* [1996] 2 FLR 241, it was held that justices were not empowered to order repayment of sums wrongly recovered by the Secretary of State under a deduction from earnings order.

9.10 Regulation 24 contains provisions to govern priority as between different deduction from earnings orders or between deduction from earnings orders and attachment of earnings orders. Deduction from earnings orders are dealt with in date order, so that the net earnings are compared with the protected earnings rate on the later order or orders after deduction of the previous order or orders. Deduction from earnings orders have priority over attachment of earnings orders; in the case of an attachment of earnings order, the net earnings to be compared with the protected earnings are calculated after deduction of the sum due under a deduction from earnings order.

9.11 Persons who fail to comply with the requirements of a deduction from earnings order will, in the last resort, be liable to criminal sanctions. Section 32(8) of the CSA 1991, which applies to liable persons and their employers, provides that:

'If any person fails to comply with the requirements of a deduction from earnings order, or with any regulation under this section which is designated for the purposes of this subsection, he shall be guilty of an offence.'

Regulation 25 provides that the designated regulations are as follows:

– reg 14(1) (payment by employer to Secretary of State);

- reg 15(1) and (2) (failure to provide details of employer, place of work, or change of employment);
- reg 16(1), (2) and (3) (employer's duty to provide information); and
- reg 19(1) (employer's duty to comply with deduction from earnings order).

'Fails' imposes an absolute liability, but some relief is afforded by s 32(10) which provides that:

> 'It shall be a defence for a person charged with an offence under subsection (8) to prove that he took all reasonable steps to comply with the requirements in question.'

Once the failure has been established, therefore, the onus of proof is on the person charged. Under s 32(11), a person guilty of an offence under s 32(8) is liable on summary conviction to a fine not exceeding level 2 on the standard scale.

4. Liability Orders

9.12 It has been seen above that deduction from earnings orders are normally available as a useful means of securing payment of the sums due under a maintenance calculation. However, this can only be used where there are earnings from employment which may be attached. The CSA 1991, therefore, has to provide other means of enforcement, and the gateway to these is the liability order. A liability order is not a means of enforcement in itself, but is a prerequisite for other forms of enforcement. By s 33(5), a liability order is registered as a judgment for the purpose of s 73 of the County Courts Act 1984.

9.13 Unlike a deduction from earnings order, a liability order can be granted only when the liable person is in default. Section 33(1) of the CSA 1991 provides that s 33, which contains the relevant provisions as to liability orders, applies where:

> '(a) a person who is liable to make payments of child support maintenance ("the liable person") fails to make one or more of those payments; and
> (b) it appears to the Secretary of State that –
> (i) it is inappropriate to make a deduction from earnings order against him (because, for example, he is not employed); or
> (ii) although such an order has been made against him, it has proved ineffective as a means of securing that payments are made in accordance with the maintenance calculation in question.'

In order for the Secretary of State to make a valid decision to apply to the court for a liability order, therefore, two conditions have to be met. First, at least one payment of child support maintenance must be in arrear. Secondly, the Secretary of State must have addressed his mind to whether a deduction from earnings order could or should be made. Where the liable person is not employed, or where a deduction from earnings order has been made and proved unsuccessful, he will have no problem. However, he is not limited to these examples; he may decide that deduction from earnings would be inappropriate for other reasons. One such reason might be that the liable person had asked for there not to be a deduction from earnings order, because, for example, it might embarrass him with his employer.

9.14 By s 33(2), the Secretary of State may apply to a magistrates' court, or, in Scotland, the sheriff, for a liability order in respect of the liable person. Section 33(3) provides that the court, or sheriff:

> '. . . shall make the order if satisfied that the payments in question have become payable by the liable person and have not been paid.'

The making of a liability order is therefore mandatory, provided the court is satisfied that the Secretary of State has proved the amount of the arrears. As in all such matters, the onus of proof is on the Secretary of State. Once the payments are in arrear, the court has to make a liability order if asked to do so. As was seen above, the Secretary of State has to go through a certain process before being able to make a valid decision as to whether to apply for a liability order; however, the magistrates, or sheriff, may not inquire into the validity of the order. Where grounds for challenge exist, they must be argued by way of an application for judicial review (see Chapter Eight).

9.15 Section 34 deals with the regulations about liability orders which the Secretary of State may make. These regulations are contained in Part IV of the CS(CE)Regs 1992. One of the most relevant here is reg 28(1), which provides that the Secretary of State must give the liable person at least seven days' notice of his intention to apply for a liability order. This notice must contain the amount of child support maintenance which it is alleged is unpaid.

Once a liability order specifying a sum of money which is unpaid has been made, it may be enforced in a variety of ways. These will now be considered.

5. Enforcement of Liability Orders by Distress

9.16 Distress means the seizure and sale of a person's goods to pay a debt. Section 35(1) provides that, where a liability order has been made against a liable person, the Secretary of State may:

> '. . . levy the appropriate amount by distress and sale of the liable person's goods.'

By s 35(2), 'appropriate amount' is defined as the aggregate of the amount in respect of which the liability order was made, to the extent that it remains unpaid, and an amount for charges. The charges are prescribed by Sch 2 to the CS(CE)Regs 1992, and include, for example, a charge of £10 for writing a warning letter, and 10p per day for 'walking possession'.

The amount to be recovered, therefore, is the outstanding balance under the liability order, and the costs of the distress.

9.17 Section 35(3) sets out what the Secretary of State may seize when levying distress. This comprises:

> '(a) any of the liable person's goods, except –
>
> (i) such tools, books, vehicles and other items of equipment as are necessary to him for use personally by him in his employment, business or vocation;
>
> (ii) such clothing, bedding, furniture, household equipment and provisions as are necessary for satisfying his basic domestic needs; and

> (b) any money, banknotes, bills of exchange, promissory notes, bonds, specialties, or securities for money belonging to the liable person.'

By s 35(4), the liable person's domestic needs are to be taken to include those of any of his family with whom he resides.

9.18 Section 35(8)(c) provides for regulations to 'provide for an appeal to a magistrates' court by any person aggrieved by the levying of, or an attempt to levy, a distress under this section'. These regulations are contained in reg 31 of the CS(CE)Regs 1992.

Regulation 31(1) provides that:

> 'A person aggrieved by the levy of, or an attempt to levy, a distress may appeal to the magistrates' court having jurisdiction in the area in which he resides.'

Regulation 31(3) and (4) provides that, if the court is satisfied that the levy was irregular, it may order the goods to be discharged, award compensation equal to the value of the goods (if sold) or require the Secretary of State to desist from levy (in the case of attempted levy). The only ground on which appeal may be brought, therefore, is that the levy is 'irregular'. This can only apply to some procedural defect, and cannot go to the root of the decision to levy. The general merits of the matter cannot be addressed.

The right to appeal is conferred on 'any person aggrieved'. This could include, for example, the spouse, cohabitant or children of the liable person.

9.19 Section 37 contains provisions as to enforcement of liability orders in Scotland.

6. Enforcement of Liability Orders in County Courts

9.20 A liability order may be enforced through a county court, as if it were a judgment or order of that court. Section 36(1) provides that, where a liability order has been made against a person, the unpaid amount in respect of which the order was made shall, if a county court so orders, be recoverable by means of a garnishee order or a charging order as if it were payable under a county court order.

The powers of the county court are, therefore, limited to the two forms of enforcement stated above. There are no special regulations under the Act, so the procedure is determined by the County Court Rules 1981, SI 1981/1687. The Secretary of State initiates the proceedings by lodging at the court an affidavit by an authorised officer proving the liability order and the unpaid balance due. Provided all is in order, the district judge makes an order nisi, and this is the first warning the liable person receives. At the stage of order nisi, all the court has to be satisfied about is the existence of the liability and of the asset which it is sought to attach or charge.

The liable person may then 'shew cause' against the order, ie seek to convince the court that an order absolute should not be made. In the case of a garnishee order this might be done by showing that the money or fund attached was not, in fact, due to the liable person. In the case of a charging order, it is only possible to charge the liable person's interest in the property; it might, therefore, be argued that the interest of a joint owner was such as to render worthless the interest of the liable person, or that there was a negative equity in the property. In answer to this, it might be said that since the charging order was only over the liable person's interest, whatever that might be, it would be unnecessary to determine the extent of the interest at this stage.

In either case, the interests of other creditors must be considered. The decision as to whether to make an order absolute is a discretionary one, which rests with the district judge; such discretion must, of course, be exercised judicially, and it would seem that the merits of the original assessment or liability order should not be considered.

Finally, although the CSA 1991 does not say so, a charging order absolute may be enforced by an order for sale of the property charged; this is normally regarded as a last resort, to be ordered only where there is no other way of recovering the sum due.

7. Disqualification from Driving and/or Imprisonment

9.21 When all other means of enforcement have failed, the Secretary of State may adopt the final and drastic sanction of applying for the liable person to be committed to prison. This remedy has existed since 1991. However, one of the novelties introduced by the CSPSSA 2000 is the addition of disqualification from driving as one of the ultimate sanctions for non-payment of child support. The possibility of either of these sanctions being imposed may arise only where the Secretary of State has sought to levy an amount by distress or to recover an amount by virtue of s 36 of the CSA 1991 (ie garnishee proceedings or a charging order application in the county court) and that amount, or any portion of it, remains unpaid. In these circumstances, the Secretary of State may apply to a magistrates' court for an order under this section.[1]

9.22 An application under this section is for:

> '... whichever the court considers most appropriate in all the circumstances of –
>
> (a) the issue of a warrant committing the liable person to prison; or
> (b) an order for him to be disqualified from holding or obtaining a driving licence.'[2]

The court will, therefore, be offered the choice of sanction. However, the Secretary of State may make representations to the court as to whether he thinks it more appropriate to commit to prison or to disqualify, and potentially liable persons will be pleased to learn that they 'may reply to those representations'.[3]

To arrive at this stage, therefore, the following conditions must have been fulfilled.

(1) A liability order must have been made in a magistrates' court or by a sheriff. The following points may be noted:

---

1 CSA 1991, s 39A(1).
2 Ibid, s 39A(2).
3 Ibid, s 39A(4).

(a) the decision to apply for a liability order must have involved a determination by the Secretary of State that a deduction from earnings order was inappropriate, either because one had been made and proved ineffective, or for some other reason;
(b) the magistrates' court may not look behind the liability order nor question its validity. Where there seems to be scope for challenge, this must be by way of judicial review.

(2) Either:

(a) distress must have been levied, and have failed to recover the whole sum due under the liability order; or
(b) there has been an unsuccessful application for a charging order or garnishee order in a county court; or
(c) a charging order or garnishee order has been made, but has failed to recover the whole sum due.

The only point to note here is that a charging order granted in a county court rarely results in immediate payment of the debt which it secured. As explained in part 6 above, orders for sale based on charging orders are quite rare; the point of a charging order is normally seen as giving a creditor some long-term or medium-term security.

(3) The amount of the sum due on the liability order, or some part of it, must still be outstanding. This will be for the Secretary of State to prove, and the magistrates are entitled to demand evidence.

Provisions applying to both remedies

9.23 Certain parts of these provisions apply both to imprisonment and to disqualification from driving. In both cases, the following must apply. The court must, in the presence of the liable person, inquire into:

(a) whether he needs a driving licence to earn his living;
(b) his means; and
(c) whether there has been wilful refusal or culpable neglect on his part.

9.24 The essential points appear to be as follows.

(1) The hearing must be in the presence of the liable person; if he is not there, it cannot proceed.

(2) The court must inquire into two matters. The first of these is the means of the liable person. It will therefore be necessary to take detailed evidence as to his income, outgoings, and liabilities. In *R v Liverpool City Justices, ex parte Lanckriet* [1977] RA 85, and *R v Richmond Justices, ex parte Atkins* [1983] RVR 148, which were cases concerned with enforcement of liability for rates and community charge, with provisions virtually identical to those in s 40, it was held that a committal is unlawful if a proper means inquiry is not carried out, or insufficient questions are put to the debtor to elicit his true financial position.

The second area of inquiry is as to whether the failure of the liable person to pay is due to his wilful refusal or culpable neglect. Here, the court must try to find out why the liable person has not paid, and make a judgment as to whether that amounts to wilful refusal or culpable neglect. Clearly, where the court is satisfied that the liable person has the funds to pay and has refused to do so, it will not be difficult to reach a decision. Similarly, where arrears have built up, but, at the date of the hearing, the liable person is without funds (eg unemployed) through no fault of his own, it would be difficult to find against him. In *R v Poole Magistrates, ex parte Benham* (1992) 156 JP 177, another community charge case, it was held that when considering whether there had been wilful refusal or culpable neglect, the court is confined to examining the conduct of the debtor between the bill and the liability order; as to means, the court may consider the debtor's means only on the day of the hearing.

As to proof of the liable person's income, CS(CE) Regs 1992, reg 33(2) provides that a statement in writing as to the liable person's earnings, purporting to be signed by or on behalf of his employer, shall be evidence of the facts stated. This means that it is admissible in evidence, not that it is conclusive evidence; it would have to be weighed against anything said in evidence by the liable person.

9.25 If the magistrates decide that the failure to pay was not due to wilful refusal or culpable neglect, but was for some other reason which could not be brought into either of those categories, that would be an end of the matter, and the application would have to be dismissed. Where they find that the failure was for one of those reasons they then have to decide what to do.

Section 40(3) of the CSA 1991 provides that they 'may' issue a warrant of commitment; in other words, they have a discretion, which must be exercised judicially.

The proper approach of justices in very similar cases was considered in *R v Luton Magistrates' Court, ex parte Sullivan* [1992] 2 FLR 196, which was concerned with the power of justices to commit under s 76 of the Magistrates' Courts Act 1980 (MCA 1980) for arrears of maintenance.

Waite J observed that the power under s 76 to issue a writ committing a spouse to prison in such cases was 'a power of extreme severity'. He continued as follows:

> 'Indeed, it might be argued that the existence of such a power in a society which long ago closed the Marshalsea Prison and abandoned imprisonment as a remedy for enforcement of debts is anomalous. Certainly, Parliament has made it plain that the power is to be exercised sparingly and only as a last resort.'

Waite J emphasised that any order of commitment must be preceded by an inquiry, in the presence of the debtor, as to whether his default did indeed amount to wilful refusal or culpable neglect and that the court was expressly prohibited from exercising the power unless satisfied that all other methods of enforcing payment had been tried or considered and had proved unsuccessful or were likely to do so. He commented adversely on the fact that the justices had not allowed the debtor to obtain legal advice.

In *R v Birmingham Justices, ex parte Mansell* [1988] *The Independent*, April 21, another community charge case, it was held that justices had erred because they had failed to consider whether other enforcement proceedings could be used. In *R v Manchester City Magistrates' Court, ex parte Davis* [1988] 1 All ER 930, it was emphasised that no one, especially someone who had never been in prison, should ever be sent to prison lightly, and that where there were no means to pay the court should bear in mind that the application could always be renewed if the debtor's financial position improved.

9.26 When the court exercises its discretion in favour of issuing a warrant of commitment, it has the choice of making an outright order or a suspended order. In the light of the judicial dicta set out above, it might be argued that a suspended order would be the natural first choice for the court.

By s 40(4), the warrant must state the amount mentioned in s 35(1) (ie the amount to be levied on distress), or so much of it as remains outstanding, plus the prescribed amount in respect of the costs of commitment. By s 40(6), a warrant must order the liable person to be imprisoned for a specified period, but to be released on payment of the amount stated on the warrant (unless in custody for some other reason).

The maximum term of imprisonment which may be imposed is to be calculated in accordance with Sch 4 to the MCA 1980, but must not exceed six weeks (s 40(7)).

Regulation 34(5) of the CS(CE)Regs 1992 provides that where, after the issue of a warrant and part payment of the amount due in it is made, the period of imprisonment shall be reduced proportionately, so that for the period of imprisonment stated in the warrant there shall be substituted a period of such number of days as bears the same proportion to the number of days specified in the warrant as the amount remaining unpaid under the warrant bears to the amount specified in the warrant.

Provisions applying only to disqualification from driving

9.27 The new s 40B provides further matters which deal only with disqualification from driving. However, before these are examined in detail, some consideration of why this new penalty has been introduced at all may be helpful. In the Second Reading debate in the House of Lords, Lord Stoddart of Swindon was clearly perplexed. He pointed out that 'the object of a driving licence is to ensure that people who drive have passed a relevant test. In my view – in many people's view, I should have thought – the withdrawal of a driving licence should not be used as a penalty for non-payment of this kind of maintenance or any other. Can the Minister explain?'[4]

The Minister was unabashed: 'We are seeking to introduce this provision at the moment because fathers who can and should pay maintenance are not doing so. For many of them, a gaol sentence is perhaps too heavy; and some of the other penalties – for example, restraint of goods (sic) or garnishee orders on their estates – take a very long time to kick in'.[5] Later, after referring to the experience of the State of Texas, the Minister said: '. . . it was not the taking away of licences that got the money flowing to children; it was the threat of taking away the driving licences that got the money flowing to children. That is what we want to ensure. If

4 Official Report (HL) 17 April 2000, col 464.
5 Ibid, per Baroness Hollis.

we have had real difficulty in some cases in getting a father who can pay to face up to his responsibilities, at the end of the day if the threat of removal of a driving licence ensures that he addresses his responsibilities for the first time, I am confident that I shall have the support of my noble friend.'[6]

9.28 The court may, but only if it is of the opinion that there has been wilful refusal or culpable neglect on the part of the liable person:

(a) order him to be disqualified for such period specified in the order but not exceeding two years from holding or obtaining a driving licence (a 'disqualification order');
(b) make a disqualification order but suspend its operation until such time and on such conditions (if any) as it thinks just.[7]

The court may not take action under both s 40 and s 40B; in other words, it may not both commit to prison and disqualify.

The disqualification order must state the amount in respect of which it is made, being, in effect, the sum stated in the liability order and costs.[8] The liable person must produce his driving licence to the court.[9]

9.29 If part of the amount due is paid, either the liable person or the Secretary of State may apply to the court for an order substituting a shorter period of disqualification or revoking the order.[10] If the amount due is paid in full, the court must make an order revoking the disqualification order.[11] The Secretary of State may make representations as to the amount which should be paid before an order is revoked.[12]

If the amount due has not been paid in full when the period of disqualification expires the Secretary of State may apply for a further disqualification order.[13]

9.30 Section 80 of the MCA 1980 applies in relation to a disqualification order.[14] The result of this is that a liable person against whom a disqualification order has been made may be searched and any money in his possession applied towards the amount due.

8. Arrears and Penalty Payments

9.31 Section 41 of the CSA 1991 Act which deals with arrears has been amended by the CSPSSA 2000. The section applies where the Secretary of State is authorised to recover child support maintenance and the non-resident parent

---

6 Official Report (HL) 17 April 2000, per Baroness Hollis.
7 CSA 1991, s 40B(1).
8 Ibid, s 40B(3).
9 Ibid, s 40B(4).
10 Ibid, s 40B(5)(a).
11 Ibid, s 40B(5)(b).
12 Ibid, s 40B(6).
13 Ibid, s 40B(7).
14 Ibid, s 40B(10).

has failed to make one or more payments due. The new provisions relate to penalty payments, which replace the former provisions for interest on arrears.

The Secretary of State may make regulations to provide for penalty payments under s 41A(1). The amount of a penalty payment may not exceed 25% of the amount of child support maintenance payable for that week, but otherwise is to be determined by regulations. [15] Payment of a penalty payment does not relieve the non-resident parent of the obligation to pay the child support maintenance.[16]

Any payments received are to be paid into the Consolidated Fund;[17] the parent with care will not benefit.

15 CSA 1991, s 41A(2).
16 Ibid, s 41A(3).
17 Ibid, s 41A(6).

CHAPTER TEN

The Role of the Courts and Maintenance Agreements

1. Introduction

10.1 One of the fundamental objectives of the CSA 1991 was the removal from the courts of the task of assessing, collecting and enforcing child maintenance and the transfer of these matters to the CSA; the reasons for this were discussed in Chapter One and need not be examined here.

However, it would be wrong to assume that the courts are left with no functions in this field. Quite apart from those areas specifically delegated to the courts by the Act, there are certain residual areas of jurisdiction which may be exercised for the time being. These will be examined in this chapter, together with the ability of parents to enter into maintenance agreements in respect of their children.

The effect of the Act on other areas, such as spousal financial provision will also be considered.

The CSPSSA 2000 has made some important changes to the position relating to court orders. The first of these has already been discussed in Chapter Two at para **2.25**. The fact that there is in force a court order made after a prescribed date no longer prevents the Secretary of State from making a maintenance calculation provided one year has elapsed from the date of the order. As has been seen, the CSPSSA 2000 amends s 4(10) of the CSA 1991.

Section 4(10), which was inserted by the CSA 1995, in effect deferred for an indefinite period any application for child support if there was a maintenance agreement in force which was made before 5 April 1993 or a maintenance order made at any time. The effect of the new provisions is that s 4(10) is amended so that it refers only to maintenance orders made before a prescribed date; this date will be prescribed once the new provisions are in force.[1] Orders made before the prescribed date will continue to operate as a bar to an application to the Secretary of State under s 4. Orders made after that date will only operate as a bar for the period of one year, after which the Secretary of State will recover jurisdiction. Orders made after the prescribed date will, inevitably, be confined to consent orders or variations of consent orders.

2. The General Principle

10.2 Section 8(3) of the CSA 1991 provides that:

'In any case where subsection (1) applies, no court shall exercise any power which it

---

1 Or not, as the case may be. Much will depend on whether the CSA is in a position to deal with the new work.

would otherwise have to make, vary or revive any maintenance order in relation to the child and absent parent concerned.'

Subsection (1) applies to any case where the Secretary of State would have jurisdiction to make an assessment (see Chapter Two). Accordingly, in cases where there is a qualifying child, a person with care and a non-resident parent, all within the United Kingdom, the Secretary of State has jurisdiction and the court may not exercise any jurisdiction which it would otherwise have.

Section 8(4) provides that these provisions do not prevent the court from revoking an order. By s 8(2), subs (1) (and, therefore, subs (3)) apply even though the circumstances of the case are such that the Secretary of State would not make a calculation if it were applied for; in other words, the courts may not be used as a fall-back position if the means of a non-resident parent are such that no calculation could be made.

10.3 On the face of it, therefore, the position is simple; the jurisdiction of the courts is excluded where the Secretary of State has jurisdiction. Unfortunately, the reality is a little more complicated. There are 11 instances where the courts may retain, or exercise, jurisdiction to make orders for child maintenance. Some of these instances are where the Secretary of State has no jurisdiction, which presents no problem, and some are where the CSA 1991 specifically confers jurisdiction on the court. In addition, some are of a more or less temporary nature, while the CSA takes its time to assume jurisdiction in all cases.

These exceptions to the rule may be summarised as follows:

(a) the Secretary of State has no jurisdiction;
(b) the child is not the adopted or 'natural' child of both parties;
(c) the child is between 17 and 19 years old and not in full-time education;
(d) the child is 19 years old or over;
(e) topping-up orders under s 8(6);
(f) orders for additional educational expenses under s 8(7);
(g) orders for expenses of a disabled or blind child under s 8(8);
(h) lump sum or property adjustment orders for child;
(i) certain consent orders;
(j) variation of existing orders;
(k) orders against the person with care.

The various exceptions will now be considered in turn.

3. Exceptions to the General Rule

(a) Secretary of State has no jurisdiction because of residence

10.4 Jurisdiction is covered by s 44 of the CSA 1991 and is dealt with in Chapter Two at para **2.3**. Briefly, the Secretary of State has jurisdiction where the qualifying child, the person with care and the non-resident parent are habitually resident within the United Kingdom. If any one of the three is not so resident, the Secretary of State lacks jurisdiction and any application will have to be brought in the courts.

(b) Stepchildren and 'children of the family'

10.5 In order to be a qualifying child, a child must be the adopted or 'natural' child of both parents. In cases to which the MCA 1973 applies, the position is different; a party to a marriage has obligations in respect of a child of whom he is not the father but has treated as a child of the family, as defined by s 52 of the MCA 1973. The most common example of a child of the family is a child of one party to a marriage who lives with her and her new husband after their marriage.

Such a child is not a qualifying child and may not be the subject of a calculation. To obtain financial relief for such a child it is therefore necessary to apply to the court under the provisions of either the MCA 1973, the CA 1989, or the DPMCA 1978.

Where a calculation is made in respect of another child or children, the CSA may arrange for the collection of maintenance for a non-qualifying child (see Chapter Nine at para **9.4**).

(c) Child aged 17 or 18

10.6 'Child' is defined by s 55(1) of the CSA 1991, which is discussed in Chapter Two at para **2.7**. A 17- or 18-year-old will be excluded from the ambit of the Act unless:

(i) he is in full-time education which is not advanced education; or
(ii) he is not in education at all.

(d) Child aged 19 or over

10.7 A person who is 19 years old or over cannot bring himself within any provision of the CSA 1991. However, it is not uncommon for such a person to be financially dependent on his parents, for example when pursuing full-time education. Local education authorities have regard to the means of parents when assessing eligibility for grants, assuming that grants are available, with the result that students have to look to their parents for support.

Any parent of a person of this age, or the person himself, who wishes to claim maintenance from a parent will, therefore, have to bring an application in the courts.

(e) Topping-up under s 8(6)

10.8 It was seen in Chapter Three that there is a 'cap' or limit on the amount of child support maintenance which can be required under a maintenance calculation. Net income of a non-resident parent exceeding £2000 per week must be disregarded, so that the maximum sum which could be required (for three or more children) would be £500. There may be circumstances where a greater figure would be reasonable, but the Government considers that the courts would be more appropriate vehicles for this kind of application.

Accordingly, the CSA 1991 permits applications to the court to 'top up'. This was permitted under the Act from the outset, but the changes to the formula have made new provisions necessary.

Section 8(6), as amended, now provides that s 8 shall not prevent a court from exercising any power which it has to make a maintenance order for a child if:

> '(a) a maintenance calculation is in force with respect to the child;

> (b) the non-resident parent's net weekly income exceeds the figure referred to in paragraph 10(3) of Schedule 1 (as it has effect from time to time pursuant to regulations made under paragraph 10A(1)(b)); and
> (c) the court is satisfied that the circumstances of the case make it appropriate for the non-resident parent to make or secure the making of periodical payments under a maintenance order in addition to the child support maintenance payable by him in accordance with the maintenance calculation.'

10.9 In order to satisfy the court that it has jurisdiction to entertain an application, therefore, the applicant must prove that there has been a maintenance calculation based on a net income for the non-resident parent of £2000 per week and that his actual net income exceeds that figure. The court would then have to proceed to deal with the application according to the statute which gave it primary jurisdiction (viz MCA 1973, DPMCA 1978 or CA 1989). The primary factors would be the needs of the child and the ability of the parents to pay; unlike in the CSA calculations, the means of the person with care would be relevant.

(f) Additional educational expenses

10.10 Section 8(7) is what might be called the 'school fees exception', although, as will be seen, it is not limited to school fees. It provides that the court shall not be prevented from exercising any power which it has to make a maintenance order in relation to a child if:

> '(a) the child is, will be or (if the order were to be made) would be receiving instruction at an educational establishment or undergoing training for a trade, profession or vocation (whether or not while in gainful employment); and
> (b) the order is made solely for the purposes of requiring the person making or securing the making of periodical payments fixed by the order to meet some or all of the expenses incurred in connection with the provision of the instruction or training.'

The first point to be noted is that there is no question of additional maintenance or topping-up involved; this subsection does not contain the prerequisite that there be a maintenance calculation to provide for everyday needs, although it may be that there will be such a calculation. Secondly, 'educational establishment' is not defined by the Act (unlike 'recognised educational establishment', which is defined by s 55(3)). Accordingly, the normal plain meaning afforded by the English language applies, and the term must mean school, college or university.

Of course, the child must be 18 years old or under; if he is aged between 16 and 18, and not attending a 'recognised educational establishment', he will be outside the ambit of the CSA 1991 in any event, so that the court would have jurisdiction anyway.

10.11 Provided the child is a child within the meaning of s 55(1), various classes of expenses seem to be claimable under s 8(7). School fees and extra expenses incurred at school are obvious examples. The subsection could also include accommodation charges, travelling expenses, or the provision of special clothing, books or computer equipment. Whatever the nature of the expenses, it would be necessary to show that they were directly attributable to the provision of the education or training.

When the expenses arise out of training for a trade, profession or vocation, the fact that the child is in gainful employment is not a bar; whatever income the child derived from such gainful employment would be one of the factors to be taken into account in assessing the child's needs.

(g) Disabled or blind child

10.12 Disabled or blind children frequently have additional special needs and expenses which cannot be accommodated within the terms of a rigid formula. Accordingly, the CSA 1991 permits application to the courts.

Section 8(8) provides that a court shall not be prevented from exercising any power which it has to make a maintenance order in relation to a child if:

> '(a) a disability living allowance is paid to or in respect of him; or
> (b) no such allowance is paid but he is disabled,
> and the order is made solely for the purpose of requiring the person making or securing the making of periodical payments fixed by the order to meet some or all of any expenses attributable to the child's disability.'

By s 8(9), a child is disabled if he is blind, deaf or dumb or is substantially and permanently handicapped by illness, injury, mental disorder or congenital deformity or such other disability as may be prescribed.

10.13 As with s 8(7), it is not a prerequisite of an application to the court that a maintenance calculation be in force. The purpose of the provision is limited to the recovery of expenses attributable to the child's disability.

(h) Lump sums or property adjustment orders

10.14 For the sake of completeness, it should be noted that s 8(1) and (3) exclude the jurisdiction of the courts in respect of 'a maintenance order in relation to a child'. The various other forms of financial relief for a child are not brought under the umbrella of the CSA 1991, and the powers of the courts in relation thereto are not affected.

The court is therefore entitled to make a lump sum order or a property adjustment order in favour of a child; such an order would be unusual (see, eg, *A v A (A Minor: Financial Provision)* [1994] 1 FLR 657).

(i) Certain consent orders

10.15 This topic is considered more fully at para **10.27**.

(j) Power to vary

10.16 The prohibition on the exercise of the court's powers contained in CSA 1991, s 8(3) extends to variation of an existing order; it might, therefore, be thought that the courts have no power to vary their orders. This is, in fact, not the case.

Paragraph 1 of the Schedule to the Child Support Act 1991 (Commencement No 3 and Transitional Provisions) Order 1992, SI 1992/2644 provided that during a transitional period between 5 April 1993 and 6 April 1997, no application for an assessment under CSA 1991, s 4 could be made where there was in force a maintenance order or maintenance agreement in respect of the qualifying child. The CSA 1995 amended the CSA 1991, in effect to postpone the 'take-up' of cases by the CSA, and to provide for resort to the courts to vary during this 'transitional' period.

From the coming into force of the CSPSSA 2000, the position will change again. As has been seen at para **10.1**, the CSPSSA 2000 amends s 4(10) of the CSA 1991 and s 8(3A), which deals with variation, is also amended. The effect of the new s 8(3A) is as follows.

(1) The existence of a maintenance calculation prevents the court from varying an order.
(2) An order may be varied provided it was made after the 'prescribed date' (see para **10.1**).
(3) Where an order was made before the prescribed date, it may be varied provided s 4(10) prevents an application being made to the Secretary of State. Otherwise, it may not be varied.

(k) Orders against the person with care

10.17 Section 8(10) provides that the section does not prevent a court exercising its power to make a maintenance order in relation to a child if that order is made against a person with care of the child. Such cases will clearly be unusual; it is difficult to think of cases where an order for periodical payments for a child would be made against the person with whom the child lived. However, the power is there, to be exercised in suitable cases.

4. The Effect of the CSA 1991 on Related Court Proceedings

10.18 The related court proceedings with which this section deals are concerned entirely with the ancillary relief proceedings between spouses or former spouses brought under the MCA 1973. On or after the grant of a decree, the court has power to make orders for periodical payments or for capital provision, and these are intended to do justice as between the parties in the light of the factors set out in s 25 of the MCA 1973.[2] The effect of the CSA 1991 is that one important aspect of the financial relations between spouses or former spouses, namely the maintenance of their children, has been removed from the jurisdiction of the court. Nevertheless, the court still has to proceed to deal with the remaining issues. The problem is, therefore, what influence the CSA 1991 should have on these remaining issues.

10.19 The first way in which the CSA 1991 impinges on the courts is the question of what relationship the calculation of orders for children in cases in which the court retains jurisdiction should have to the amounts which the formula calculation would produce. Should the courts have regard to the formula when assessing child maintenance?

In principle, the answer must be that the court cannot be guided by a statute other than that under which the application before it is brought. The various statutes under which an application for child maintenance may be made (MCA

---

2 The timing of such orders may change if the provisions of the Family Law Act 1996, Part II are implemented, but the general principles will remain the same.

1973, DPMCA 1978, CA 1989) all have provisions which direct the court to have regard to certain matters. It might be argued that it would not be proper for the court to look beyond for guidance.

However, the position is not entirely clear-cut. When deciding the amount of the needs of the child, the court has to use some 'raw material'; the court cannot exist in a vacuum and has to have some figures, such as income support or foster-care rates, to decide how much it costs to keep a child. It might be argued that the method of calculating the maintenance requirement prescribed by the CSA 1991 is as good a means as any of working out what the financial needs of the child are. However, this could only be a starting point.

10.20 Some guidance under the previous formula was provided by the decision of Douglas Brown J in *E v C (Child Maintenance)* [1996] 1 FLR 472. In this case, a family proceedings court made orders reducing a maintenance order against a father from £5 per week for each of two children to £1 per year each. He was unemployed and in receipt of benefit. On the appeal, the judge allowed the appeal. He said that the CSA would have produced a nil assessment in this case. While that assessment was not binding on the justices, it would have been strongly persuasive had they known about it. It was the practice of professional judges to ask about a CSA assessment, and it would be helpful to justices to do likewise.

From this case, one can draw high judicial approval for the proposition that a maintenance calculation which the CSA would make is a material factor in all cases involving maintenance of children, and should be produced in all such cases. It would, of course, then be open to the parties to argue that such calculation should be altered in the light of the facts of the case, and the statutory matters to which the court was directed to have regard.

10.21 One matter which caused concern when the CSA 1991 was in its infancy was the problem of the parent, normally a father, who had transferred his share of a matrimonial home to the other parent to secure a roof over the heads of the family, and whose liability for maintenance of the other parent had been dismissed, with a fairly nominal order for the children. The Act, as originally enacted, made little or no provision for such parents, and there is no doubt that injustice resulted; this is recognised by the fact that the Government has introduced the departure scheme (now 'variations') to take account of such cases.

Some of these arguments have come before the courts, and the more important decisions will now be set out.

In *Crozier v Crozier* [1994] 1 FLR 126, a consent order for ancillary relief was made in 1989; this provided for the transfer of the husband's interest in the former matrimonial home to the wife, in full and final settlement of all claims against him, save for child maintenance which was agreed in a nominal sum. The wife was in receipt of income support. In 1993, the Secretary of State applied to the magistrates for a contribution from the husband towards the child's maintenance; the husband was ordered to pay £4 per week; it was common ground that an application would be made to the CSA, and that the husband would then have to pay £29 per week. The husband applied to set aside or vary the consent order, to enable him to recoup his half-share in the house to meet his liabilities.

Booth J refused leave to appeal out of time. She said that the parties may never have reached the agreement they did had the husband known that he would have to pay for the child. However, although the clean break was available to spouses, different considerations applied to child maintenance. The ongoing responsibilities of parents remained a basic factor, and parents could not achieve a clean break in respect of their child. Furthermore, at the time of the consent order, the State was empowered to recover maintenance for the child under the Social Security Act 1986. The State was never bound by the parents' agreement. Accordingly, neither the existence of the order in 1993, nor the anticipated liability under the CSA 1991 constituted a new event in fact or law sufficient to invalidate the basis of the agreed order.

10.22 In *Mawson v Mawson* [1994] 2 FLR 985, the facts were that during an application for ancillary relief, the wife withdrew her claim for financial provision for the child pending an application to the CSA for an assessment. The assessment was for £596.70 per month, which was manifestly more than would have been ordered by the court. In the light of this, the district judge ordered the transfer to her of the matrimonial home and a lump sum of £2000, but only allowed a three-month term for periodical payments at the rate of £150 per month, with no right to make any further application. The wife appealed.

Thorpe J said that a s 28(1A) direction, prohibiting the wife from making any further application, was inappropriate where there was a young child, and that part of the order should be deleted. There should be a limited term order, which should be for nine months. Apart from that, the order of the district judge was unchanged.

10.23 Thorpe J was also the judge in *Smith v McInerney* [1994] 2 FLR 1077. Ostensibly, this case was concerned with the effects of a maintenance agreement on a subsequent application for ancillary relief. In 1990, the husband and wife made a separation agreement, pursuant to which the husband transferred his interest in the former matrimonial home to the wife; in return, he was released from any obligation to maintain the wife or the children, although, in fact, he continued to make payments for the children. He was subsequently made redundant, and, in 1993, applied for a property adjustment order. The district judge ordered that the property be charged with 35% of its net value in favour of the husband. The wife appealed.

Thorpe J asserted the general principle that what the parties had agreed at the time of separation should be upheld by the court; the circumstances of the present case fell far short of those which would justify the court in imposing terms other than those agreed. The appeal should therefore be allowed. However, that was not an end of the matter; since the wife asserted her rights under the agreement, the husband was also entitled to the benefits for which he had contracted. He was entitled to the money he had advanced prior to his redundancy. More significantly, from the point of view of this book, the judge accepted that, since the wife was now in receipt of State benefits, it was likely that the husband would be the subject of an assessment by the CSA. The judge said:

> 'It seems to me manifestly fair that if the husband parted with capital in February 1990, in part in commutation of his future obligations to maintain [the child], then he should have the right to look to the wife for indemnity in respect of any sums which are extracted from him in respect of [the child]'s maintenance. In reality, he would be paying twice to discharge the same obligation; once by capital, and secondly by periodical payments. While the wife would not herself have laid claim to that second payment, she would indirectly have triggered it by her application for income support for herself.'

The judge therefore adjourned the husband's application for a property adjustment order generally, for the single purpose of providing a means of pursuing a claim for indemnity if, and only if, the CSA extracted from him substantive periodical payments in respect of the child between the date of the order and the date of the child ceasing to be dependent. The quantification of the claim could not sensibly be attempted until the child was 'off cost'. At that stage, in the absence of agreement, the court could quantify the sums paid by the husband and do justice to him by fixing some percentage interest, or charge, in relation to the capital from which he parted in February 1990 to settle his obligations in respect of the child in part.

10.24 This case may seem, at first, to be contrary to the spirit of *Crozier*. However, the essential point seems to be that in *Crozier* there was an application to set aside a consent order of the court, which had to be considered in the light of the authorities on that subject, particularly *Barder v Caluori* [1988] AC 20; in *Smith v McInerney* (above), there was not yet a court order, and the issue before the court was the weight to be attached to an agreement, the relevant leading case being *Edgar v Edgar* (1981) FLR 19. The arguments which may be taken on behalf of parties in such cases may, therefore, depend on the substantive nature of the application under consideration.

10.25 The final case to be considered is a decision of a judge in a county court which, although not a binding authority, has some persuasive weight. In *B v M (Child Support: Revocation of Order)* [1994] 1 FLR 342, a father had been ordered in 1986 to pay maintenance for two children at the rate of £41 per month per child. In 1993, the mother sought the help of the CSA, and was told that she could apply for an assessment if the order were revoked. She applied for revocation, and the district judge revoked the order. The father appealed.

His Honour Judge Bryant said that an application to revoke an order was governed by s 31(7) of the MCA 1973, which set out a list of factors to be considered. He accepted that a CSA assessment would probably be higher than the court order. However, it did not follow that an assessment under the CSA 1991 was necessarily in the best interests of the child. It might be that other matters would outweigh the financial advantage. For example, a high maintenance figure might inhibit the father from exercising his right to contact. The result could only be reached by the court weighing up all relevant factors, bearing in mind the welfare of the children. It was not enough to come to the court and say 'I wish to go to the Child Support Agency. Please revoke the existing order'. In the present case, he had heard nothing to take it out of the ordinary run of cases for which the transitional provisions were designed.

10.26 It would be difficult to give a definitive summary of the way in which the CSA 1991 has impinged on the conduct of applications for ancillary relief. This may be partly because, despite the fears of many when the Act first came into force, the CSA has only impinged on the lives of a limited number of people, since its 'take-up' has not been as extensive as had been anticipated.[3]

However, the fact that future orders, once made after the prescribed date, will last for only one year before they can be overtaken by a maintenance calculation, indicates that orders for children should, so far as possible, be based on the new formula contained in Sch 1.

5. Maintenance Agreements and Consent Orders

10.27 It has always been possible for parents to make agreements to regulate the maintenance payable in respect of their children. Such agreements could be incorporated into orders of the court but, if not, they established contractual obligations which could be sued upon like any other contract. The CSA 1991 does not affect the ability of parents to make maintenance agreements, but certain restrictions are placed on their enforceability.

10.28 Section 9(1) defines a maintenance agreement as:

> ' . . . any agreement for the making, or for securing the making, of periodical payments by way of maintenance, or in Scotland aliment, to or for the benefit of any child.'

Section 9(2) sets out the general principle:

> 'Nothing in this Act shall be taken to prevent any person from entering into a maintenance agreement.'

Freedom of contract still exists. However, the CSA 1991 goes on to ensure that the jurisdiction of the CSA is not ousted, and that parents are unable to contract out of the Act.

Section 9(3) provides that:

> '. . . the existence of a maintenance agreement shall not prevent any party to the agreement, or any other person, from applying for a maintenance calculation with respect to any child to or for whose benefit periodical payments are to be made or secured under the agreement.'

This is followed by s 9(4), which provides that any clause in an agreement purporting to restrict the right of any person to apply for a maintenance calculation shall be void. A person who makes a maintenance agreement may therefore resile from it at any time and apply to the CSA; where someone is in receipt of benefit she may be compelled to do so.

---

3 It is also possible that, as a result of economic recession and decline in property prices, separating or divorcing couples have had less to argue about than in the mid-1980s. There has certainly been a decline in the numbers of applications for ancillary relief coming before the courts. Perhaps, like death, the Child Support Agency is something which most people know will come one day, but prefer not to think about now.

Finally, while parents are entitled to make agreements, they may not apply to the court to vary the agreement. Section 9(5)(b) prevents any such application where the Secretary of State has jurisdiction. Anyone dissatisfied with the amount payable under an agreement has no remedy except for an application for a calculation.

10.29 The CSA 1991 is also modified, again, ostensibly, on a temporary basis, by its provisions for consent order based on agreements. It will be remembered that s 8 purports to oust the jurisdiction of the court in all cases where the Secretary of State has jurisdiction. On the face of it, this prevents parties from applying to the court for a consent order for ancillary relief including an order for children. However, the rigour of this provision is modified by s 8(5) which empowers the Lord Chancellor (and, in Scotland, the Lord Advocate), to provide by order that the court shall not be prevented from exercising its powers if:

> '(a) a written agreement (whether or not enforceable) provides for the making, or securing, by a non-resident parent of the child of periodical payments to or for the benefit of the child; and
> (b) the maintenance order which the court makes is, in all material respects, in the same terms as that agreement.'

The order envisaged by the CSA 1991 is the Child Maintenance (Written Agreements) Order 1993, SI 1993/620.

The court may, therefore, make a maintenance order in respect of a child if there is before it an agreement in writing, and the order sought is in the same amounts as the amounts provided for in the agreement.[4] Most such applications will be by consent. However, notwithstanding the use of the word 'consent' in the title of the order, there seems to be no reason why one party could not seek an order against the wishes of the other party, provided the order sought was in the same terms as those in the agreement.

It is to be noted that an order under s 8(5) does not require that the agreement was made before 5 April 1993; the agreement may be made at any time.

The Lord Chancellor's Department said originally that s 8(5) is intended to be a temporary provision, pending the assumption by the CSA of full jurisdiction in all cases. However, it remains intact after the changes effected by the CSPSSA 2000.

6. The Relationship Between Maintenance Calculations and Court Orders

10.30 Section 30 of the CSA 1991, and the regulations made thereunder, which deal with the power of the Secretary of State to collect some forms of child

4 Most courts require the agreement to be produced before making an order. Opinion is divided as to whether a separate agreement is necessary, or whether the agreement can be incorporated in the recitals in the consent application. The general practice (as adopted in the PRFD) is not to require such evidence of separate agreement.

maintenance in addition to child support maintenance, have already been considered in Chapter Nine at **9.4**. This section of this chapter is concerned with the way in which maintenance calculations and court orders impinge on each other, and the statutory provisions and regulations which govern this relationship.

The basic position under the existing regulations may be summarised as follows.

(1) Certain types of court orders are prescribed by reg 3(1) of the CS(MAJ) Regs 1992 as coming within the regulations for the purpose of s 10(1). Twenty-six such types of order are prescribed; they are, in effect, any court order which might be made for, or in respect of, a child (a complete list of the statutes is set out in the regulation).
(2) By reg 3(2), when a maintenance calculation is made in respect of all the children with respect to whom a prescribed order has been made, or in respect of one or more but not all such children and the amount payable under the order to or for the benefit of each child is separately stated, the order shall cease to have effect insofar as it relates to the child or children.
(3) The exceptions to the rule set out in (2) above, are:
   (a) where the order was made under s 8(7) or (8) (ie for educational expenses or where the child is disabled); and
   (b) an exception relating to Scotland.
(4) Where reg 3(1) and (2) apply, the maintenance calculation takes effect two days after it is made, and the order will cease to have effect on that day (reg 3(5) and (6)).
(5) Similar provisions to those set out above exist in relation to maintenance agreements. By reg 4(2), where a maintenance calculation is made with respect to all the children with respect to whom an agreement is in force, or to one or more but not all such children but the amount payable to or for the benefit of each child is separately specified, the agreement shall become unenforceable insofar as it relates to the children who are the subject of the assessment from the effective date of the calculation. The agreement will remain unenforceable until such date as the Secretary of State no longer has jurisdiction to make a maintenance calculation with respect to that child (reg 4(3)).

10.31 Provision had to be made for the overlapping jurisdiction of the CSA and the courts. This is contained in the Maintenance Orders (Backdating) Order 1993, SI 1993/623. Its effect may be summarised as follows.

(1) Amendments were made to s 29(5) of the MCA 1973, s 5(5) of the DPMCA 1978, and Sch 1, para 3(5) to the CA 1989, to enable a court to backdate any order made under s 8(6) (the top-up provisions) to the date of any maintenance calculation. However, as some protection for the non-resident parent, it was also provided that the backdating provision shall only apply where the application for the top-up order is made within six months of the assessment.
(2) Amendments were made to s 31(2) of the MCA 1973, and s 20(9B) of the DPMCA 1978, to deal with the position where an order has been made for children and spouse, and a calculation supersedes the order insofar as it

relates to the children. In such circumstances, one of the spouses might wish to apply to vary the spousal maintenance. It was provided that any variation may be backdated to the date of the calculation, with the same time-limit of six months.

(3) Amendments were made to s 29(7) of the MCA 1973, s 5(7) of the DPMCA 1978, and Sch 1, para 3(7) to the CA 1989, to provide for the position where cases move out of the jurisdiction of the CSA and are either terminated automatically or cancelled by the Secretary of State. In such circumstances, any subsequent court order might be backdated to the date of cancellation or termination, with a time-limit of six months.

(4) Amendments were made to s 31(11) of the MCA 1973, s 20(9A) of the DPMCA 1978, and Sch 1, para 6(9) to the CA 1989, to govern the position where a non-resident parent applies to vary an order covering more than one child following a calculation in respect of one or more but not all the children. The onus was on the non-resident parent to apply to vary, and, if a variation order is made, it may be backdated to the date when the calculation took effect.

10.32 Finally, procedures have been devised to deal with the position where there is a dispute as to whether the court or the Secretary of State has jurisdiction; these are contained in rr 10.24–10.26 of the FPR 1991. When a parent applies to a county court for a periodical payments order for a child, court staff sift and check the application. The form on which the application is made, normally Form A in App 1A of the FPR 1991, contains a 'tick box' checklist to identify which of the exceptions to the general rule in s 8 applies. Where either the proper officer or the district judge considers that the court does not have jurisdiction, the applicant is informed to that effect.

If the applicant persists with the application, the proper officer, if it was he who made the original decision, refers the matter to the district judge, who either informs the applicant that there appears to be no jurisdiction or gives directions for a hearing, which may be ex parte. At the hearing, if the district judge declines jurisdiction, the parties are given reasons in writing. That decision is subject to appeal to a circuit judge.

10.33 A practice has arisen of making orders for periodical payments in favour of a spouse, such sums to be reduced *pro tanto* by any sums payable under a CSA assessment or calculation. In *Dorney-Kingdom v Dorney-Kingdom* [2000] 2 FLR 855, CA, it was held that such a device was legitimate, since it did not seek to oust the CSA's jurisdiction, but it was crucial that there be a substantial element of spousal support in such an order.

CHAPTER ELEVEN

Transitional Provisions and Miscellaneous Matters

1. Transitional Provisions

11.1 The CSPSSA 2000 contains the usual provision that the Secretary of State may in regulations make such transitional and transitory provisions as he considers necessary or expedient in connection with the coming into force of Part I of the Act.[1] The matters for which these regulations may in particular provide are then set out.[2] They may be summarised as follows.

(a) There may be provision for the amount of child support maintenance payable by or to any person to be at a transitional rate.
(b) There may be more than one transitional rate, successively.
(c) There may be a phasing-in process by way of prescribed steps. This may result in an increase or a decrease in the amount payable.
(d) If a departure direction has been given under the previous arrangements, there may be regulations to ensure that this is taken into account under the new system.

11.2 The Government has stated that the new scheme will deal with new applications first. It is intended that existing cases will be transferred at a later date and the new rates will be phased in over a period of time.[3] It seems, therefore, that for some time the present system and the new system will run in tandem, after which there will be a period of phasing-in for old cases to be adapted to the new system.

It has already been seen (in Chapter Ten) that the Secretary of State will prescribe a date after which orders made by a court will only prevent the Secretary of State assuming jurisdiction for one year. This will add another factor to the equation.

2. The Child Maintenance Bonus

11.3 The CSA 1995 introduced a 'child maintenance bonus' to have effect as from April 1997. This was based on the 'back to work' bonus in the jobseeker's allowance and was intended to ensure that a person with care who was in receipt of income support would receive a credit for some of the child maintenance paid.

1 CSPSSA 2000, s 29(2).
2 In ibid, s 29(2)(a) and (b).
3 See Notes for Guidance, p 55.

This has now been abolished.[4] The Government intends to replace it by a child maintenance premium which would allow families in receipt of income support or jobseeker's allowance to keep up to £10 per week of the child maintenance paid.

3. Pilot Schemes

11.4 Section 28 of the CSPSSA 2000 provides a power for pilot schemes to be set up for specific elements of the child support provisions. This will enable the CSA to test certain elements of the new scheme on a small scale before launching them nationwide. It is not yet known which, if any, parts of the new scheme will be tested in this way.

---

4 By CSPSSA 2000, s 23.

APPENDIX

STATUTES

Child Support Act 1991, including prospective amendments by the Child Support, Pensions and Social Security Act 2000

ARRANGEMENT OF SECTIONS

Decisions and appeals dependent on other cases

Cases of error

Variations

Voluntary payments

Collection and enforcement

Special cases

Jurisdiction

Miscellaneous and supplemental

The basic principles

1 The duty to maintain

(1) For the purposes of this Act, each parent of a qualifying child is responsible for maintaining him.

(2) For the purposes of this Act, a non-resident parent shall be taken to have met his responsibility to maintain any qualifying child of his by making periodical payments of maintenance with respect to the child of such amount, and at such intervals, as may be determined in accordance with the provisions of this Act.

(3) Where a maintenance calculation made under this Act requires the making of periodical payments, it shall be the duty of the non-resident parent with respect to whom the calculation was made to make those payments.

Amendments—Child Support, Pensions and Social Security Act 2000, s 1(2), Sch 3, para 11(2) – in force from a date to be appointed.

2 Welfare of children: the general principle

Where, in any case which falls to be dealt with under this Act, the Secretary of State is considering the exercise of any discretionary power conferred by this Act, he shall have regard to the welfare of any child likely to be affected by his decision.

Amendments—Social Security Act 1998, s 86(1), Sch 7, para 18.

3 Meaning of certain terms used in this Act

(1) A child is a 'qualifying child' if –

(a) one of his parents is, in relation to him, a non-resident parent; or
(b) both of his parents are, in relation to him, non-resident parents.

(2) The parent of any child is a 'non-resident parent', in relation to him, if –

(a) that parent is not living in the same household with the child; and
(b) the child has his home with a person who is, in relation to him, a person with care.

(3) A person is a 'person with care', in relation to any child, if he is a person –

(a) with whom the child has his home;
(b) who usually provides day to day care for the child (whether exclusively or in conjunction with any other person); and
(c) who does not fall within a prescribed category of person.

(4) The Secretary of State shall not, under subsection (3)(c), prescribe as a category –

(a) parents;
(b) guardians;
(c) persons in whose favour residence orders under section 8 of the Children Act 1989 are in force;
(d) (*applies to Scotland only*)

(5) For the purposes of this Act there may be more than one person with care in relation to the same qualifying child.

(6) Periodical payments which are required to be paid in accordance with a maintenance calculation are referred to in this Act as 'child support maintenance'.

(7) Expressions are defined in this section only for the purposes of this Act.

Amendments—Child Support, Pensions and Social Security Act 2000, s 1(2), Sch 3, para 11(2) – in force from a date to be appointed.

4 Child support maintenance

(1) A person who is, in relation to any qualifying child or any qualifying children, either the person with care or the non-resident parent may apply to the Secretary of State for a maintenance calculation to be made under this Act with respect to that child, or any of those children.

(2) Where a maintenance calculation has been made in response to an application under this section the Secretary of State may, if the person with care or non-resident parent with respect to whom the calculation was made applies to him under this subsection, arrange for –

(a) the collection of the child support maintenance payable in accordance with the calculation;
(b) the enforcement of the obligation to pay child support maintenance in accordance with the calculation.

(3) Where an application under subsection (2) for the enforcement of the obligation mentioned in subsection (2)(b) authorises the Secretary of State to take steps to enforce that obligation whenever he considers it necessary to do so, the Secretary of State may act accordingly.

(4) A person who applies to the Secretary of State under this section shall, so far as that person reasonably can, comply with such regulations as may be made by the Secretary of State with a view to the Secretary of State being provided with the information which is required to enable –

(a) the non-resident parent to be identified or traced (where that is necessary);
(b) the amount of child support maintenance payable by the non-resident parent to be calculated; and
(c) that amount to be recovered from the non-resident parent.

(5) Any person who has applied to the Secretary of State under this section may at any time request him to cease acting under this section.

(6) It shall be the duty of the Secretary of State to comply with any request made under subsection (5) (but subject to any regulations made under subsection (8)).

(7) The obligation to provide information which is imposed by subsection (4) –

(a) shall not apply in such circumstances as may be prescribed; and
(b) may, in such circumstances as may be prescribed, be waived by the Secretary of State.

(8) The Secretary of State may by regulation make such incidental, supplemental or transitional provision as he thinks appropriate with respect to cases in which he is requested to cease to act under this section.

(9) No application may be made under this section if there is in force with respect to the person with care and non-resident parent in question a maintenance calculation made in response to an application treated as made under section 6.

(10) No application may be made at any time under this section with respect to a qualifying child or any qualifying children if –

(a) there is in force a written maintenance agreement made before 5th April 1993, or a maintenance order made before a prescribed date, in respect of that child or those children and the person who is, at that time, the non-resident parent; or
(aa) a maintenance order made on or after the date prescribed for the purposes of paragraph (a) is in force in respect of them, but has been so for less than the period of one year beginning with the date on which it was made; or
(b) benefit is being paid to, or in respect of, a parent with care of that child or those children.

(11) In subsection (10) 'benefit' means any benefit which is mentioned in, or prescribed by regulations under, section 6(1).

Amendments—Child Support Act 1995, s 18(1); Social Security Act 1998, s 86(1), Sch 7, para 19; Child Support, Pensions and Social Security Act 2000, ss 1(2), 2, Sch 3, para 11(2), (3) – in force from a date to be appointed.

5 Child support maintenance: supplemental provisions

(1) Where –

(a) there is more than one person with care of a qualifying child; and
(b) one or more, but not all, of them have parental responsibility for the child;

no application may be made for a maintenance calculation with respect to the child by any of those persons who do not have parental responsibility for the child.

(2) Where more than one application for a maintenance calculation is made with respect to the child concerned, only one of them may be proceeded with.

(3) The Secretary of State may by regulation make provision as to which of two or more applications for a maintenance calculation with respect to the same child is to be proceeded with.

Amendments—Children (Scotland) Act 1995, s 105(4), Sch 4, para 52(1), (3); Child Support, Pensions and Social Security Act 2000, s 1(2) – in force from a date to be appointed.

6 Applications by those claiming or receiving benefit

(1) This section applies where income support, an income-based jobseeker's allowance or any other benefit of a prescribed kind is claimed by or in respect of, or paid to or in respect of, the parent of a qualifying child who is also a person with care of the child.

(2) In this section, that person is referred to as 'the parent'.

(3) The Secretary of State may –

- (a) treat the parent as having applied for a maintenance calculation with respect to the qualifying child and all other children of the non-resident parent in relation to whom the parent is also a person with care; and
- (b) take action under this Act to recover from the non-resident parent, on the parent's behalf, the child support maintenance so determined.

(4) Before doing what is mentioned in subsection (3), the Secretary of State must notify the parent in writing of the effect of subsections (3) and (5) and section 46.

(5) The Secretary of State may not act under subsection (3) if the parent asks him not to (a request which need not be in writing).

(6) Subsection (1) has effect regardless of whether any of the benefits mentioned there is payable with respect to any qualifying child.

(7) Unless she has made a request under subsection (5), the parent shall, so far as she reasonably can, comply with such regulations as may be made by the Secretary of State with a view to the Secretary of State's being provided with the information which is required to enable –

- (a) the non-resident parent to be identified or traced;
- (b) the amount of child support maintenance payable by him to be calculated; and
- (c) that amount to be recovered from him.

(8) The obligation to provide information which is imposed by subsection (7) –

- (a) does not apply in such circumstances as may be prescribed; and
- (b) may, in such circumstances as may be prescribed, be waived by the Secretary of State.

(9) If the parent ceases to fall within subsection (1), she may ask the Secretary of State to cease acting under this section, but until then he may continue to do so.

(10) The Secretary of State must comply with any request under subsection (9) (but subject to any regulations made under subsection (11)).

(11) The Secretary of State may by regulations make such incidental or transitional provisions as he thinks appropriate with respect to cases in which he is asked under subsection (9) to cease to act under this section.

(12) The fact that a maintenance calculation is in force with respect to a person with care does not prevent the making of a new maintenance calculation with respect to her as a result of the Secretary of State's acting under subsection (3).

Amendments—Child Support, Pensions and Social Security Act 2000, s 3 – in force from a date to be appointed.

7 *(applies to Scotland only)*

8 Role of the courts with respect to maintenance for children

(1) This subsection applies in any case where the Secretary of State would have jurisdiction to make a maintenance calculation with respect to a qualifying child and a non-resident parent of his on an application duly made (or treated as made) by a person entitled to apply for such a calculation with respect to that child.

(2) Subsection (1) applies even though the circumstances of the case are such that the Secretary of State would not make a calculation if it were applied for.

(3) Except as provided in subsection (3A), in any case where subsection (1) applies, no court shall exercise any power which it would otherwise have to make, vary or revive any maintenance order in relation to the child and non-resident parent concerned.

(3A) Unless a maintenance calculation has been made with respect to the child concerned, subsection (3) does not prevent a court from varying a maintenance order in relation to that child and the non-resident parent concerned –

- (a) if the maintenance order was made on or after the date prescribed for the purposes of section 4(1)(a) or 7(1)(a); or
- (b) where the order was made before then, in any case in which section 4(10) or 7(10) prevents the making of an application for a maintenance calculation with respect to or by that child.

(4) Subsection (3) does not prevent a court from revoking a maintenance order.

(5) The Lord Chancellor or in relation to Scotland the Lord Advocate may by order provide that, in such circumstances as may be specified by the order, this section shall not prevent a court from exercising any power which it has to make a maintenance order in relation to a child if –

- (a) a written agreement (whether or not enforceable) provides for the making, or securing, by a non-resident parent of the child of periodical payments to or for the benefit of the child; and
- (b) the maintenance order which the court makes is, in all material respects, in the same terms as that agreement.

(6) This section shall not prevent a court from exercising any power which it has to make a maintenance order in relation to a child if –

- (a) a maintenance calculation is in force with respect to the child;
- (b) the non-resident parent's net weekly income exceeds the figure referred to in paragraph 10(3) of Schedule 1 (as it has effect from time to time pursuant to regulations made under paragraph 10A(1)(b));
- (c) the court is satisfied that the circumstances of the case make it appropriate for the non-resident parent to make or secure the making of periodical payments under a maintenance order in addition to the child support maintenance payable by him in accordance with the maintenance calculation.

(7) This section shall not prevent a court from exercising any power which it has to make a maintenance order in relation to a child if –

(a) the child is, will be or (if the order were to be made) would be receiving instruction at an educational establishment or undergoing training for a trade, profession or vocation (whether or not while in gainful employment); and
(b) the order is made solely for the purposes of requiring the person making or securing the making of periodical payments fixed by the order to meet some or all of the expenses incurred in connection with the provision of the instruction or training.

(8) This section shall not prevent a court from exercising any power which it has to make a maintenance order in relation to a child if –

(a) a disability living allowance is paid to or in respect of him; or
(b) no such allowance is paid but he is disabled,

and the order is made solely for the purpose of requiring the person making or securing the making of periodical payments fixed by the order to meet some or all of any expenses attributable to the child's disability.

(9) For the purposes of subsection (8), a child is disabled if he is blind, deaf or dumb or is substantially and permanently handicapped by illness, injury, mental disorder or congenital deformity or such other disability as may be prescribed.

(10) This section shall not prevent a court from exercising any power which it has to make a maintenance order in relation to a child if the order is made against a person with care of the child.

(11) In this Act 'maintenance order', in relation to any child, means an order which requires the making or securing of periodical payments to or for the benefit of the child and which is made under –

(a) Part II of the Matrimonial Causes Act 1973;
(b) the Domestic Proceedings and Magistrates' Courts Act 1978;
(c) Part III of the Matrimonial and Family Proceedings Act 1984;
(d) the Family Law (Scotland) Act 1985;
(e) Schedule 1 to the Children Act 1989; or
(f) any other prescribed enactment,

and includes any order varying or reviving such an order.

Amendments—Child Support Act 1995, s 18(3); Social Security Act 1998, s 86(1), Sch 7, para 22; Child Support, Pensions and Social Security Act 2000, s 1(2), Sch 3, para 11(2), (5) – in force from a date to be appointed.

9 Agreements about maintenance

(1) In this section 'maintenance agreement' means any agreement for the making, or for securing the making, of periodical payments by way of maintenance, or in Scotland aliment, to or for the benefit of any child.

(2) Nothing in this Act shall be taken to prevent any person from entering into a maintenance agreement.

(3) Subject to section 4(10)(a) and section 7(10), the existence of a maintenance agreement shall not prevent any party to the agreement, or any other person, from

applying for a maintenance calculation with respect to any child to or for whose benefit periodical payments are to be made or secured under the agreement.

(4) Where any agreement contains a provision which purports to restrict the right of any person to apply for a maintenance calculation, that provision shall be void.

(5) Where section 8 would prevent any court from making a maintenance order in relation to a child and a non-resident parent of his, no court shall exercise any power that it has to vary any agreement so as –

- (a) to insert a provision requiring that non-resident parent to make or secure the making of periodical payments by way of maintenance, or in Scotland aliment, to or for the benefit of that child; or
- (b) to increase the amount payable under such a provision.

(6) In any case in which section 4(10) or 7(10) prevents the making of an application for a maintenance calculation, and –

- (a) no parent has been treated under section 6(3) as having applied for a maintenance calculation with respect to the child; or
- (b) a parent has been so treated but no maintenance calculation has been made,

subsection (5) shall have effect with the omission of paragraph (b).

Amendments—Child Support Act 1995, s 18(4); Child Support, Pensions and Social Security Act 2000, s 1(2), Sch 3, para 11(2), (6) – in force from a date to be appointed.

10 Relationship between maintenance calculations and certain court orders and related matters

(1) Where an order of a kind prescribed for the purposes of this subsection is in force with respect to any qualifying child with respect to whom a maintenance calculation is made, the order –

- (a) shall, so far as it relates to the making or securing of periodical payments, cease to have effect to such extent as may be determined in accordance with regulations made by the Secretary of State; or
- (b) where the regulations so provide, shall, so far as it so relates, have effect subject to such modifications as may be so determined.

(2) Where an agreement of a kind prescribed for the purposes of this subsection is in force with respect to any qualifying child with respect to whom a maintenance calculation is made, the agreement –

- (a) shall, so far as it relates to the making or securing of periodical payments, be unenforceable to such extent as may be determined in accordance with regulations made by the Secretary of State; or
- (b) where the regulations so provide, shall, so far as it so relates, have effect subject to such modifications as may be determined.

(3) Any regulations under this section may, in particular, make such provision with respect to –

- (a) any case where any person with respect to whom an order or agreement of a kind prescribed for the purposes of subsection (1) or (2) has effect applies to the prescribed court, before the end of the prescribed period, for the order or agreement to be varied in the light of the maintenance calculation and of the provisions of this Act;

(b) the recovery of any arrears under the order or agreement which fell due before the coming into force of the maintenance calculation,

as the Secretary of State considers appropriate and may provide that, in prescribed circumstances, an application to any court which is made with respect to an order of a prescribed kind relating to the making or securing of periodical payments to or for the benefit of a child shall be treated by the court as an application for the order to be revoked.

(4) The Secretary of State may by regulation make provision for –

(a) notification to be given by the Secretary of State to the prescribed person in any case where he considers that the making of a maintenance calculation has affected, or is likely to affect, any order of a kind prescribed for the purposes of this subsection;
(b) notification to be given by the prescribed person to the Secretary of State in any case where a court makes an order which it considers has affected, or is likely to affect, a maintenance calculation.

(5) Rules may be made under section 144 of the Magistrates' Courts Act 1980 (rules of procedure) requiring any person who, in prescribed circumstances, makes an application to a magistrates' court for a maintenance order to furnish the court with a statement in a prescribed form, and signed by an officer of the Secretary of State, as to whether or not, at the time when the statement is made, there is a maintenance calculation in force with respect to that person or the child concerned.

In this subsection –

'maintenance order' means an order of a prescribed kind for the making or securing of periodical payments to or for the benefit of a child; and
'prescribed' means prescribed by the rules.

Amendments—Social Security Act 1998, s 86(1), Sch 7, para 23(1)(a), (b), (2); Child Support, Pensions and Social Security Act 2000, s 1(2) – in force from a date to be appointed.

Maintenance calculations

11 Maintenance calculations

(1) An application for a maintenance calculation made to the Secretary of State shall be dealt with by him in accordance with the provison made by or under this Act.

(2) The Secretary of State shall (unless he decides not to make a maintenance calculation in response to the application, or makes a decision under section 12) determine the application by making a decision under this section about whether any child support maintenance is payable and, if so, how much.

(3) Where –

(a) a parent is treated under section 6(3) as having applied for a maintenance calculation; but
(b) the Secretary of State becomes aware before determining the application that the parent has ceased to fall within section 6(1),

he shall, subject to subsection (4), cease to treat that parent as having applied for a maintenance calculation.

(4) If it appears to the Secretary of State that subsection (10) of section 4 would not have prevented the parent with care concerned from making an application for a maintenance calculation under that section he shall –

(a) notify her of the effect of this subsection; and
(b) if, before the end of the period of one month beginning with the day on which notice was sent to her, she asks him to do so, treat her as having applied not under section 6 but under section 4.

(5) Where subsection (3) applies but subsection (4) does not, the Secretary of State shall notify –

(a) the parent with care concerned; and
(b) the non-resident parent (or alleged non-resident parent), where it appears to him that that person is aware that the parent with care has been treated as having applied for a maintenance calculation.

(6) The amount of child support maintenance to be fixed by a maintenance calculation shall be determined in accordance with Part I of Schedule 1 unless an application for a variation has been made and agreed.

(7) If the Secretary of State has agreed to a variation, the amount of child support maintenance to be fixed shall be determined on the basis he determines under section 28F(4).

(8) Part II of Schedule 1 makes further provision with respect to maintenance calculations.

Amendments—Child Support, Pensions and Social Security Act 2000, s 1(1) – in force from a date to be appointed.

12 Default and interim maintenance decisions

(1) Where the Secretary of State –

(a) is required to make a maintenance calculation; or
(b) is proposing to make a decision under section 16 or 17,

and it appears to him that he does not have sufficient information to enable him to do so, he may make a default maintenance decision.

(2) Where an application for a variation has been made under section 28A(1) in connection with an application for a maintenance calculation (or in connection with such an application which is treated as having been made), the Secretary of State may make an interim maintenance decision.

(3) The amount of child support maintenance fixed by an interim maintenance decision shall be determined in accordance with Part I of Schedule 1.

(4) The Secretary of State may by regulations make provision as to default and interim maintenance decisions.

(5) The regulations may, in particular, make provision as to –

(a) the procedure to be followed in making a default or an interim maintenance decision; and
(b) a default rate of child support maintenance to apply where a default maintenance decision is made.

Amendments—Child Support, Pensions and Social Security Act 2000, s 4 – in force from a date to be appointed.

13 . . .

Amendments—Social Security Act 1998, s 86(1), Sch 7, para 26.

Information

14 Information required by Secretary of State

(1) The Secretary of State may make regulations requiring any information or evidence needed for the determination of any application made or treated as made under this Act, or any question arising in connection with such an application (or application treated as made), or needed for the making of any decision or in connection with the imposition of any condition or requirement under this Act, or needed in connection with the collection or enforcement of child support or other maintenance under this Act, to be furnished –

- (a) by such persons as may be determined in accordance with regulations made by the Secretary of State; and
- (b) in accordance with the regulations.

(1A) Regulations under subsection (1) may make provision for notifying any person who is required to furnish any information or evidence under the regulations of the possible consequences of failing to do so.

(2)–(2A) ...

(3) The Secretary of State may by regulation make provision authorising the disclosure by him, in such circumstances as may be prescribed, of such information held by him for purposes of this Act as may be prescribed.

(4) The provisions of Schedule 2 (which relate to information which is held for purposes other than those of this Act but which is required by the Secretary of State) shall have effect.

Amendments—Child Support Act 1995, s 30(5), Sch 3, paras 2, 3(1), (2); Social Security Act 1998, s 86(1), Sch 7, para 27(a), (b); Child Support, Pensions and Social Security Act 2000, s 12, Sch 3, para 11(7) – in force from a date to be appointed.

14A Information – offences

(1) This section applies to –

- (a) persons who are required to comply with regulations under section 4(4) or 7(5); and
- (b) persons specified in regulations under section 14(1)(a).

(2) Such a person is guilty of an offence if, pursuant to a request for information under or by virtue of those regulations –

- (a) he makes a statement or representation which he knows to be false; or
- (b) he provides, or knowingly causes or knowingly allows to be provided, a document or other information which he knows to be false in a material particular.

(3) Such a person is guilty of an offence if, following such a request, he fails to comply with it.

(4) It is a defence for a person charged with an offence under subsection (3) to prove that he had a reasonable excuse for failing to comply.

(5) A person guilty of an offence under this section is liable on summary conviction to a fine not exceeding level 3 on the standard scale.

Amendments—Child Support, Pensions and Social Security Act 2000, s 13 – in force from a date to be appointed.

15 Powers of inspectors

(1) The Secretary of State may appoint, on such terms as he thinks fit, persons to act as inspectors under this section.

(2) The function of inspectors is to acquire information which the Secretary of State needs for any of the purposes of this Act.

(3) Every inspector is to be given a certificate of his appointment.

(4) An inspector has power, at any reasonable time and either alone or accompanied by such other persons as he thinks fit, to enter any premises which –

(a) are liable to inspection under this section; and
(b) are premises to which it is reasonable for him to require entry in order that he may exercise his functions under this section,

and may there make such examination and inquiry as he considers appropriate.

(4A) Premises liable to inspection under this section are those which are not used wholly as a dwelling house and which the inspector has reasonable grounds for suspecting are –

(a) premises at which a non-resident parent is or has been employed;
(b) premises at which a non-resident parent carries out, or has carried out, a trade, profession, vocation or business;
(c) premises at which there is information held by a person ('A') whom the inspector has reasonable grounds for suspecting has information about a non-resident parent acquired in the course of A's own trade, profession, vocation or business.

(5) An inspector exercising his powers may question any person aged 18 or over whom he finds on the premises.

(6) If required to do so by an inspector exercising his powers, any such person shall furnish to the inspector all such information and documents as the inspector may reasonably require.

(7) No person shall be required under this section to answer any question or to give any evidence tending to incriminate himself or, in the case of a person who is married, his or her spouse.

(8) On applying for admission to any premises in the exercise of his powers, an inspector shall, if so required, produce his certificate.

(9) If any person –

(a) intentionally delays or obstructs any inspector exercising his powers; or
(b) without reasonable excuse, refuses or neglects to answer any question or furnish any information or to produce any document when required to do so under this section,

he shall be guilty of an offence and liable on summary conviction to a fine not exceeding level 3 on the standard scale.

(10) In this section –

'certificate' means a certificate of appointment issued under this section;
'inspector' means an inspector appointed under this section;
'powers' means powers conferred by this section.

(11) In this section, 'premises' includes –

(a) moveable structures and vehicles, vessels, aircraft and hovercraft;

(b) installations that are offshore installations for the purposes of the Mineral Workings (Offshore Installations) Act 1971; and
(c) places of all other descriptions whether or not occupied as land or otherwise,

and references in this section to the occupier of premises are to be construed, in relation to premises that are not occupied as land, as references to any person for the time being present at the place in question.

Amendments—Social Security Act 1998, s 86(1), Sch 7, para 28; Child Support, Pensions and Social Security Act 2000, s 14(2)–(4) – in force from a date to be appointed.

Reviews and appeals

16 Revision of decisions

(1) Any decision to which subsection (1A) applies may be revised by the Secretary of State –

(a) either within the prescribed period or in prescribed cases or circumstances; and
(b) either on an application made for the purpose or on his own initiative;

and regulation may prescribe the procedure by which a decision of the Secretary of State may be so revised.

(1A) This subsection applies to –

(a) a decision of the Secretary of State under section 11, 12 or 17;
(b) a reduced benefit decision under section 46;
(c) a decision of an appeal tribunal on a referral under section 28D(1)(b).

(1B) Where the Secretary of State revises a decision under section 12(1) –

(a) he may (if appropriate) do so as if he were revising a decision under section 11; and
(b) if he does that, his decision as revised is to be treated as one under section 11 instead of section 12(1) (and, in particular, is to be so treated for the purposes of an appeal against it under section 20).

(2) In making a decision under subsection (1), the Secretary of State need not consider any issue that is not raised by the application or, as the case may be, did not cause him to act on his own initiative.

(3) Subject to subsections (4) and (5) and section 28ZC, a revision under this section shall take effect as from the date on which the original decision took (or was to take) effect.

(4) Regulations may provide that, in prescribed cases or circumstances, a revision under this section shall take effect as from such other date as may be prescribed.

(5) Where a decision is revised under this section, for the purpose of any rule as to the time allowed for bringing an appeal, the decision shall be regarded as made on the date on which it is so revised.

(6) Except in prescribed circumstances, an appeal against a decision of the Secretary of State shall lapse if the decision is revised under this section before the appeal is determined.

Amendments—Social Security Act 1998, s 40; Child Support, Pensions and Social Security Act 2000, s 8 – in force from a date to be appointed.

17 Decisions superseding earlier decisions

(1) Subject to subsection (2), the following, namely –

- (a) any decision of the Secretary of State under section 11 or 12 or this section, whether as originally made or as revised under section 16;
- (b) any decision of an appeal tribunal under section 20;
- (c) any reduced benefit decision under section 46;
- (d) any decision of an appeal tribunal on a referral under section 28D(1)(b);
- (e) any decision of a Child Support Commissioner on an appeal from such a decision as is mentioned in paragraph (b) or (d),

may be superseded by a decision made by the Secretary of State, either on an application made for the purpose or on his own initiative.

(2) In making a decision under subsection (1), the Secretary of State need not consider any issue that is not raised by the application or, as the case may be, did not cause him to act on his own initiative.

(3) Regulations may prescribe the cases and circumstances in which, and the procedure by which, a decision may be made under this section.

(4) Subject to subsection (5) and section 28ZC, a decision under this section shall take effect as from the beginning of the maintenance period in which it is made or, where applicable, the beginning of the maintenance period in which the application was made.

(4A) In subsection (4), a 'maintenance period' is (except where a different meaning is prescribed for prescribed cases) a period of seven days, the first one beginning on the effective date of the first decison made by the Secretary of State under section 11 or (if earlier) his first default or interim maintenance decision (under section 12) in relation to the non-resident parent in question, and each subsequent one beginning on the day after the last day of the previous one.

(5) Regulations may provide that, in prescribed cases or circumstances, a decision under this section shall take effect as from such other date as may be prescribed.

Amendments—Social Security Act 1998, s 41; Child Support, Pensions and Social Security Act 2000, s 9, Sch 9 – in force from a date to be appointed.

18–19 ...

Amendments—Social Security Act 1998, s 41.

20 Appeals to appeal tribunals

(1) A qualifying person has a right of appeal to an appeal tribunal against –

- (a) a decision of the Secretary of State under section 11, 12 or 17 (whether as originally made or as revised under section 16);
- (b) a decision of the Secretary of State not to make a maintenance calculation under section 11 or not to supersede a decision under section 17;
- (c) a reduced benefit decision under section 46;
- (d) the imposition (by virtue of section 41A) of a requirement to make penalty payments, or their amount;
- (e) the imposition (by virtue of section 47) of a requirement to pay fees.

(2) In subsection (1), 'qualifying person' means –

(a) in relation to paragraphs (a) and (b) –
  (i) the person with care, or non-resident parent, with respect to whom the Secretary of State made the decision, or
  (ii) in a case relating to a maintenance calculation which was applied for under section 7, either of those persons or the child concerned;
(b) in relation to paragraph (c), the person in respect of whom the benefits are payable;
(c) in relation to paragraph (d), the parent who has been required to make penalty payments; and
(d) in relation to paragraph (e), the person required to pay fees.

(3) A person with a right of appeal under this section shall be given such notice as may be prescribed of –

(a) that right; and
(b) the relevant decision, or the imposition of the requirement.

(4) Regulations may make –

(a) provision as to the manner in which, and the time within which, appeals are to be brought; and
(b) such provision with respect to proceedings before appeal tribunals as the Secretary of State considers appropriate.

(5) The regulations may in particular make any provision of a kind mentioned in Schedule 5 to the Social Security Act 1998.

(6) No appeal lies by virtue of subsection (1)(c) unless the amount of the person's benefit is reduced in accordance with the reduced benefit decision; and the time within which such an appeal may be brought runs from the date of notification of the reduction.

(7) In deciding an appeal under this section, an appeal tribunal –

(a) need not consider any issue that is not raised by the appeal; and
(b) shall not take into account any circumstances not obtaining at the time when the Secretary of State made the decision or imposed the requirement.

(8) If an appeal under this section is allowed, the appeal tribunal may –

(a) itself make such decision as it considers appropriate; or
(b) remit the case to the Secretary of State, together with such directions (if any) as it considers appropriate.

Amendments—Child Support, Pensions and Social Security Act 2000, s 10 – in force from a date to be appointed.

20A, 21 . . .

Amendments—Social Security Act 1998, s 42.

22 Child Support Commissioners

(1) Her Majesty may from time to time appoint a Chief Child Support Commissioner and such number of other Child Support Commissioners as she may think fit.

(2) The Chief Child Support Commissioner and the other Child Support Commissioners shall be appointed from among persons who –

(a) have a 10 year general qualification; or
(b) *(applies to Scotland only)*

(3) The Lord Chancellor, after consulting the Lord Advocate, may make such regulation with respect to proceedings before Child Support Commissioners as he considers appropriate.

(4) The regulations –

(a) may, in particular, make any provision of a kind mentioned in Schedule 5 to the Social Security Act 1998; and
(b) shall provide that any hearing before a Child Support Commissioner shall be in public except in so far as the Commissioner for special reasons directs otherwise.

(5) Schedule 4 shall have effect with respect to Child Support Commissioners.

Amendments—Social Security Act 1998, s 86(1), Sch 7, para 29.

23 *(applies to Northern Ireland only)*

23A Redetermination of appeals

(1) This section applies where an application is made to a person under section 24(6)(a) for leave to appeal from a decision of an appeal tribunal.

(2) If the person who constituted, or was the chairman of, the appeal tribunal considers that the decision was erroneous in law, he may set aside the decision and refer the case either for redetermination by the tribunal or for determination by a differently constituted tribunal.

(3) If each of the principal parties to the case expresses the view that the decision was erroneous in point of law, the person shall set aside the decision and refer the case for determination by a differently constituted tribunal.

(4) The 'principal parties' are –

(a) the Secretary of State; and
(b) those who are qualifying persons for the purposes of section 20(2) in relation to the decision in question.

Amendments—Child Support, Pensions and Social Security Act 2000, s 11 – in force from a date to be appointed.

24 Appeal to Child Support Commissioner

(1) Any person who is aggrieved by a decision of an appeal tribunal, and the Secretary of State, may appeal to a Child Support Commissioner on a question of law.

(1A) ...

(2) Where, on an appeal under this section, a Child Support Commissioner holds that the decision appealed against was wrong in law he shall set it aside.

(3) Where a decision is set aside under subsection (2), the Child Support Commissioner may –

(a) if he can do so without making fresh or further findings of fact, give the decision which he considers should have been given by the appeal tribunal;

(b) if he considers it expedient, make such findings and give such decision as he considers appropriate in the light of those findings; or
(c) on an appeal by the Secretary of State, refer the case to an appeal tribunal with directions for its determination; or
(d) on any other appeal, refer the case to the Secretary of State or, if he considers it appropriate, to an appeal tribunal with directions for its determination.

(4) The reference under subsection (3) to the Secretary of State shall, subject to any direction of the Child Support Commissioner, be to an officer of his, or a person providing him with services, who has taken no part in the decision originally appealed against.

(5) On a reference under subsection (3) to an appeal tribunal, the tribunal shall, subject to any direction of the Child Support Commissioner, consist of persons who were not members of the tribunal which gave the decision which has been appealed against.

(6) No appeal lies under this section without the leave –

(a) of the person who constituted, or was the chairman of, the appeal tribunal when the decision appealed against was given or of such other person as may be determined in accordance with regulations made by the Lord Chancellor; or
(b) subject to and in accordance with regulations so made, of a Child Support Commissioner.

(7) The Lord Chancellor may by regulation make provision as to the manner in which, and the time within which, appeals under this section are to be brought and applications for leave under this section are to be made.

(8) Where a question which would otherwise fall to be determined by the Secretary of State first arises in the course of an appeal to a Child Support Commissioner, he may, if he thinks fit, determine it even though it has not been considered by the Secretary of State.

(9) Before making any regulations under subsection (6) or (7), the Lord Chancellor shall consult the Lord Advocate.

Amendments—Child Support Act 1995, s 30(5), Sch 3, paras 2, 7(2), (3); Social Security Act 1998, s 86(1), Sch 7, para 30(1), (2), (3)(a)–(c), (4)–(6)(a), (b), (7).

25 Appeal from Child Support Commissioner on question of law

(1) An appeal on a question of law shall lie to the appropriate court from any decision of a Child Support Commissioner.

(2) No such appeal may be brought except –

(a) with leave of the Child Support Commissioner who gave the decision or, where regulations made by the Lord Chancellor so provide, of a Child Support Commissioner selected in accordance with the regulations; or
(b) if the Child Support Commissioner refuses leave, with the leave of the appropriate court.

(3) An application for leave to appeal under this section against a decision of a Child Support Commissioner ('the appeal decision') may only be made by –

(a) a person who was a party to the proceedings in which the original decision, or appeal decision, was given;
(b) the Secretary of State; or
(c) any other person who is authorised to do so by regulations made by the Lord Chancellor.

(3A) The Child Support Commissioner to whom an application for leave to appeal under this section is made shall specify as the appropriate court either the Court of Appeal or the Court of Session.

(3B) In determining the appropriate court, the Child Support Commissioner shall have regard to the circumstances of the case, and in particular the convenience of the persons who may be parties to the appeal.

(4) In this section –

'appropriate court', except in subsections (3A) and (3B), means the court specified in accordance with those subsections; and
'original decision' means the decision to which the appeal decision in question relates.

(5) The Lord Chancellor may by regulation make provision with respect to –

(a) the manner in which and the time within which applications must be made to a Child Support Commissioner for leave under this section; and
(b) the procedure for dealing with such applications.

(6) Before making any regulations under subsection (2), (3) or (5), the Lord Chancellor shall consult the Lord Advocate.

Amendments—Child Support Act 1995, s 30(5), Sch 3, paras 2, 8(1), (2).

26 Disputes about parentage

(1) Where a person who is alleged to be a parent of the child with respect to whom an application for a maintenance calculation has been made or treated as made ('the alleged parent') denies that he is one of the child's parents, the Secretary of State shall not make a maintenance calculation on the assumption that the alleged parent is one of the child's parents unless the case falls within one of those set out in subsection (2).

(2) The Cases are –

CASE A1

Where –

(a) the child is habitually resident in England and Wales;
(b) the Secretary of State is satisfied that the alleged parent was married to the child's mother at some time in the period beginning with the conception and ending with the birth of the child; and
(c) the child has not been adopted.

CASE A2

Where –

(a) the child is habitually resident in England and Wales;
(b) the alleged parent has been registered as father of the child under section 10 or 10A of the Births and Deaths Registration Act 1953, or in any register kept under section 13 (register of births and still-births) or section 44 (Register of Corrections Etc) of the Registration of Births, Deaths and Marriages (Scotland) Act 1965, or under Article 14 or 18(1)(b)(ii) of the Births and Deaths Registration (Northern Ireland) Order 1976; and
(c) the child has not subsequently been adopted.

Case A3

Where the result of a scientific test (within the meaning of section 27A) taken by the alleged parent would be relevant to determining the child's parentage, and the alleged parent –

(a) refuses to take such a test; or
(b) has submitted to such a test, and it shows that there is no reasonable doubt that the alleged parent is a parent of the child.

Case A

Where the alleged parent is a parent of the child in question by virtue of having adopted him.

Case B

Where the alleged parent is a parent of the child in question by virtue of an order under section 30 of the Human Fertilisation and Embryology Act 1990 (parental orders in favour of gamete donors).

Case B1

Where the Secretary of State is satisfied that the alleged parent is a parent of the child in question by virtue of section 27 or 28 of that Act (meaning of 'mother' and of 'father' respectively).

Case C

Where –

(a) either –
  (i) a declaration that the alleged parent is a parent of the child in question (or a declaration which has that effect) is in force under section 55A or 56 of the Family Law Act 1986 or Article 32 of the Matrimonial and Family Proceedings (Northern Ireland) Order 1989 (declarations of parentage); or
  (ii) (*applies to Scotland only*); and
(b) the child has not subsequently been adopted.

Case D

Where –

(a) a declaration to the effect that the alleged parent is one of the parents of the child in question has been made under section 27; and
(b) the child has not subsequently been adopted.

Case E

Where –

(a) the child is habitually resident in Scotland;
(b) the Secretary of State is satisfied that one or other of the presumptions set out in section 5(1) of the Law Reform (Parent and Child) (Scotland) Act 1986 applies; and
(c) the child has not subsequently been adopted.

CASE F

Where –

(a) the alleged parent has been found, or adjudged, to be the father of the child in question –

(i) in proceedings before any court in England and Wales which are relevant proceedings for the purposes of section 12 of the Civil Evidence Act 1968 or in proceedings before any court in Northern Ireland which are relevant proceedings for the purposes of section 8 of the Civil Evidence Act (Northern Ireland) 1971; or

(ii) in affiliation proceedings before any court in the United Kingdom,

(whether or not he offered any defence to the allegation of paternity) and that finding or adjudication still subsists; and

(b) the child has not subsequently been adopted.

(3) In this section –

'adopted' means adopted within the meaning of Part IV of the Adoption Act 1976 or, in relation to Scotland, Part IV of the Adoption (Scotland) Act 1978; and

'affiliation proceedings', in relation to Scotland, means any action of affiliation and aliment.

Amendments—Children (Northern Ireland Consequential Amendments) Order 1995, SI 1995/756; Social Security Act 1998, s 86(1), Sch 7, para 31(1), (2); Child Support, Pensions and Social Security Act 2000, ss 1(2), 15, Sch 3, para 11(8), Sch 8, para 12 – in force from a date to be appointed.

27 Applications for declaration of parentage under Family Law Act 1986

(1) This section applies where –

(a) an application for a maintenance calculation has been made (or is treated as having been made), or a maintenance calculation is in force, with respect to a person ('the alleged parent') who denies that he is a parent of a child with respect to whom the application or calculation was made or treated as made;

(b) the Secretary of State is not satisfied that the case falls within one of those set out in section 26(2); and

(c) the Secretary of State or the person with care makes an application for a declaration under section 55A of the Family Law Act 1986 as to whether or not the alleged parent is one of the child's parents.

(2) Where this section applies –

(a) if it is the person with care who makes the application, she shall be treated as having a sufficient personal interest for the purposes of subsection (3) of that section; and

(b) if it is the Secretary of State who makes the application, that subsection shall not apply.

(3) This section does not apply to Scotland.

Amendments—Child Support, Pensions and Social Security Act 2000, Sch 8, para 13.

27A Recovery of fees for scientific tests

(1) This section applies in any case where –

(a) an application for a maintenance calculation has been made or treated as made or a maintenance calculation is in force;
(b) scientific tests have been carried out (otherwise than under a direction or in response to a request) in relation to bodily samples obtained from a person who is alleged to be a parent of a child with respect to whom the application or calculation is made or, as the case may be, treated as made;
(c) the results of the tests do not exclude the alleged parent from being one of the child's parents; and
(d) one of the conditions set out in subsection (2) is satisfied.

(2) The conditions are that –

(a) the alleged parent does not deny that he is one of the child's parents;
(b) in proceedings under section 55A of the Family Law Act 1986, a court has made a declaration that the alleged parent is a parent of the child in question; or
(c) (*applies to Scotland only*).

(3) In any case to which this section applies, any fee paid by the Secretary of State in connection with scientific tests may be recovered by him from the alleged parent as a debt due to the Crown.

(4) In this section –

'bodily sample' means a sample of bodily fluid or bodily tissue taken for the purpose of scientific tests;
'direction' means a direction given by a court under section 20 of the Family Law Reform Act 1969 (tests to determine paternity);
'request' means a request made by a court under section 70 of the Law Reform (Miscellaneous Provisions) (Scotland) Act 1990 (blood and other samples in civil proceedings); and
'scientific tests' means scientific tests made with the object of ascertaining the inheritable characteristics of bodily fluids or bodily tissue.

(5) Any sum recovered by the Secretary of State under this section shall be paid by him into the Consolidated Fund.

Amendments—Child Support Act 1995, s 21; Child Support, Pensions and Social Security Act 2000, s 1(2), Sch 3, para 11(9) – in force from a date to be appointed.

28 (*applies to Scotland only*)

Decisions and appeals dependent on other cases

28ZA Decisions involving issues that arise on appeal in other cases

(1) This section applies where –

(a) a decision by the Secretary of State falls to be made under section 11, 12, 16 or 17 or with respect to a reduced benefit decision under section 46; and
(b) an appeal is pending against a decision given in relation to a different matter by a Child Support Commissioner or a court.

(2) If the Secretary of State considers it possible that the result of the appeal will be such that, if it were already determined, it would affect the decision in some way –

(a) he need not, except in such cases or circumstances as may be prescribed, make the decision while the appeal is pending;
(b) he may, in such cases or circumstances as may be prescribed, make the decision on such basis as may be prescribed.

(3) Where the Secretary of State acts in accordance with subsection (2)(b), following the determination of the appeal he shall if appropriate revise his decision (under section 16) in accordance with that determination.

(4) For the purposes of this section, an appeal against a decision is pending if –

(a) an appeal against the decision has been brought but not determined;
(b) an application for leave to appeal against the decision has been made but not determined; or
(c) in such circumstances as may be prescribed, an appeal against the decision has not been brought (or, as the case may be, an application for leave to appeal against the decision has not been made) but the time for doing so has not yet expired.

(5) In paragraphs (a), (b) and (c) of subsection (4), any reference to an appeal, or an application for leave to appeal, against a decision includes a reference to –

(a) an application for, or for leave to apply for, judicial review of the decision under section 31 of the Supreme Court Act 1981; or
(b) an application to the supervisory jurisdiction of the Court of Session in respect of the decision.

Amendments—Social Security Act 1998, s 43; Child Support, Pensions and Social Security Act 2000, s 1(2), Sch 3, para 11(11) – in force from a date to be appointed.

28ZB Appeals involving issues that arise on appeal in other cases

(1) This section applies where –

(a) an appeal ('appeal A') in relation to a decision or the imposition of a requirement falling within section 20(1), is made to an appeal tribunal, or from an appeal tribunal to a Child Support Commissioner; and
(b) an appeal ('appeal B') is pending against a decision given in a different case by a Child Support Commissioner or a court.

(2) If the Secretary of State considers it possible that the result of appeal B will be such that, if it were already determined, it would affect the determination of appeal A, he may serve notice requiring the tribunal or Child Support Commissioner –

(a) not to determine appeal A but to refer it to him; or
(b) to deal with the appeal in accordance with subsection (4).

(3) Where appeal A is referred to the Secretary of State under subsection (2)(a), following the determination of appeal B and in accordance with that determination, he shall if appropriate –

(a) in a case where appeal A has not been determined by the tribunal, revise (under section 16) his decision which gave rise to that appeal; or
(b) in a case where appeal A has been determined by the tribunal, make a decision (under section 17) superseding the tribunal's decision.

(4) Where appeal A is to be dealt with in accordance with this subsection, the appeal tribunal or Child Support Commissioner shall either –

(a) stay appeal A until appeal B is determined; or
(b) if the tribunal or Child Support Commissioner considers it to be in the interests of the appellant to do so, determine appeal A as if –
  (i) appeal B had already been determined; and
  (ii) the issues arising on appeal B had been decided in the way that was most unfavourable to the appellant.

In this subsection 'the appellant' means the person who appealed or, as the case may be, first appealed against the decision or the imposition of the requirement mentioned in subsection (1)(a).

(5) Where the appeal tribunal or Child Support Commissioner acts in accordance with subsection (4)(b), following the determination of appeal B the Secretary of State shall, if appropriate, make a decision (under section 17) superseding the decision of the tribunal or Child Support Commissioner in accordance with that determination.

(6) For the purposes of this section, an appeal against a decision is pending if –

(a) an appeal against the decision has been brought but not determined;
(b) an application for leave to appeal against the decision has been made but not determined; or
(c) in such circumstances as may be prescribed, an appeal against the decision has not been brought (or, as the case may be, an application for leave to appeal against the decision has not been made) but the time for doing so has not yet expired.

(7) In this section –

(a) the reference in subsection (1)(a) to an appeal to a Child Support Commissioner includes a reference to an application for leave to appeal to a Child Support Commissioner; and
(b) any reference in paragraph (a), (b) or (c) of subsection (6) to an appeal, or to an application for leave to appeal, against a decision includes a reference to –
  (i) an application for, or for leave to apply for, judicial review of the decision under section 31 of the Supreme Court Act 1981; or
  (ii) an application to the supervisory jurisdiction of the Court of Session in respect of the decision.

(8) Regulations may make provision supplementing that made by this section.

Amendments—Social Security Act 1998, s 43; Child Support, Pensions and Social Security Act 2000, Sch 3, para 11(12).

Cases of error

28ZC Restrictions on liability in certain cases of error

(1) Subject to subsection (2), this section applies where –

(a) the effect of the determination, whenever made, of an appeal to a Child Support Commissioner or the court ('the relevant determination') is that the adjudicating authority's decision out of which the appeal arose was erroneous in point of law; and
(b) after the date of the relevant determination a decision falls to be made by the Secretary of State in accordance with that determination (or would, apart from this section, fall to be so made) –

(i) with respect to an application for a maintenance calculation (made after the commencement date or one treated as having been so made, or under section 46 as to the reduction of benefit);
(ii) as to whether to revise, under section 16, any decision (made after the commencement date) referred to in section 16(1A); or
(iii) on an application under section 17 (made after the commencement date) for any decision (made after the commencement date) referred to in section 17(1).

(2) This section does not apply where the decision of the Secretary of State mentioned in subsection (1)(b)–

(a) is one which, but for section 28ZA(2)(a), would have been made before the date of the relevant determination; or
(b) is one made in pursuance of section 28ZB(3) or (5).

(3) In so far as the decision relates to a person's liability or the reduction of a person's benefit in respect of a period before the date of the relevant determination, it shall be made as if the adjudicating authority's decision had been found by the Commissioner or court not to have been erroneous in point of law.

(4) Subsection (1)(a) shall be read as including a case where –

(a) the effect of the relevant determination is that part or all of a purported regulation or order is invalid; and
(b) the error of law made by the adjudicating authority was to act on the basis that the purported regulation or order (or the part held to be invalid) was valid.

(5) It is immaterial for the purposes of subsection (1)–

(a) where such a decision as is mentioned in paragraph (b)(i) falls to be made; or
(b) where such a decision as is mentioned in paragraph (b)(ii) or (iii) falls to be made on an application under section 16 or (as the case may be) section 17,

whether the application was made before or after the date of the relevant determination.

(6) In this section –

'adjudicating authority' means the Secretary of State, or a child support officer or, in the case of a decision made on a referral under section 28D(1)(b), an appeal tribunal;

'the commencement date' means the date of the coming into force of section 44 of the Social Security Act 1998; and

'the court' means the High Court, the Court of Appeal, the Court of Session, the High Court or Court of Appeal in Northern Ireland, the House of Lords or the Court of Justice of the European Community.

(7) The date of the relevant determination shall, in prescribed cases, be determined for the purposes of this section in accordance with any regulation made for that purpose.

(8) Regulations made under subsection (7) may include provision –

(a) for a determination of a higher court to be treated as if it had been made on the date of a determination of a lower court or a Child Support Commissioner; or
(b) for a determination of a lower court or a Child Support Commissioner to be treated as if it had been made on the date of a determination of a higher court.

Amendments—Social Security Act 1998, s 44; Child Support, Pensions and Social Security Act 2000, Sch 3, para 11(13).

28ZD Correction of errors and setting aside of decisions

(1) Regulations may make provision with respect to –

(a) the correction of accidental errors in any decision or record of a decision given under this Act; and
(b) the setting aside of any such decision in a case where it appears just to set the decision aside on the ground that –
    (i) a document relating to the proceedings in which the decision was given was not sent to, or was not received at an appropriate time by, a party to the proceedings or a party's representative or was not received at an appropriate time by the body or person who gave the decision; or
    (ii) a party to the proceedings or a party's representative was not present at a hearing related to the proceedings.

(2) Nothing in subsection (1) shall be construed as derogating from any power to correct errors or set aside decisions which is exercisable apart from regulation made by virtue of that subsection.

Amendments—Social Security Act 1998, s 44.

Variations

28A Application for variation of usual rules for calculating maintenance

(1) Where an application for a maintenance calculation is made under section 4 or 7, or treated as made under section 6, the person with care or the non-resident parent or (in the case of an application under section 7) either of them or the child concerned may apply to the Secretary of State for the rules by which the calculation is made to be varied in accordance with this Act.

(2) Such an application is referred to in this Act as an 'application for a variation'.

(3) An application for a variation may be made at any time before the Secretary of State has reached a decision (under section 11 or 12(1)) on the application for a maintenance calculation (or the application treated as having been made under section 6).

(4) A person who applies for a variation –

(a) need not make the application in writing unless the Secretary of State directs in any case that he must; and
(b) must say upon what grounds the application is made.

(5) In other respects an application for a variation is to be made in such manner as may be prescribed.

(6) Schedule 4A has effect in relation to applications for a variation.

Amendments—Child Support, Pensions and Social Security Act 2000, s 5(2) – in force from a date to be appointed.

28B Preliminary consideration of applications

(1) Where an application for a variation has been duly made to the Secretary of State, he may give it a preliminary consideration.

(2) Where he does so he may, on completing the preliminary consideration, reject the application (and proceed to make his decision on the application for a maintenance calculation without any variation) if it appears to him –

(a) that there are no grounds on which he could agree to a variation;
(b) that he has insufficient information to make a decision on the application for the maintenance calculation under section 11 (apart from any information needed in relation to the application for a variation), and therefore that his decision would be made under section 12(1); or
(c) that other prescribed circumstances apply.

Amendments—Child Support, Pensions and Social Security Act 2000, s 5(2) – in force from a date to be appointed.

28C Imposition of regular payments condition

(1) Where –

(a) an application for a variation is made by the non-resident parent; and
(b) the Secretary of State makes an interim maintenance decision,

the Secretary of State may also, if he has completed his preliminary consideration (under section 28B) of the application for a variation and has not rejected it under that section, impose on the non-resident parent one of the conditions mentioned in subsection (2) (a 'regular payments condition').

(2) The conditions are that –

(a) the non-resident parent must make the payments of child support maintenance specified in the interim maintenance decision;
(b) the non-resident parent must make such lesser payments of child support maintenance as may be determined in accordance with regulations made by the Secretary of State.

(3) Where the Secretary of State imposes a regular payments condition, he shall give written notice of the imposition of the condition and of the effect of failure to comply with it to –

(a) the non-resident parent;
(b) all the persons with care concerned; and
(c) if the application for the maintenance calculation was made under section 7, the child who made the application.

(4) A regular payments condition shall cease to have effect –

(a) when the Secretary of State has made a decision on the application for a maintenance calculation under section 11 (whether he agrees to a variation or not);
(b) on the withdrawal of the application for a variation.

(5) Where a non-resident parent has failed to comply with a regular payments condition, the Secretary of State may in prescribed circumstances refuse to consider the application for a variation, and instead reach his decision under section 11 as if no such application had been made.

(6) The question whether a non-resident parent has failed to comply with a regular payments condition is to be determined by the Secretary of State.

(7) Where the Secretary of State determines that a non-resident parent has failed to comply with a regular payments condition he shall give written notice of his determination to –

(a) that parent;

(b) all the persons with care concerned; and
(c) if the application for the maintenance calculation was made under section 7, the child who made the application.

Amendments—Child Support, Pensions and Social Security Act 2000, s 5(2) – in force from a date to be appointed.

28D Determination of applications

(1) Where an application for a variation has not failed, the Secretary of State shall, in accordance with the relevant provisions of, or made under, this Act –

(a) either agree or not to a variation, and make a decision under section 11 or 12(1); or
(b) refer the application to an appeal tribunal for the tribunal to determine what variation, if any, is to be made.

(2) For the purposes of subsection (1), an application for a variation has failed if –

(a) it has been withdrawn; or
(b) the Secretary of State has rejected it on completing a preliminary consideration under section 28B; or
(c) the Secretary of State has refused to consider it under section 28C(5).

(3) In dealing with an application for a variation which has been referred to it under subsection (1)(b), an appeal tribunal shall have the same powers, and be subject to the same duties, as would the Secretary of State if he were dealing with the application.

Amendments—Child Support Act 1995, s 4; Social Security Act 1998, s 86(1), Sch 7, para 36; Child Support, Pensions and Social Security Act 2000, s 5(3) – in force from a date to be appointed.

28E Matters to be taken into account

(1) In determining whether to agree to a variation, the Secretary of State shall have regard both to the general principles set out in subsection (2) and to such other considerations as may be prescribed.

(2) The general principles are that –

(a) parents should be responsible for maintaining their children whenever they can afford to do so;
(b) where a parent has more than one child, his obligation to maintain any one of them should be no less of an obligation than his obligation to maintain any other of them.

(3) In determining whether to agree to a variation, the Secretary of State shall take into account any representations made to him –

(a) by the person with care or non-resident parent concerned; or
(b) (*applies to Scotland only*)

(4) In determining whether to agree to a variation, no account shall be taken of the fact that –

(a) any part of the income of the person with care concerned is, or would be if the Secretary of State agreed to a variation, derived from any benefit; or
(b) some or all of any child support maintenance might be taken into account in any manner in relation to any entitlement to benefit.

(5) In this section 'benefit' has such meaning as may be prescribed.

Amendments—Child Support Act 1998, s 5; Child Support, Pensions and Social Security Act 2000, s 5(4), Sch 3, para 11(2) – in force from a date to be appointed.

28F Agreement to a variation

(1) The Secretary of State may agree to a variation if –

(a) he is satisfied that the case is one which falls within one or more of the cases set out in Part I of Schedule 4B or in regulations made under that Part; and
(b) it is his opinion that, in all the circumstances of the case, it would be just and equitable to agree to a variation.

(2) In considering whether it would be just and equitable in any case to agree to a variation, the Secretary of State –

(a) must have regard, in particular, to the welfare of any child likely to be affected if he did agree to a variation; and
(b) must, or as the case may be must not, take any prescribed factors into account, or must take them into account (or not) in prescribed circumstances.

(3) The Secretary of State shall not agree to a variation (and shall proceed to make his decision on the application for a maintenance calculation without any variation) if he is satisfied that –

(a) he has insufficient information to make a decision on the application for the maintenance calculation under section 11, and therefore that his decision would be made under section 12(1); or
(b) other prescribed circumstances apply.

(4) Where the Secretary of State agrees to a variation, he shall –

(a) determine the basis on which the amount of child support maintenance is to be calculated in response to the application for a maintenance calculation (including an application treated as having been made); and
(b) make a decision under section 11 on that basis.

(5) If the Secretary of State has made an interim maintenance decision, it is to be treated as having been replaced by his decision under section 11, and except in prescribed circumstances any appeal connected with it (under section 20) shall lapse.

(6) In determining whether or not to agree to a variation, the Secretary of State shall comply with regulations made under Part II of Schedule 4B.

Amendments—Child Support, Pensions and Social Security Act 2000, s 5(5) – in force from a date to be appointed.

28G Variations: revision and supersession

(1) An application for a variation may also be made when a maintenance calculation is in force.

(2) The Secretary of State may by regulations provide for –

(a) sections 16, 17 and 20; and
(b) sections 28A to 28F and Schedules 4A and 4B,

to apply with prescribed modifications in relation to such applications.

(3) The Secretary of State may by regulations provide that, in prescribed cases (or except in prescribed cases), a decision under section 17 made otherwise than pursuant to an application for a variation may be made on the basis of a variation agreed to for the purposes of an earlier decision without a new application for a variation having to be made.

Amendments—Child Support, Pensions and Social Security Act 2000, s 7 – in force from a date to be appointed.

28H, 28I ...

Amendments—Child Support, Pensions and Social Security Act 2000, Sch 3, para 11(14) – in force from a date to be appointed.

Voluntary payments

28J Voluntary payments

(1) This section applies where –

(a) a person has applied for a maintenance calculation under section 4(1) or 7(1), or is treated as having applied for one by virtue of section 6;
(b) the Secretary of State has neither made a decision under section 11 or 12 on the application, nor decided not to make a maintenance calculation; and
(c) the non-resident parent makes a voluntary payment.

(2) A 'voluntary payment' is a payment –

(a) on account of child support maintenance which the non-resident parent expects to become liable to pay following the determination of the application (whether or not the amount of the payment is based on any estimate of his potential liability which the Secretary of State has agreed to give); and
(b) made before the maintenance calculation has been notified to the non-resident parent or (as the case may be) before the Secretary of State has notified the non-resident parent that he has decided not to make a maintenance calculation.

(3) In such circumstances and to such extent as may be prescribed –

(a) the voluntary payment may be set off against arrears of child support maintenance which accrued by virtue of the maintenance calculation taking effect on a date earlier than that on which it was notified to the non-resident parent;
(b) the amount payable under a maintenance calculation may be adjusted to take account of the voluntary payment.

(4) A voluntary payment shall be made to the Secretary of State unless he agrees, on such conditions as he may specify, that it may be made to the person with care, or to or through another person.

(5) The Secretary of State may by regulations make provision as to voluntary payments, and the regulations may in particular –

(a) prescribe what payments or descriptions of payment are, or are not, to count as 'voluntary payments';
(b) prescribe the extent to which and circumstances in which a payment, or a payment of a prescribed description, counts.

Amendments—Child Support, Pensions and Social Security Act 2000, s 20 – in force from a date to be appointed.

Collection and enforcement

29 Collection of child support maintenance

(1) The Secretary of State may arrange for the collection of any child support maintenance payable in accordance with a maintenance calculation where –

(a) the calculation is made by virtue of section 6; or
(b) an application has been made to the Secretary of State under section 4(2) or 7(3) for him to arrange for its collection.

(2) Where a maintenance calculation is made under this Act, payments of child support maintenance under the calculation shall be made in accordance with regulations made by the Secretary of State.

(3) The regulation may, in particular, make provision –

(a) for payments of child support maintenance to be made –
  (i) to the person caring for the child or children in question;
  (ii) to, or through, the Secretary of State; or
  (iii) to, or through, such other person as the Secretary of State may, from time to time, specify;
(b) as to the method by which payments of child support maintenance are to be made;
(c) as to the intervals at which such payments are to be made;
(d) as to the method and timing of the transmission of payments which are made, to or through the Secretary of State or any other person, in accordance with the regulations;
(e) empowering the Secretary of State to direct any person liable to make payments in accordance with the calculation –
  (i) to make them by standing order or by any other method which requires one person to give his authority for payments to be made from an account of his to an account of another's on specific dates during the period for which the authority is in force and without the need for any further authority from him;
  (ii) to open an account from which payments under the calculation may be made in accordance with the method of payment which that person is obliged to adopt;
(f) providing for the making of representations with respect to matters with which the regulations are concerned.

Amendments—Child Support, Pensions and Social Security Act 2000, s 1(2) – in force from a date to be appointed.

30 Collection and enforcement of other forms of maintenance

(1) Where the Secretary of State is arranging for the collection of any payments under section 29 or subsection (2), he may also arrange for the collection of any periodical payments, or secured periodical payments, of a prescribed kind which are payable to or for the benefit of any person who falls within a prescribed category.

(2) The Secretary of State may, except in prescribed cases, arrange for the collection of any periodical payments, or secured periodical payments, of a prescribed kind which are payable for the benefit of a child even though he is not arranging for the collection of child support maintenance with respect to that child.

(3) Where –

(a) the Secretary of State is arranging, under this Act, for the collection of different payments ('the payments') from the same non-resident parent;
(b) an amount is collected by the Secretary of State from the non-resident parent which is less than the total amount due in respect of the payments; and
(c) the non-resident parent has not stipulated how that amount is to be allocated by the Secretary of State as between the payments,

the Secretary of State may allocate that amount as he sees fit.

(4) In relation to England and Wales, the Secretary of State may by regulation make provision for sections 29 and 31 to 40 to apply, with such modifications (if any) as he considers necessary or expedient, for the purpose of enabling him to enforce any obligation to pay any amount which he is authorised to collect under this section.

(5) (*applies to Scotland only*)

(5A) Regulations made under subsection (1) or (2) prescribing payments which may be collected by the Secretary of State may make provision for the payment to him by such person or persons as may be prescribed of such fees as may be prescribed.

Amendments—Child Support, Pensions and Social Security Act 2000, Sch 3, para 11(2), (15) – in force from a date to be appointed.

31 Deduction from earnings orders

(1) This section applies where any person ('the liable person') is liable to make payments of child support maintenance.

(2) The Secretary of State may make an order ('a deduction from earnings order') against a liable person to secure the payment of any amount due under the maintenance calculation in question.

(3) A deduction from earnings order may be made so as to secure the payment of –

(a) arrears of child support maintenance payable under the calculation;
(b) amounts of child support maintenance which will become due under the calculation; or
(c) both such arrears and such future amounts.

(4) A deduction from earnings order –

(a) shall be expressed to be directed at a person ('the employer') who has the liable person in his employment; and
(b) shall have effect from such date as may be specified in the order.

(5) A deduction from earnings order shall operate as an instruction to the employer to –

(a) make deductions from the liable person's earnings; and
(b) pay the amounts deducted to the Secretary of State.

(6) The Secretary of State shall serve a copy of any deduction from earnings order which he makes under this section on –

(a) the person who appears to the Secretary of State to have the liable person in question in his employment; and
(b) the liable person.

(7) Where –

(a) a deduction from earnings order has been made; and
(b) a copy of the order has been served on the liable person's employer,

it shall be the duty of that employer to comply with the order; but he shall not be under any liability for non-compliance before the end of the period of 7 days beginning with the date on which the copy was served on him.

(8) In this section and in section 32 'earnings' has such meaning as may be prescribed.

Amendments—Child Support, Pensions and Social Security Act 2000, s 1(2) – in force from a date to be appointed.

32 Regulations about deduction from earnings orders

(1) The Secretary of State may by regulation make provision with respect to deduction from earnings orders.

(2) The regulation may, in particular, make provision –

(a) as to the circumstances in which one person is to be treated as employed by another;
(b) requiring any deduction from earnings under an order to be made in the prescribed manner;
(bb) for the amount or amounts which are to be deducted from the liable person's earnings not to exceed a prescribed proportion of his earnings (as determined by the employer);
(c) requiring an order to specify the amount or amounts to which the order relates and the amount or amounts which are to be deducted from the liable person's earnings in order to meet his liabilities under the maintenance calculation in question;
(d) requiring the intervals between deductions to be made under an order to be specified in the order;
(e) as to the payment of sums deducted under an order to the Secretary of State;
(f) allowing the person who deducts and pays any amount under an order to deduct from the liable person's earnings a prescribed sum towards his administrative costs;
(g) with respect to the notification to be given to the liable person of amounts deducted, and amounts paid, under the order;
(h) requiring any person on whom a copy of an order is served to notify the Secretary of State in the prescribed manner and within a prescribed period if he does not have the liable person in his employment or if the liable person ceases to be in his employment;
(i) as to the operation of an order where the liable person is in the employment of the Crown;
(j) for the variation of orders;
(k) similar to that made by section 31(7), in relation to any variation of an order;
(l) for an order to lapse when the employer concerned ceases to have the liable person in his employment;
(m) as to the revival of an order in such circumstances as may be prescribed;
(n) allowing or requiring an order to be discharged;
(o) as to the giving of notice by the Secretary of State to the employer concerned that an order has lapsed or has ceased to have effect.

(3) The regulation may include provision that while a deduction from earnings order is in force –

(a) the liable person shall from time to time notify the Secretary of State, in the prescribed manner and within a prescribed period, of each occasion on which he leaves any employment or becomes employed, or re-employed, and shall include in such a notification a statement of his earnings and expected earnings from the employment concerned and of such other matters as may be prescribed;
(b) any person who becomes the liable person's employer and knows that the order is in force shall notify the Secretary of State, in the prescribed manner and within a prescribed period, that he is the liable person's employer, and shall include in such a notification a statement of the liable person's earnings and expected earnings from the employment concerned and of such other matters as may be prescribed.

(4) The regulation may include provision with respect to the priority as between a deduction from earnings order and –

(a) any other deduction from earnings order;
(b) any order under any other enactment relating to England and Wales which provides for deductions from the liable person's earnings;
(c) any diligence against earnings.

(5) The regulation may include a provision that a liable person may appeal to a magistrates' court (or in Scotland to the sheriff) if he is aggrieved by the making of a deduction from earnings order against him, or by the terms of any such order, or there is a dispute as to whether payments constitute earnings or as to any other prescribed matter relating to the order.

(6) On an appeal under subsection (5) the court or (as the case may be) the sheriff shall not question the maintenance calculation by reference to which the deduction from earnings order was made.

(7) Regulations made by virtue of subsection (5) may include provision as to the powers of a magistrates' court, or in Scotland of the sheriff, in relation to an appeal (which may include provision as to the quashing of a deduction from earnings order or the variation of the terms of such an order).

(8) If any person fails to comply with the requirements of a deduction from earnings order, or with any regulation under this section which is designated for the purposes of this subsection, he shall be guilty of an offence.

(9) In subsection (8) 'designated' means designated by the regulation.

(10) It shall be a defence for a person charged with an offence under subsection (8) to prove that he took all reasonable steps to comply with the requirements in question.

(11) Any person guilty of an offence under subsection (8) shall be liable on summary conviction to a fine not exceeding level two on the standard scale.

Amendments—Child Support, Pensions and Social Security Act 2000, s 1(2), Sch 3, para 11(16) – in force from a date to be appointed.

33 Liability orders

(1) This section applies where –

(a) a person who is liable to make payments of child support maintenance ('the liable person') fails to make one or more of those payments; and
(b) it appears to the Secretary of State that –
  (i) it is inappropriate to make a deduction from earnings order against him (because, for example, he is not employed); or

(ii) although such an order has been made against him, it has proved ineffective as a means of securing that payments are made in accordance with the maintenance calculation in question.

(2) The Secretary of State may apply to a magistrates' court or, in Scotland, to the sheriff for an order ('a liability order') against the liable person.

(3) Where the Secretary of State applies for a liability order, the magistrates' court or (as the case may be) sheriff shall make the order if satisfied that the payments in question have become payable by the liable person and have not been paid.

(4) On an application under subsection (2), the court or (as the case may be) the sheriff shall not question the maintenance calculation under which the payments of child support maintenance fell to be made.

(5) If the Secretary of State designates a liability order for the purposes of this subsection it shall be treated as a judgment entered in a county court for the purposes of section 73 of the County Courts Act 1984 (register of judgments and orders).

(6) Where regulations have been made under section 29(3)(a) –

(a) the liable person fails to make a payment (for the purposes of subsection (1)(a) of this section); and
(b) a payment is not paid (for the purposes of subsection (3)),

unless the payment is made to, or through, the person specified in or by virtue of those regulations for the case of the liable person in question.

Amendments—Child Support Act 1995, s 30(5), Sch 3, para 10; Child Support, Pensions and Social Security Act 2000, s 1(2), Sch 3, para 11(17) – in force from a date to be appointed.

34 Regulations about liability orders

(1) The Secretary of State may make regulation in relation to England and Wales –

(a) prescribing the procedure to be followed in dealing with an application by the Secretary of State for a liability order;
(b) prescribing the form and contents of a liability order; and
(c) providing that where a magistrates' court has made a liability order, the person against whom it is made shall, during such time as the amount in respect of which the order was made remains wholly or partly unpaid, be under a duty to supply relevant information to the Secretary of State.

(2) In subsection (1) 'relevant information' means any information of a prescribed description which is in the possession of the liable person and which the Secretary of State has asked him to supply.

35 Enforcement of liability orders by distress

(1) Where a liability order has been made against a person ('the liable person'), the Secretary of State may levy the appropriate amount by distress and sale of the liable person's goods.

(2) In subsection (1), 'the appropriate amount' means the aggregate of –

(a) the amount in respect of which the order was made, to the extent that it remains unpaid; and
(b) an amount, determined in such manner as may be prescribed, in respect of the charges connected with the distress.

(3) The Secretary of State may, in exercising his powers under subsection (1) against the liable person's goods, seize –

(a) any of the liable person's goods except –
   (i) such tools, books, vehicles and other items of equipment as are necessary to him for use personally by him in his employment, business or vocation;
   (ii) such clothing, bedding, furniture, household equipment and provisions as are necessary for satisfying his basic domestic needs; and
(b) any money, banknotes, bills of exchange, promissory notes, bonds, specialties or securities for money belonging to the liable person.

(4) For the purposes of subsection (3), the liable person's domestic needs shall be taken to include those of any member of his family with whom he resides.

(5) No person levying a distress under this section shall be taken to be a trespasser –

(a) on that account; or
(b) from the beginning, on account of any subsequent irregularity in levying the distress.

(6) A person sustaining special damage by reason of any irregularity in levying a distress under this section may recover full satisfaction for the damage (and no more) by proceedings in trespass or otherwise.

(7) The Secretary of State may make regulation supplementing the provisions of this section.

(8) The regulation may, in particular –

(a) provide that a distress under this section may be levied anywhere in England and Wales;
(b) provide that such a distress shall not be deemed unlawful on account of any defect or want of form in the liability order;
(c) provide for an appeal to a magistrates' court by any person aggrieved by the levying of, or an attempt to levy, a distress under this section;
(d) make provision as to the powers of the court on an appeal (which may include provision as to the discharge of goods distrained or the payment of compensation in respect of goods distrained and sold).

36 Enforcement in county courts

(1) Where a liability order has been made against a person, the amount in respect of which the order was made, to the extent that it remains unpaid, shall, if a county court so orders, be recoverable by means of garnishee proceedings or a charging order, as if it were payable under a county court order.

(2) In subsection (1) 'charging order' has the same meaning as in section 1 of the Charging Orders Act 1979.

37, 38 (*apply to Scotland only*)

39 Liability orders: enforcement throughout United Kingdom

(1) The Secretary of State may by regulation provide for –

(a) any liability order made by a court in England and Wales; or
(b) any corresponding order made by a court in Northern Ireland,

to be enforced in Scotland as if it had been made by the Sheriff.

(2) The power conferred on the Court of Session by section 32 of the Sheriff Courts (Scotland) Act 1971 (power of Court of Session to regulate civil procedure in the sheriff court) shall extend to making provision for the registration in the sheriff court for enforcement of any such order as is referred to in subsection (1).

(3) The Secretary of State may by regulation make provision for, or in connection with, the enforcement in England and Wales of –

(a) any liability order made by the sheriff in Scotland; or
(b) any corresponding order made by a court in Northern Ireland,

as if it had been made by a magistrates' court in England and Wales.

(4) Regulations under subsection (3) may, in particular, make provision for the registration of any such order as is referred to in that subsection in connection with its enforcement in England and Wales.

39A Commitment to prison and disqualification from driving

(1) Where the Secretary of State has sought –

(a) in England and Wales to levy an amount by distress under this Act; or
(b) to recover an amount by virtue of section 36 or 38,

and that amount, or any portion of it, remains unpaid he may apply to the court under this section.

(2) An application under this section is for whichever the court considers appropriate in all the circumstances of –

(a) the issue of a warrant committing the liable person to prison; or
(b) an order for him to be disqualified from holding or obtaining a driving licence.

(3) On any such application the court shall (in the presence of the liable person) inquire as to –

(a) whether he needs a driving licence to earn his living;
(b) his means; and
(c) whether there has been wilful refusal or culpable neglect on his part.

(4) The Secretary of State may make representations to the court as to whether he thinks it more appropriate to commit the liable person to prison or to disqualify him from holding or obtaining a driving licence; and the liable person may reply to those representations.

(5) In this section and section 40B, 'driving licence' means a licence to drive a motor vehicle granted under Part III of the Road Traffic Act 1988.

(6) In this section 'the court' means –

(a) in England and Wales, a magistrates' court;
(b) in Scotland, the sheriff.

Amendments—Child Support, Pensions and Social Security Act 2000, s 16(1) – in force from a date to be appointed.

40 Commitment to prison

(1), (2) . . .

(3) If, but only if, the court is of the opinion that there has been wilful refusal or culpable neglect on the part of the liable person it may –

(a) issue a warrant of commitment against him; or
(b) fix a term of imprisonment and postpone the issue of the warrant until such time and on such conditions (if any) as it thinks just.

(4) Any such warrant –

(a) shall be made in respect of an amount equal to the aggregate of –
  (i) the amount mentioned in section 35(1) or so much of it as remains outstanding; and
  (ii) an amount (determined in accordance with regulations made by the Secretary of State) in respect of the costs of commitment; and
(b) shall state that amount.

(5) No warrant may be issued under this section against a person who is under the age of 18.

(6) A warrant issued under this section shall order the liable person –

(a) to be imprisoned for a specified period; but
(b) to be released (unless he is in custody for some other reason) on payment of the amount stated in the warrant.

(7) The maximum period of imprisonment which may be imposed by virtue of subsection (6) shall be calculated in accordance with Schedule 4 to the Magistrates' Courts Act 1980 (maximum periods of imprisonment in default of payment) but shall not exceed six weeks.

(8) The Secretary of State may by regulation make provision for the period of imprisonment specified in any warrant issued under this section to be reduced where there is part payment of the amount in respect of which the warrant was issued.

(9) A warrant issued under this section may be directed to such person or persons as the court issuing it thinks fit.

(10) Section 80 of the Magistrates' Courts Act 1980 (application of money found on defaulter) shall apply in relation to a warrant issued under this section against a liable person as it applies in relation to the enforcement of a sum mentioned in subsection (1) of that section.

(11) The Secretary of State may by regulation make provision –

(a) as to the form of any warrant issued under this section;
(b) allowing an application under this section to be renewed where no warrant is issued or term of imprisonment is fixed;
(c) that a statement in writing to the effect that wages of any amount have been paid to the liable person during any period, purporting to be signed by or on behalf of his employer, shall be evidence of the facts stated;
(d) that, for the purposes of enabling an inquiry to be made as to the liable person's conduct and means, a justice of the peace may issue a summons to him to appear before a magistrates' court and (if he does not obey) may issue a warrant for his arrest;
(e) that for the purpose of enabling such an inquiry, a justice of the peace may issue a warrant for the liable person's arrest without issuing a summons;
(f) as to the execution of a warrant for arrest.

(12) This section does not apply to Scotland.

Amendments—Child Support, Pensions and Social Security Act 2000, ss 16(2), 17(1) – in force from a date to be appointed.

40A *(applies to Scotland only)*

40B Disqualification from driving: further provision

(1) If, but only if, the court is of the opinion that there has been wilful refusal or culpable neglect on the part of the liable person, it may –

(a) order him to be disqualified, for such period specified in the order but not exceeding two years as it thinks fit, from holding or obtaining a driving licence (a 'disqualification order'); or
(b) make a disqualification order but suspend its operation until such time and on such conditions (if any) as it thinks just.

(2) The court may not take action under both section 40 and this section.

(3) A disqualification order must state the amount in respect of which it is made, which is to be the aggregate of –

(a) the amount mentioned in section 35(1), or so much of it as remains outstanding; and
(b) an amount (determined in accordance with regulations made by the Secretary of State) in respect of the costs of the application under section 39A.

(4) A court which makes a disqualification order shall require the person to whom it relates to produce any driving licence held by him, and its counterpart (within the meaning of section 108(1) of the Road Traffic Act 1988).

(5) On an application by the Secretary of State or the liable person, the court –

(a) may make an order substituting a shorter period of disqualification, or make an order revoking the disqualification order, if part of the amount referred to in subsection (3) (the 'amount due') is paid to any person authorised to receive it; and
(b) must make an order revoking the disqualification order if all of the amount due is so paid.

(6) The Secretary of State may make representations to the court as to the amount which should be paid before it would be appropriate to make an order revoking the disqualification order under subsection (5)(a), and the person liable may reply to those representations.

(7) The Secretary of State may make a further application under section 39A if the amount due has not been paid in full when the period of disqualification specified in the disqualification order expires.

(8) Where a court –

(a) makes a disqualification order;
(b) makes an order under subsection (5); or
(c) allows an appeal against a disqualification order,

it shall send notice of that fact to the Secretary of State; and the notice shall contain such particulars and be sent in such manner and to such address as the Secretary of State may determine.

(9) Where a court makes a disqualification order, it shall also send the driving licence and its counterpart, on their being produced to the court, to the Secretary of State at such address as he may determine.

(10) Section 80 of the Magistrates' Courts Act 1980 (application of money found on defaulter) shall apply in relation to a disqualification order under this section in relation to a liable person as it applies in relation to the enforcement of a sum mentioned in subsection (1) of that section.

(11) The Secretary of State may by regulations make provision in relation to disqualification orders corresponding to the provision he may make under section 40(11).

(12) (*applies to Scotland only*)

Amendments—Child Support, Pensions and Social Security Act 2000, s 16(3) – in force from a date to be appointed.

41 Arrears of child support maintenance

(1) This section applies where –

- (a) the Secretary of State is authorised under section 4, 6 or 7 to recover child support maintenance payable by a non-resident parent in accordance with the maintenance calculation; and
- (b) the non-resident parent has failed to make one or more payments of child support maintenance due from him in accordance with that calculation.

(2) Where the Secretary of State recovers any such arrears he may, in such circumstances as may be prescribed and to such extent as may be prescribed, retain them if he is satisfied that the amount of any benefit paid to or in respect of the person with care of the child or children in question would have been less had the non-resident parent made the payment or payments of child support maintenance in question.

(2A) In determining for the purposes of subsection (2) whether the amount of any benefit paid would have been less at any time than the amount which was paid at that time, in a case where the maintenance calculation had effect from a date earlier than that on which it was made, the calculation shall be taken to have been in force at that time.

(3)–(5) ...

(6) Any sums retained by the Secretary of State by virtue of this section shall be paid by him into the Consolidated Fund.

Amendments—Child Support Act 1995, s 30(3), Sch 3, para 11; Child Support, Pensions and Social Security Act 2000, ss 1(2), 18(1), Sch 3, para 11(2) – in force from a date to be appointed.

41A Penalty payments

(1) The Secretary of State may by regulations make provision for the payment to him by non-resident parents who are in arrears with payments of child support maintenance of penalty payments determined in accordance with the regulations.

(2) The amount of a penalty payment in respect of any week may not exceed 25% of the amount of child support maintenance payable for that week, but otherwise is to be determined by the Secretary of State.

(3) The liability of a non-resident parent to make a penalty payment does not affect his liability to pay the arrears of child support maintenance concerned.

(4) Regulations under subsection (1) may, in particular, make provision –

- (a) as to the time at which a penalty payment is to be payable;
- (b) for the Secretary of State to waive a penalty payment, or part of it.

(5) The provisions of this Act with respect to –

(a) the collection of child support maintenance;
(b) the enforcement of an obligation to pay child support maintenance,

apply equally (with any necessary modifications) to penalty payments payable by virtue of regulations under this section.

(6) The Secretary of State shall pay penalty payments received by him into the Consolidated Fund.

Amendments—Child Support, Pensions and Social Security Act 2000, s 18(2) – in force from a date to be appointed.

41B Repayment of overpaid child support maintenance

(1) This section applies where it appears to the Secretary of State that a non-resident parent has made a payment by way of child support maintenance which amounts to an overpayment by him of that maintenance and that –

(a) it would not be possible for the non-resident parent to recover the amount of the overpayment by way of an adjustment of the amount payable under a maintenance calculation; or
(b) it would be inappropriate to rely on an adjustment of the amount payable under a maintenance calculation as the means of enabling the non-resident parent to recover the amount of the overpayment.

(1A) This section also applies where the non-resident parent has made a voluntary payment and it appears to the Secretary of State –

(a) that he is not liable to pay child support maintenance; or
(b) that he is liable, but some or all of the payment amounts to an overpayment,

and, in a case falling within paragraph (b), it also appears to him that subsection (1)(a) or (b) applies.

(2) The Secretary of State may make such payment to the non-resident parent by way of reimbursement, or partial reimbursement, of the overpayment as the Secretary of State considers appropriate.

(3) Where the Secretary of State has made a payment under this section he may, in such circumstances as may be prescribed, require the relevant person to pay him the whole, or a specified proportion, of the amount of that payment.

(4) Any such requirement shall be imposed by giving the relevant person a written demand for the amount which the Secretary of State wishes to recover from him.

(5) Any sum which a person is required to pay to the Secretary of State under this section shall be recoverable from him by the Secretary of State as a debt due to the Crown.

(6) The Secretary of State may by regulation make provision in relation to any case in which –

(a) one or more overpayments of child support maintenance are being reimbursed to the Secretary of State by the relevant person; and
(b) child support maintenance has continued to be payable by the non-resident parent concerned to the person with care concerned, or again becomes so payable.

(7) For the purposes of this section –

(a) a payment made by a person under a maintenance calculation which was not validly made; and
(b) a voluntary payment made in the circumstances set out in subsection (1A)(a),

shall be treated as an overpayment of child support maintenance made by a non-resident parent.

(8) In this section 'relevant person', in relation to an overpayment, means the person with care to whom the overpayment was made.

(9) Any sum recovered by the Secretary of State under this section shall be paid by him into the Consolidated Fund.

Amendments—Child Support Act 1995, s 23; Child Support, Pensions and Social Security Act 2000, ss 1(2), 20(3), (4), Sch 3 – in force from a date to be appointed.

Special cases

42 Special cases

(1) The Secretary of State may by regulation provide that in prescribed circumstances a case is to be treated as a special case for the purposes of this Act.

(2) Those regulation may, for example, provide for the following to be special cases –

(a) each parent of a child is a non-resident parent in relation to the child;
(b) there is more than one person who is a person with care in relation to the same child;
(c) there is more than one qualifying child in relation to the same non-resident parent but the person who is the person with care in relation to one of those children is not the person who is the person with care in relation to all of them;
(d) a person is a non-resident parent in relation to more than one child and the other parent of each of those children is not the same person;
(e) the person with care has care of more than one qualifying child and there is more than one non-resident parent in relation to those children;
(f) a qualifying child has his home in two or more separate households.

(3) The Secretary of State may by regulation make provision with respect to special cases.

(4) Regulations made under subsection (3) may, in particular –

(a) modify any provision made by or under this Act, in its application to any special case or any special case falling within a prescribed category;
(b) make new provision for any such case; or
(c) provide for any prescribed provision made by or under this Act not to apply to any such case.

Amendments—Child Support, Pensions and Social Security Act 2000, Sch 3, para 11(2) – in force from a date to be appointed.

43 Recovery of child support maintenance by deduction from benefit

(1) This section applies where –

(a) a non-resident parent is liable to pay a flat rate of child support maintenance (or would be so liable but for a variation having been agreed to), and that rate applies (or would have applied) because he falls within paragraph 4(1)(b) or (c) or 4(2) of Schedule 1; and
(b) such conditions as may be prescribed for the purposes of this section are satisfied.

(2) The power of the Secretary of State to make regulations under section 5 of the Social Security Administration Act 1992 by virtue of subsection (1)(p) (deductions from benefits) may be exercised in relation to cases to which this section applies with a view to securing that payments in respect of child support maintenance are made or that arrears of child support maintenance are recovered.

(3) For the purposes of this section, the benefits to which section 5 of the 1992 Act applies are to be taken as including war disablement pensions and war widows' pensions (within the meaning of section 150 of the Social Security Contributions and Benefits Act 1992 (interpretation)).

Amendments—Child Support, Pensions and Social Security Act 2000, s 21 – in force from a date to be appointed.

Jurisdiction

44 Jurisdiction

(1) The Secretary of State shall have jurisdiction to make a maintenance calculation with respect to a person who is –

- (a) a person with care;
- (b) a non-resident parent; or
- (c) a qualifying child,

only if that person is habitually resident in the United Kingdom, except in the case of a non-resident parent who falls within subsection (2A).

(2) Where the person with care is not an individual, subsection (1) shall have effect as if paragraph (a) were omitted.

(2A) A non-resident parent falls within this subsection if he is not habitually resident in the United Kingdom, but is –

- (a) employed in the civil service of the Crown, including Her Majesty's Diplomatic Service and Her Majesty's Overseas Civil Service;
- (b) a member of the naval, military or air forces of the Crown, including any person employed by an association established for the purposes of Part XI of the Reserve Forces Act 1996;
- (c) employed by a company of a prescribed description registered under the Companies Act 1985 in England and Wales or in Scotland, or under the Companies (Northern Ireland) Order 1986; or
- (d) employed by a body of a prescribed description.

(3) . . .

Amendments—Social Security Act 1998, s 86(1), Sch 7, para 41; Child Support, Pensions and Social Security Act 2000, ss 1(2), 22, Sch 3, para 11(2) – in force from a date to be appointed.

45 Jurisdiction of courts in certain proceedings under this Act

(1) The Lord Chancellor or, in relation to Scotland, the Lord Advocate may by order make such provision as he considers necessary to secure that appeals, or such class of appeals as may be specified in the order –

- (a) shall be made to a court instead of being made to an appeal tribunal; or
- (b) shall be so made in such circumstances as may be so specified.

(2) In subsection (1), 'court' means –

(a) in relation to England and Wales and subject to any provision made under Schedule 11 to the Children Act 1989 (jurisdiction of courts with respect to certain proceedings relating to children) the High Court, a county court or a magistrates' court; and
(b) in relation to Scotland, the Court of Session or the sheriff.

(3) Schedule 11 to the Act of 1989 shall be amended in accordance with subsections (4) and (5).

(4) The following sub-paragraph shall be inserted in paragraph 1, after sub-paragraph (2) –

'(2A) Sub-paragraph (1) and (2) shall also apply in relation to proceedings –

(a) under section 27 of the Child Support Act 1991 (reference to court for declaration of parentage); or
(b) which are to be dealt with in accordance with an order made under section 45 of that Act (jurisdiction of courts in certain proceedings under that Act)'.

(5) In paragraphs 1(3) and 2(3), the following shall be inserted after 'Act 1976' –

'(bb) section 20 (appeals) or 27 (reference to court for declaration of parentage) of the Child Support Act 1991;'

(6) Where the effect of any order under subsection (1) is that there are no longer any appeals which fall to be dealt with by appeal tribunals, the Lord Chancellor after consultation with the Lord Advocate may by order provide for the abolition of those tribunals.

(7) Any order under subsection (1) or (6) may make –

(a) such modifications of any provision of this Act or of any other enactment; and
(b) such transitional provision,

as the Minister making the order considers appropriate in consequence of any provision made by the order.

Amendments—Social Security Act 1998, s 86(1), Sch 7, para 42(1).

Miscellaneous and supplemental

46 Reduced benefit decisions

(1) This section applies where any person ('the parent') –

(a) has made a request under section 6(5);
(b) fails to comply with any regulation made under section 6(7); or
(c) having been treated as having applied for a maintenance calculation under section 6, refuses to take a scientific test (within the meaning of section 27A).

(2) The Secretary of State may serve written notice on the parent requiring her, before the end of a specified period –

(a) in a subsection (1)(a) case, to give him her reasons for making the request;
(b) in a subsection (1)(b) case, to give him her reasons for failing to do so; or
(c) in a subsection (1)(c) case, to give him her reasons for her refusal.

(3) When the specified period has expired, the Secretary of State shall consider whether, having regard to any reasons given by the parent, there are reasonable grounds for believing that –

(a) in a subsection (1)(a) case, if the Secretary of State were to do what is mentioned in section 6(3);
(b) in a subsection (1)(b) case, if she were to be required to comply; or
(c) in a subsection (1)(c) case, if she took the scientific test,

there would be a risk of her, or of any children living with her, suffering harm or undue distress as a result of his taking such action, or her complying or taking the test.

(4) If the Secretary of State considers that there are such reasonable grounds, he shall –

(a) take no further action under this section in relation to the request, the failure or the refusal in question; and
(b) notify the parent, in writing, accordingly.

(5) If the Secretary of State considers that there are no such reasonable grounds, he may, except in prescribed circumstances, make a reduced benefit decision with respect to the parent.

(6) In a subsection (1)(a) case, the Secretary of State may from time to time serve written notice on the parent requiring her, before the end of a specified period –

(a) to state whether her request under section 6(5) still stands; and
(b) if so, to give him her reasons for maintaining her request,

and subsections (3) to (5) have effect in relation to such a notice and any response to it as they have effect in relation to a notice under subsection (2)(a) and any response to it.

(7) Where the Secretary of State makes a reduced benefit decision he must send a copy of it to the parent.

(8) A reduced benefit decision is to take effect on such date as may be specified in the decision.

(9) Reasons given in response to a notice under subsection (2) or (6) need not be given in writing unless the Secretary of State directs in any case that they must.

(10) In this section –

(a) 'comply' means to comply with the requirement or with the regulation in question; and 'complied' and 'complying' are to be construed accordingly;
(b) 'reduced benefit decision' means a decision that the amount payable by way of any relevant benefit to, or in respect of, the parent concerned be reduced by such amount, and for such period, as may be prescribed;
(c) 'relevant benefit' means income support or an income-based jobseeker's allowance or any other benefit of a kind prescribed for the purposes of section 6; and
(d) 'specified', in relation to a notice served under this section, means specified in the notice; and the period to be specified is to be determined in accordance with regulations made by the Secretary of State.

Amendments—Child Support, Pensions and Social Security Act 2000, s 19 – in force from a date to be appointed.

46A Finality of decisions

(1) Subject to the provisions of this Act, any decision of the Secretary of State or an appeal tribunal made in accordance with the foregoing provisions of this Act shall be final.

(2) If and to the extent that regulations so provide, any finding of fact or other determination embodied in or necessary to such a decision, or on which such a decision is based, shall be conclusive for the purposes of –

(a) further such decisions;
(b) decisions made in accordance with sections 8 to 16 of the Social Security Act 1998, or with regulations under section 11 of that Act; and
(c) decisions made under the Vaccine Damage Payments Act 1979.

Amendments—Social Security Act 1998, s 86(1), Sch 7, para 44.

46B Matters arising as respects decisions

(1) Regulations may make provision as respects matters arising pending –

(a) any decision of the Secretary of State under section 11, 12 or 17;
(b) any decision of an appeal tribunal under section 20; or
(c) any decision of a Child Support Commissioner under section 24.

(2) Regulations may also make provision as respects matters arising out of the revision under section 16, or on appeal, of any such decision as is mentioned in subsection (1).

(3) . . .

Amendments—Social Security Act 1998, s 86(1), Sch 7, para 44; Child Support, Pensions and Social Security Act 2000, Sch 9, Part I.

47 Fees

(1) The Secretary of State may by regulation provide for the payment, by the non-resident parent or the person with care (or by both), such fees as may be prescribed in cases where the Secretary of State takes any action under section 4 or 6.

(2) The Secretary of State may by regulation provide for the payment, by the non-resident parent, the person with care or the child concerned (or by any or all of them), of such fees as may be prescribed in cases where the Secretary of State takes action under section 7.

(3) Regulations made under this section –

(a) may require any information which is needed for the purpose of determining the amount of any such fee to be furnished, in accordance with the regulations, by such person as may be prescribed;
(b) shall provide that no such fees shall be payable by any person to or in respect of whom income support, an income-based jobseeker's allowance, working families' tax credit or any other benefit of a prescribed kind is paid; and
(c) may, in particular, make provision with respect to the recovery by the Secretary of State of any fees payable under the regulations.

(4) The provisions of this Act with respect to –

(a) the collection of child support maintenance;
(b) the enforcement of any obligation to pay child support maintenance,

shall apply equally (with any necessary modifications) to fees payable by virtue of regulations made under this section.

Amendments—Jobseekers Act 1995, s 41(4), Sch 2, para 20; Tax Credits Act 1999, s 1(2), Sch 1, para 6(f)(i); Child Support, Pensions and Social Security Act 2000, Sch 3, para 11(2), (18).

48 Right of audience

(1) Any officer of the Secretary of State who is authorised by the Secretary of State for the purposes of this section shall have, in relation to any proceedings under this Act before a magistrates' court, a right of audience and the right to conduct litigation.

(2) In this section 'right of audience' and 'right to conduct litigation' have the same meaning as in section 119 of the Courts and Legal Services Act 1990.

Amendments—Child Support Act 1995, s 30(5), Sch 3, para 14.

49 (*applies to Scotland only*)

50 Unauthorised disclosure of information

(1) Any person who is, or has been, employed in employment to which this section applies is guilty of an offence if, without lawful authority, he discloses any information which –

(a) was acquired by him in the course of that employment; and
(b) relates to a particular person.

(2) It is not an offence under this section –

(a) to disclose information in the form of a summary or collection of information so framed as not to enable information relating to any particular person to be ascertained from it; or
(b) to disclose information which has previously been disclosed to the public with lawful authority.

(3) It is a defence for a person charged with an offence under this section to prove that at the time of the alleged offence –

(a) he believed that he was making the disclosure in question with lawful authority and had no reasonable cause to believe otherwise; or
(b) he believed that the information in question had previously been disclosed to the public with lawful authority and had no reasonable cause to believe otherwise.

(4) A person guilty of an offence under this section shall be liable –

(a) on conviction on indictment, to imprisonment for a term not exceeding two years or a fine or both; or
(b) on summary conviction, to imprisonment for a term not exceeding six months or a fine not exceeding the statutory maximum or both.

(5) This section applies to employment as –

(a) the Chief Child Support Officer;
(b) any other child support officer;
(c) any clerk to, or other officer of, an appeal tribunal or a child support appeal tribunal;
(d) any member of the staff of such a tribunal;
(e) a civil servant in connection with the carrying out of any functions under this Act,

and to employment of any other kind which is prescribed for the purposes of this section.

(6) For the purposes of this section a disclosure is to be regarded as made with lawful authority if, and only if, it is made –

(a) by a civil servant in accordance with his official duty; or
(b) by any other person either –
  (i) for the purposes of the function in the exercise of which he holds the information and without contravening any restriction duly imposed by the responsible person; or
  (ii) to, or in accordance with an authorisation duly given by, the responsible person;
(c) in accordance with any enactment or order of a court;
(d) for the purpose of instituting, or otherwise for the purposes of, any proceedings before a court or before any tribunal or other body or person mentioned in this Act; or
(e) with the consent of the appropriate person.

(7) 'The responsible person' means –

(a) the Lord Chancellor;
(b) the Secretary of State;
(c) any person authorised by the Lord Chancellor, or Secretary of State, for the purposes of this subsection; or
(d) any other prescribed person, or person falling within a prescribed category.

(8) 'The appropriate person' means the person to whom the information in question relates, except that if the affairs of that person are being dealt with –

(a) under a power of attorney;
(b) by a receiver appointed under section 99 of the Mental Health Act 1983;
(c) (*applies to Scotland only*); or
(d) by a mental health appointee, that is to say –
  (i) a person directed or authorised as mentioned in sub-paragraph (a) of rule 41(1) of the Court of Protection Rules 1984; or
  (ii) a receiver ad interim appointed under sub-paragraph (b) of that rule;

the appropriate person is the attorney, receiver, custodian or appointee (as the case may be) or, in a case falling within paragraph (a), the person to whom the information relates.

Amendments—Social Security Act 1998, s 86(1), Sch 7, para 45.

51 Supplementary powers to make regulations

(1) The Secretary of State may by regulation make such incidental, supplemental and transitional provision as he considers appropriate in connection with any provision made by or under this Act.

(2) The regulation may, in particular, make provision –

(a) as to the procedure to be followed with respect to –
  (i) the making of applications for maintenance calculations;
  (ii) the making of decisions under section 11;
  (iii) the making of decisions under section 16 or 17;
(b) extending the categories of case to which section 16, 17 or 20 applies;
(c) as to the date on which an application for a maintenance calculation is to be treated as having been made;
(d) for attributing payments made under maintenance calculations to the payment of arrears;
(e) for the adjustment, for the purpose of taking account of the retrospective effect of a maintenance calculation, of amounts payable under the calculation;

(f) for the adjustment, for the purpose of taking account of over-payments or under-payments of child support maintenance, of amounts payable under a maintenance calculation;
(g) as to the evidence which is to be required in connection with such matters as may be prescribed;
(h) as to the circumstances in which any official record or certificate is to be conclusive (or in Scotland, sufficient) evidence;
(i) with respect to the giving of notices or other documents;
(j) for the rounding up or down of any amounts calculated, estimated or otherwise arrived at in applying any provision made by or under this Act.

(3) No power to make regulations conferred by any other provision of this Act shall be taken to limit the powers given to the Secretary of State by this section.

Amendments—Social Security Act 1998, s 86(1), Sch 7, para 46(a), (b); Child Support, Pensions and Social Security Act 2000, s 1(2), Sch 3, para 11(19) – in force from a date to be appointed.

52 Regulations and orders

(1) Any power conferred on the Lord Chancellor, or Lord Advocate or the Secretary of State by this Act to make regulations or orders (other than a deduction from earnings order) shall be exercisable by statutory instrument.

(2) No statutory instrument containing (whether alone or with other provisions) regulations made under –

(a) section 6(1), 12(4) (so far as the regulations make provision for the default rate of child support maintenance mentioned in section 12(5)(b)), 28C(2)(b), 28F(2)(b), 30(5A), 41(2), 41A, 41B(6), 43(1), 44(2A)(d), 46 or 47;
(b) paragraph 3(2) or 10A(1) of Part I of Schedule 1; or
(c) Schedule 4B,

or an order made under section 45(1) or (6), shall be made unless a draft of the instrument has been laid before Parliament and approved by a resolution of each House of Parliament.

(2A) No statutory instrument containing (whether alone or with other provisions) the first set of regulations made under paragraph 10(1) of Part I of Schedule 1 as substituted by section 1(3) of the Child Support, Pensions and Social Security Act 2000 shall be made unless a draft of the instrument has been laid before Parliament and approved by a resolution of each House of Parliament.

(3) Any other statutory instrument made under this Act (except an order made under section 58(2)) shall be subject to annulment in pursuance of a resolution of either House of Parliament.

(4) Any power of a kind mentioned in subsection (1) may be exercised –

(a) in relation to all cases to which it extends, in relation to those cases but subject to specified exceptions or in relation to any specified cases or classes of case;
(b) so as to make, as respects the cases in relation to which it is exercised –
   (i) the full provision to which it extends or any lesser provision (whether by way of exception or otherwise);
   (ii) the same provision for all cases, different provision for different cases or classes of case or different provision as respects the same case or class of case but for different purposes of this Act;

(iii) provision which is either unconditional or is subject to any specified condition;

(c) so to provide for a person to exercise a discretion in dealing with any matter.

Amendments—Child Support, Pensions and Social Security Act 2000, s 25 – in force from a date to be appointed.

53 Financial provisions

Any expenses of the Lord Chancellor or the Secretary of State under this Act shall be payable out of money provided by Parliament.

54 Interpretation

In this Act –

'non-resident parent', has the meaning given in section 3(2);
'appeal tribunal' means an appeal tribunal constituted under Chapter I of Part I of the Social Security Act 1998;
'application for a variation' means an application under section 28A or 28G;
'benefit Acts' means the Social Security Contributions and Benefits Act 1992 and the Social Security Administration Act 1992;
'child benefit' has the same meaning as in the Child Benefit Act 1975;
'child support maintenance' has the meaning given in section 3(6);
'deduction from earnings order' has the meaning given in section 31(2);
'default maintenance decision' has the meaning given in section 12;
'disabled person's tax credit' has the same meaning as in the benefit Acts;
'working families' tax credit' has the same meaning as in the benefit Acts;
'general qualification' shall be construed in accordance with section 71 of the Courts and Legal Services Act 1990 (qualification for judicial appointments);
'income support' has the same meaning as in the benefit Acts;
'income-based jobseeker's allowance' has the same meaning as in the Jobseekers Act 1995;
'interim maintenance decision' has the meaning given in section 12;
'liability order' has the meaning given in section 33(2);
'maintenance agreement' has the meaning given in section 9(1);
'maintenance calculation' means a calculation of maintenance made under this Act and, except in prescribed circumstances, includes a default maintenance decision and an interim maintenance decision;
'maintenance order' has the meaning given in section 8(11);
'parent', in relation to any child, means any person who is in law the mother or father of the child;
'parent with care' means a person who is, in relation to a child, both a parent and a person with care;
'parental responsibility', in the application of this Act –

(a) to England and Wales, has the same meaning as in the Children Act 1989; and

(b) (*applies to Scotland only*);

'person with care' has the meaning given in section 3(3);
'prescribed' means prescribed by regulations made by the Secretary of State;
'qualifying child' has the meaning given in section 3(1);
'voluntary payment' has the meaning given in section 28J.

Amendments—Social Security (Consequential Provisions) Act 1992, s 4, Sch 2, para 114; Child (Scotland) Act 1995, s 105(4), Sch 4, para 52(1), (4); Jobseekers Act 1995, s 41(4), Sch 2, para 20;

Child Support Act 1995, s 30(5), Sch 3, para 16; Social Security Act 1998, s 86(1), Sch 7, para 47(a), (b); Tax Credits Act 1999, s 1(2), Sch 1, paras 1, 6(i); Child Support, Pensions and Social Security Act 2000, Sch 3, para 11(2), (20) – in force from a date to be appointed.

55 Meaning of 'child'

(1) For the purposes of this Act a person is a child if –

- (a) he is under the age of 16;
- (b) he is under the age of 19 and receiving full-time education (which is not advanced education) –
  - (i) by attendance at a recognised educational establishment; or
  - (ii) elsewhere, if the education is recognised by the Secretary of State; or
- (c) he does not fall within paragraph (a) or (b) but –
  - (i) he is under the age of 18, and
  - (ii) prescribed conditions are satisfied with respect to him.

(2) A person is not a child for the purposes of this Act if he –

- (a) is or has been married;
- (b) has celebrated a marriage which is void; or
- (c) has celebrated a marriage in respect of which a decree of nullity has been granted.

(3) In this section –

'advanced education' means education of a prescribed description; and
'recognised educational establishment' means an establishment recognised by the Secretary of State for the purposes of this section as being, or as comparable to, a university, college or school.

(4) Where a person has reached the age of 16, the Secretary of State may recognise education provided for him otherwise than at a recognised educational establishment only if the Secretary of State is satisfied that education was being so provided for him immediately before he reached the age of 16.

(5) The Secretary of State may provide that in prescribed circumstances education is or is not to be treated for the purposes of this section as being full-time.

(6) In determining whether a person falls within subsection (1)(b), no account shall be taken of such interruptions in his education as may be prescribed.

(7) The Secretary of State may by regulation provide that a person who ceases to fall within subsection (1) shall be treated as continuing to fall within that subsection for a prescribed period.

(8) No person shall be treated as continuing to fall within subsection (1) by virtue of regulations made under subsection (7) after the end of the week in which he reaches the age of 19.

56 (*applies to Northern Ireland only*)

57 Application to Crown

(1) The power of the Secretary of State to make regulations under section 14 requiring prescribed persons to furnish information may be exercised so as to require information to be furnished by persons employed in the service of the Crown or otherwise in the discharge of Crown functions.

(2) In such circumstances, and subject to such conditions, as may be prescribed, an inspector appointed under section 15 may enter any Crown premises for the purpose of exercising any powers conferred on him by that section.

(3) Where such an inspector duly enters any Crown premises for those purposes, section 15 shall apply in relation to persons employed in the service of the Crown or otherwise in the discharge of Crown functions as it applies in relation to other persons.

(4) Where a liable person is in the employment of the Crown, a deduction from earnings order may be made under section 31 in relation to that person; but in such a case subsection (8) of section 32 shall apply only in relation to the failure of that person to comply with any requirement imposed on him by regulations made under section 32.

58 Short title, commencement and extent, etc

(1) This Act may be cited as the Child Support Act 1991.

(2) Section 56(1) and subsections (1) to (11) and (14) of this section shall come into force on the passing of this Act but otherwise this Act shall come into force on such date as may be appointed by order made by the Lord Chancellor, the Secretary of State or Lord Advocate, or by any of them acting jointly.

(3) Different dates may be appointed for different provisions of this Act and for different purposes (including, in particular, for different cases or categories of case).

(4) An order under subsection (2) may make such supplemental, incidental or transitional provision as appears to the person making the order to be necessary or expedient in connection with the provisions brought into force by the order, including such adaptations or modifications of –

(a) the provisions so brought into force;
(b) any provisions of this Act then in force; or
(c) any provision of any other enactment,

as appear to him to be necessary or expedient.

(5) Different provision may be made by virtue of subsection (4) with respect to different periods.

(6) Any provision made by virtue of subsection (4) may, in particular, include provision for –

(a) the enforcement of a maintenance calculation (including the collection of sums payable under the calculation) as if the calculation were a court order of a prescribed kind;
(b) the registration of maintenance calculations with the appropriate court in connection with any provision of a kind mentioned in paragraph (a);
(c) the variation, on application made to a court, of the provisions of a maintenance calculation relating to the method of making payments fixed by the calculation or the intervals at which such payments are to be made;
(d) a maintenance calculation, or an order of a prescribed kind relating to one or more children, to be deemed, in prescribed circumstances, to have been validly made for all purposes or for such purposes as may be prescribed.

In paragraph (c) 'court' includes a single justice.

(7) The Lord Chancellor, the Secretary of State or the Lord Advocate may by order make such amendments or repeals in, or such modifications of, such enactments as may be

specified in the order, as appear to him to be necessary or expedient in consequence of any provision made by or under this Act (including any provision made by virtue of subsection (4)).

(8) This Act shall, in its application to the Isles of Scilly, have effect subject to such exceptions, adaptations and modifications as the Secretary of State may by order prescribe.

(9) Sections 27, 35, 40 and 48 and paragraph 7 of Schedule 5 do not extend to Scotland.

(10) Sections 7, 28, 40A and 49 extend only to Scotland.

(11) With the exception of sections 23 and 56(1), subsections (1) to (3) of this section and Schedules 2 and 4, and (in so far as it amends any enactment extending to Northern Ireland) Schedule 5, this Act does not extend to Northern Ireland.

(12) Until Schedule 1 to the Disability Living Allowance and Disability Working Allowance Act 1991 comes into force, paragraph 1(1) of Schedule 3 shall have effect with the omission of the words 'and disability appeal tribunals' and the insertion, after 'social security appeal tribunals', of the word 'and'.

(13) The consequential amendments set out in Schedule 5 shall have effect.

(14) In Schedule 1 to the Children Act 1989 (financial provision for children), paragraph 2(6)(b) (which is spent) is hereby repealed.

Amendments—Child Support, Pensions and Social Security Act 2000, s 1(2), Sch 3, para 11(21) – in force from a date to be appointed.

SCHEDULE 1

MAINTENANCE CALCULATIONS

PART I

CALCULATION OF WEEKLY AMOUNT OF CHILD SUPPORT MAINTENANCE

1 General rule

(1) The weekly rate of child support maintenance is the basic rate unless a reduced rate, a flat rate or the nil rate applies.

(2) Unless the nil rate applies, the amount payable weekly to a person with care is –

- (a) the applicable rate, if paragraph 6 does not apply; or
- (b) if paragraph 6 does apply, that rate as apportioned between the persons with care in accordance with paragraph 6,

as adjusted, in either case, by applying the rules about shared care in paragraph 7 or 8.

2 Basic rate

(1) The basic rate is the following percentage of the non-resident parent's net weekly income –

15% where he has one qualifying child;
20% where he has two qualifying children;

25% where he has three or more qualifying children.

(2) If the non-resident parent also has one or more relevant other children, the appropriate percentage referred to in sub-paragraph (1) is to be applied instead to his net weekly income less –

15% where he has one relevant other child;
20% where he has two relevant other children;
25% where he has three or more relevant other children.

3 Reduced rate

(1) A reduced rate is payable if –

(a) neither a flat rate nor the nil rate applies; and
(b) the non-resident parent's net weekly income is less than £200 but more than £100.

(2) The reduced rate payable shall be prescribed in, or determined in accordance with, regulations.

(3) The regulations may not prescribe, or result in, a rate of less than £5.

4 Flat rate

(1) Except in a case falling within sub-paragraph (2), a flat rate of £5 is payable if the nil rate does not apply and –

(a) the non-resident parent's net weekly income is £100 or less; or
(b) he receives any benefit, pension or allowance prescribed for the purposes of this paragraph of this sub-paragraph; or
(c) he or his partner (if any) receives any benefit prescribed for the purposes of this paragraph of this sub-paragraph.

(2) A flat rate of a prescribed amount is payable if the nil rate does not apply and –

(a) the non-resident parent has a partner who is also a non-resident parent;
(b) the partner is a person with respect to whom a maintenance calculation is in force; and
(c) the non-resident parent or his partner receives any benefit prescribed under sub-paragraph (1)(c).

(3) The benefits, pensions and allowances which may be prescribed for the purposes of sub-paragraph (1)(b) include ones paid to the non-resident parent under the law of a place outside the United Kingdom.

5 Nil rate

The rate payable is nil if the non-resident parent –

(a) is of a prescribed description; or
(b) has a net weekly income of below £5.

6 Apportionment

(1) If the non-resident parent has more than one qualifying child and in relation to them there is more than one person with care, the amount of child support maintenance payable

is (subject to paragraph 7 or 8) to be determined by apportioning the rate between the persons with care.

(2) The rate of maintenance liability is to be divided by the number of qualifying children, and shared among the persons with care according to the number of qualifying children in relation to whom each is a person with care.

7 Shared care – basic and reduced rate

(1) This paragraph applies only if the rate of child support maintenance payable is the basic rate or a reduced rate.

(2) If the care of a qualifying child is shared between the non-resident parent and the person with care, so that the non-resident parent from time to time has care of the child overnight, the amount of child support maintenance which he would otherwise have been liable to pay the person with care, as calculated in accordance with the preceding paragraphs of this Part of this Schedule, is to be decreased in accordance with this paragraph.

(3) First, there is to be a decrease according to the number of such nights which the Secretary of State determines there to have been, or expects there to be, or both during a prescribed twelve-month period.

(4) The amount of that decrease for one child is set out in the following Table –

Number of nights	Fraction to subtract
52 to 103	One-seventh
104 to 155	Two-sevenths
156 to 174	Three-sevenths
175 or more	One-half

(5) If the person with care is caring for more than one qualifying child of the non-resident parent, the applicable decrease is the sum of the appropriate fractions in the Table divided by the number of such qualifying children.

(6) If the applicable fraction is one-half in relation to any qualifying child in the care of the person with care, the total amount payable to the person with care is then to be further decreased by £7 for each such child.

(7) If the application of the preceding provisons of this paragraph would decrease the weekly amount of child support maintenance (or the aggregate of all such amounts) payable by the non-resident parent to the person with care (or all of them) to less than £5, he is instead liable to pay child support maintenance at the rate of £5 a week, apportioned (if appropriate) in accordance with paragraph 6.

8 Shared care – flat rate

(1) This paragraph applies only if –

(a) the rate of child support maintenance payable is a flat rate; and
(b) that rate applies because the non-resident parent falls within paragraph 4(1)(b) or (c) or 4(2).

(2) If the care of a qualifying child is shared as mentioned in paragraph 7(2) for at least 52 nights during a prescribed 12-month period, the amount of child support maintenance payable by the non-resident parent to the person with care of that child is nil.

9 Regulations about shared care

The Secretary of State may by regulations provide –

(a) for which nights are to count for the purposes of shared care under paragraphs 7 and 8, or for how it is to be determined whether a night counts;
(b) for what counts, or does not count, as 'care' for those purposes; and
(c) for paragraph 7(3) or 8(2) to have effect, in prescribed circumstances, as if the period mentioned there were other than 12 months, and in such circumstances for the Table in paragraph 7(4) (or that Table as modified pursuant to regulations made under paragraph 10A(2)(a)), or the period mentioned in paragraph 8(2), to have effect with prescribed adjustments.

10 Net weekly income

(1) For the purposes of this Schedule, net weekly income is to be determined in such manner as is provided for in regulations.

(2) The regulations may, in particular, provide for the Secretary of State to estimate any income or make an assumption as to any fact where, in his view, the information at his disposal is unreliable, insufficient, or relates to an atypical period in the life of the non-resident parent.

(3) Any amount of net weekly income (calculated as above) over £2,000 is to be ignored for the purposes of this Schedule.

10A Regulations about rates, figures, etc.

(1) The Secretary of State may by regulations provide that –

(a) paragraph 2 is to have effect as if different percentages were substituted for those set out there;
(b) paragraph 3(1) or (3), 4(1), 5, 7(7) or 10(3) is to have effect as if different amounts were substituted for those set out there.

(2) The Secretary of State may by regulations provide that –

(a) the Table in paragraph 7(4) is to have effect as if different numbers of nights were set out in the first column and different fractions were substituted for those set out in the second column;
(b) paragraph 7(6) is to have effect as if a different amount were substituted for that mentioned there, or as if the amount were an aggregate amount and not an amount for each qualifying child, or both.

10B Regulations about income

The Secretary of State may by regulations provide that, in such circumstances and to such extent as may be prescribed –

(a) where the Secretary of State is satisfied that a person has intentionally deprived himself of a source of income with a view to reducing the amount of his net weekly income, his net weekly income shall be taken to include income from that source of an amount estimated by the Secretary of State;
(b) a person is to be treated as possessing income which he does not possess;
(c) income which a person does possess is to be disregarded.

10C References to various terms

(1) References in this Part of this Schedule to 'qualifying children' are to those qualifying children with respect to whom the maintenance calculation falls to be made.

(2) References in this Part of this Schedule to 'relevant other children' are to –

(a) children other than qualifying children in respect of whom the non-resident parent or his partner receives child benefit under Part IX of the Social Security Contributions and Benefits Act 1992; and
(b) such other description of children as may be prescribed.

(3) In this Part of this Schedule, a person 'receives' a benefit, pension, or allowance for any week if it is paid or due to be paid to him in respect of that week.

(4) In this Part of this Schedule, a person's 'partner' is –

(a) if they are a couple, the other member of that couple;
(b) if the person is a husband or wife by virtue of a marriage entered into under a law which permits polygamy, another party to the marriage who is of the opposite sex and is a member of the same household.

(5) In sub-paragraph (4)(a), 'couple' means a man and a woman who are –

(a) married to each other and are members of the same household; or
(b) not married to each other but are living together as husband and wife.

PART II

GENERAL PROVISIONS ABOUT MAINTENANCE CALCULATIONS

11 Effective date of calculation

(1) A maintenance calculation shall take effect on such date as may be determined in accordance with regulations made by the Secretary of State.

(2) That date may be earlier than the date on which the calculation is made.

12 Form of calculation

Every maintenance calculation shall be made in such form and contain such information as the Secretary of State may direct.

13 . . .

14 Consolidated applications and calculations

(1) The Secretary of State may by regulation provide –

(a) for two or more applications for maintenance calculations to be treated, in prescribed circumstances, as a single application; and
(b) for the replacement, in prescribed circumstances, of a maintenance calculation made on the application of one person by a later maintenance calculation made on the application of that or any other person.

(2) In sub-paragraph (1), the references (however expressed) to applications for maintenance calculations include references to applications treated as made.

15 Separate calculation for different periods

Where the Secretary of State is satisfied that the circumstances of a case require different amounts of child support maintenance to be calculated in respect of different periods, he may make separate maintenance calculations each expressed to have effect in relation to a different specified period.

16 Termination of calculations

(1) A maintenance calculation shall cease to have effect –

- (a) on the death of the non-resident parent, or of the person with care, with respect to whom it was made;
- (b) on there no longer being any qualifying child with respect to whom it would have effect;
- (c) on the non-resident parent with respect to whom it was made ceasing to be a parent of –
  - (i) the qualifying child with respect to whom it was made; or
  - (ii) where it was made with respect to more than one qualifying child, all of the qualifying children with respect to whom it was made.

(2)–(9) . . .

(10) A person with care with respect to whom a maintenance calculation is in force shall provide the Secretary of State with such information, in such circumstances, as may be prescribed, with a view to assisting the Secretary of State in determining whether the calculation has ceased to have effect.

(11) The Secretary of State may by regulation make such supplemental, incidental or transitional provision as he thinks necessary or expedient in consequence of the provisions of this paragraph.

Amendments—Child Support Act 1995, s 14; Social Security Act 1998, s 86(1), Sch 7, para 48(3), (4), (5)(a)(c); Child Support, Pensions and Social Security Act 2000, s 1(2), Sch 1, Sch 3, para 11(2), (22) – in force from a date to be appointed.

SCHEDULE 2

PROVISION OF INFORMATION TO SECRETARY OF STATE

1 Inland Revenue records

(1) This paragraph applies where the Secretary of State or the Department of Health and Social Services for Northern Ireland requires information for the purpose of tracing –

- (a) the current address of a non-resident parent; or
- (b) the current employer of a non-resident parent.

(2) In such a case, no obligation as to secrecy imposed by statute or otherwise on a person employed in relation to the Inland Revenue shall prevent any information obtained or held in connection with the calculation or collection of income tax from being disclosed to –

- (a) the Secretary of State;
- (b) the Department of Health and Social Services for Northern Ireland; or
- (c) an officer of either of them authorised to receive such information in connection with the operation of this Act or of any corresponding Northern Ireland legislation.

(3) This paragraph extends only to disclosure by or under the authority of the Commissioners of Inland Revenue.

(4) Information which is the subject of disclosure to any person by virtue of this paragraph shall not be further disclosed to any person except where the further disclosure is made –

(a) to a person to whom disclosure could be made by virtue of sub-paragraph (2); or
(b) for the purposes of any proceedings (civil or criminal) in connection with the operation of this Act or of any corresponding Northern Ireland legislation.

1A Supply of information for child support purposes

(1) This paragraph applies to any information which –

(a) relates to any earnings or other income of a non-resident parent in respect of a tax year in which he is or was a self-employed earner, and
(b) is required by the Secretary of State or the Department of Health and Social Services for Northern Ireland for any purposes of this Act.

(2) No obligation as to secrecy imposed by statute or otherwise on a person employed in relation to the Inland Revenue shall prevent any such information obtained or held in connection with the calculation or collection of income tax from being disclosed to –

(a) the Secretary of State;
(b) the Department of Health and Social Services for Northern Ireland; or
(c) an officer of either of them authorised to receive such information in connection with the operation of this Act.

(3) This paragraph extends only to disclosure by or under the authority of the Commissioners of Inland Revenue.

(4) Information which is the subject of disclosure to any person by virtue of this paragraph shall not be further disclosed to any person except where the further disclosure is made –

(a) to a person to whom disclosure could be made by virtue of sub-paragraph (2); or
(b) for the purposes of any proceedings (civil or criminal) in connection with the operation of this Act.

(5) For the purposes of this paragraph 'self-employed earner' and 'tax year' have the same meaning as in Parts I to VI of the Social Security Contributions and Benefits Act 1992.

2 . . .

Amendments—Social Security Act 1998, s 86(1), Sch 7, para 49; Welfare Reform and Pensions Act 1999, s 80; Child Support, Pensions and Social Security Act 2000, s 1(2), Sch 3, para 11(2) – in force from a date to be appointed.

SCHEDULE 3

. . .

Amendments—Social Security Act 1998, s 86, Sch 7, para 50.

SCHEDULE 4

CHILD SUPPORT COMMISSIONERS

1 Tenure of office

(1) Every Child Support Commissioner shall vacate his office on the date on which he reaches the age of 70; but this sub-paragraph is subject to section 26(4) to (6) of the Judicial Pensions and Retirement Act 1993 (power to authorise continuance in office up to the age of 75).

(2) . . .

(3) A Child Support Commissioner may be removed from office by the Lord Chancellor on the ground of misbehaviour or incapacity.

2 Commissioners' remuneration and their pensions

(1) The Lord Chancellor may pay, or make such payments towards the provision of such remuneration, pension, allowances or gratuities to or in respect of persons appointed as Child Support Commissioners as, with the consent of the Treasury, he may determine.

(2) The Lord Chancellor shall pay to a Child Support Commissioner such expenses incurred in connection with his work as such a Commissioner as may be determined by the Treasury.

(3) Sub-paragraph (1), so far as relating to pensions, allowances or gratuities, shall not have effect in relation to any person to whom Part I of the Judicial Pensions and Retirement Act 1993 applies, except to the extent provided by or under that Act.

2A Expenses of other persons

(1) The Lord Chancellor or, in Scotland, the Secretary of State may pay to any person who attends any proceedings before a Child Support Commissioner such travelling and other allowances as he may determine.

(2) In sub-paragraph (1), references to travelling and other allowances include references to compensation for loss of remunerative time.

(3) No compensation for loss of remunerative time shall be paid to any person under this paragraph in respect of any time during which he is in receipt of other remuneration so paid.

3 Commissioners barred from legal practice

Section 75 of the Courts and Legal Services Act 1990 (judges etc barred from legal practice) shall apply to any person appointed as a Child Support Commissioner as it applies to any person holding as a full-time appointment any of the offices listed in Schedule 11 to that Act.

4 Deputy Child Support Commissioners

(1) The Lord Chancellor may appoint persons to act as Child Support Commissioners (but to be known as deputy Child Support Commissioners) in order to facilitate the disposal of the business of Child Support Commissioners.

(2) A deputy Child Support Commissioner shall be appointed –

- (a) from among persons who have a 10 year general qualification or are advocates or solicitors in Scotland of 10 years' standing; and

(b) for such period or on such occasions as the Lord Chancellor thinks fit.

(3) Paragraph 2 applies to deputy Child Support Commissioners as if the reference to pensions were omitted and paragraph 3 does not apply to them.

4A Determination of questions by other officers

(1) The Lord Chancellor may by regulation provide –

(a) for officers authorised –
   (i) by the Lord Chancellor; or
   (ii) (*applies to Scotland only*),
   to determine any question which is determinable by a Child Support Commissioner and which does not involve the determination of any appeal, application for leave to appeal or reference;

(b) for the procedure to be followed by any such officer in determining any such question;

(c) for the manner in which determinations of such questions by such officers may be called in question.

(2) A determination which would have the effect of preventing an appeal, application for leave to appeal or reference being determined by a Child Support Commissioner is not a determination of the appeal, application or reference for the purposes of sub-paragraph (1).

5 Tribunals of Commissioners

(1) If it appears to the Chief Child Support Commissioner (or, in the case of his inability to act, to such other of the Child Support Commissioners as he may have nominated to act for the purpose) that –

(a) an application for leave under section 24(6)(b); or
(b) an appeal,

falling to be heard by one of the Child Support Commissioners involves a question of law of special difficulty, he may direct that the application or appeal be dealt with by a tribunal consisting of any three or more of the Child Support Commissioners.

(2) If the decision of such a tribunal is not unanimous, the decision of the majority shall be the decision of the tribunal; and the presiding Child Support Commissioner shall have a casting vote if the votes are equally divided.

(3) Where a direction is given under sub-paragraph (1)(a), section 24(6)(b) shall have effect as if the reference to a Child Support Commissioner were a reference to such a tribunal as is mentioned in sub-paragraph (1).

6 Finality of decisions

(1) Subject to section 25, the decision of any Child Support Commissioner shall be final.

(2) If and to the extent that regulations so provide, any finding of fact or other determination which is embodied in or necessary to a decision, or on which a decision is based, shall be conclusive for the purposes of any further decision.

7 Consultation with Lord Advocate

(1) Before exercising any of his powers under paragraph 1(2) or (3), 4(1) or (2)(b) or 4A(1), the Lord Chancellor shall consult the Lord Advocate.

8 (*applies to Northern Ireland only*)

SCHEDULE 4A

APPLICATIONS FOR A VARIATION

1 Interpretation

In this Schedule, 'regulations' means regulations made by the Secretary of State.

2 Applications for a variation

Regulations may make provision –

(a) as to the procedure to be followed in considering an application for a variation;
(b) as to the procedure to be followed when an application for a variation is referred to an appeal tribunal under section 28D(1)(b).

3 Completion of preliminary consideration

Regulations may provide for determining when the preliminary consideration of an application for a variation is to be taken to have been completed.

4 Information

If any information which is required (by regulations under this Act) to be furnished to the Secretary of State in connection with an application for a variation has not been furnished within such period as may be prescribed, the Secretary of State may nevertheless proceed to consider the application.

5 Joint consideration of applications for a variation and appeals

(1) Regulations may provide for two or more applications for a variation with respect to the same application for a maintenance calculation to be considered together.

(2) In sub-paragraph (1), the reference to an application for a maintenance calculation includes an application treated as having been made under section 6.

(3) An appeal tribunal considering an application for a variation under section 28D(1)(b) may consider it at the same time as an appeal under section 20 in connection with an interim maintenance decision, if it considers that to be appropriate.

Amendments—Child Support, Pensions and Social Security Act 2000, s 6(1) – in force from a date to be appointed.

SCHEDULE 4B

APPLICATIONS FOR A VARIATION: THE CASES AND CONTROLS

PART I

THE CASES

1 General

(1) The cases in which a variation may be agreed are those set out in this Part of this Schedule or in regulations made under this Part.

(2) In this Schedule 'applicant' means the person whose application for a variation is being considered.

2 Special expenses

(1) A variation applied for by a non-resident parent may be agreed with respect to his special expenses.

(2) In this paragraph 'special expenses' means the whole, or any amount above a prescribed amount, or any prescribed part, of expenses which fall within a prescribed description of expenses.

(3) In prescribing descriptions of expenses for the purposes of this paragraph, the Secretary of State may, in particular, make provision with respect to –

(a) costs incurred by a non-resident parent in maintaining contact with the child, or with any of the children, with respect to whom the application for a maintenance calculation has been made (or treated as made);
(b) costs attributable to a long-term illness or disability of a relevant other child (within the meaning of paragraph 10C(2) of Schedule 1);
(c) debts of a prescribed description incurred, before the non-resident parent became a non-resident parent in relation to a child with respect to whom the maintenance calculation has been applied for (or treated as having been applied for) –

(i) for the joint benefit of both parents;
(ii) for the benefit of any such child; or
(iii) for the benefit of any other child falling within a prescribed category;

(d) boarding school fees for a child in relation to whom the application for a maintenance calculation has been made (or treated as made);
(e) the cost to the non-resident parent of making payments in relation to a mortgage on the home he and the person with care shared, if he no longer has an interest in it, and she and a child in relation to whom the application for a maintenance calculation has been made (or treated as made) still live there.

(4) For the purposes of sub-paragraph (3)(b) –

(a) 'disability' and 'illness' have such meaning as may be prescribed; and
(b) the question whether an illness or disability is long-term shall be determined in accordance with regulations made by the Secretary of State.

(5) For the purposes of sub-paragraph (3)(d), the Secretary of State may prescribe –

(a) the meaning of 'boarding school fees'; and
(b) components of such fees (whether or not itemised as such) which are, or are not, to be taken into account,

and may provide for estimating any such component.

3 Property or capital transfers

(1) A variation may be agreed in the circumstances set out in sub-paragraph (2) if before 5th April 1993 –

(a) a court order of a prescribed kind was in force with respect to the non-resident parent and either the person with care with respect to the application for the maintenance calculation or the child, or any of the children, with respect to whom that application was made; or
(b) an agreement of a prescribed kind between the non-resident parent and any of those persons was in force.

(2) The circumstances are that in consequence of one or more transfers of property of a prescribed kind and exceeding (singly or in aggregate) a prescribed minimum value –

- (a) the amount payable by the non-resident parent by way of maintenance was less than would have been the case had that transfer or those transfers not been made; or
- (b) no amount was payable by the non-resident parent by way of maintenance.

(3) For the purposes of sub-paragraph (2), 'maintenance' means periodical payments of maintenance made (otherwise than under this Act) with respect to the child, or any of the children, with respect to whom the application for a maintenance calculation has been made.

4 Additional cases

(1) The Secretary of State may by regulations prescribe other cases in which a variation may be agreed.

(2) Regulations under this paragraph may, for example, make provision with respect to cases where –

- (a) the non-resident parent has assets which exceed a prescribed value;
- (b) a person's lifestyle is inconsistent with his income for the purposes of a calculation made under Part I of Schedule 1;
- (c) a person has income which is not taken into account in such a calculation;
- (d) a person has unreasonably reduced the income which is taken into account in such a calculation.

PART II

REGULATORY CONTROLS

5—(1) The Secretary of State may by regulations make provision with respect to the variations from the usual rules for calculating maintenance which may be allowed when a variation is agreed.

(2) No variations may be made other than those which are permitted by the regulations.

(3) Regulations under this paragraph may, in particular, make provision for a variation to result in –

- (a) a person's being treated as having more, or less, income than would be taken into account witout the variation in a calculation under Part I of Schedule 1;
- (b) a person's being treated as liable to pay a higher, or a lower, amount of child support maintenance than would result without the variation from a calculation under that Part.

(4) Regulations may provide for the amount of any special expenses to be taken into account in a case falling within paragraph 2, for the purposes of a variation, not to exceed such amounts as may be prescribed or as may be determined in accordance with the regulations.

(5) Any regulations under this paragraph may in particular make different provision with respect to different levels of income.

6 The Secretary of State may by regulations provide for the application, in connection with child support maintenance payable following a variation, of paragraph 7(2) to (7) of Schedule 1 (subject to any prescribed modifications).

Amendments—Child Support, Pensions and Social Security Act 2000, s 6(2) – in force from a date to be appointed.

SCHEDULE 4C

. . .

Amendments—Child Support, Pensions and Social Security Act 2000, Sch 9, Part I – in force from a date to be appointed.

SCHEDULE 5

CONSEQUENTIAL AMENDMENTS

1 The Tribunals and Inquiries Act 1971 (c 62)

(1) In section 7(3) of the Tribunals and Inquiries Act 1971 (chairman of certain tribunals to be drawn from panels) after 'paragraph' there shall be inserted '4A'.

(2) In Schedule 1 to that Act (tribunals under the general supervision of the Council on Tribunals) the following entry shall be inserted at the appropriate place –

'Child support maintenance	4A (a) The child support appeal tribunals established under section 21 of the Child Support Act 1991. (b) A Child Support Commissioner appointed under section 22 of the Child Support Act 1991 and any tribunal presided over by such a Commissioner.'

2 (*applies to Northern Ireland only*)

3 The House of Commons Disqualification Act 1975 (c 24)

(1) The House of Commons Disqualification Act 1975 shall be amended as follows.

(2) In Part I (disqualifying judicial offices), the following entries shall be inserted at the appropriate places –

'Chief or other Child Support Commissioner (excluding a person appointed under paragraph 4 of Schedule 4 to the Child Support Act 1991).'

'Chief or other Child Support Commissioner for Northern Ireland (excluding a person appointed under paragraph 4 of Schedule 4 to the Child Support Act 1991).'

(3) In Part III (other disqualifying offices), the following entry shall be inserted at the appropriate place –

'Regional or other full-time chairman of a child support appeal tribunal established under section 21 of the Child Support Act 1991'.

4 (*applies to Northern Ireland only*)

5 (*applies to Scotland only*)

6 (*applies to Scotland only*)

7 The Insolvency Act 1986 (c 45)

In section 281(5)(b) of the Insolvency Act 1986 (effect of discharge of bankrupt), after 'family proceedings' there shall be inserted 'or under a maintenance calculation made under the Child Support Act 1991'.

8 (*applies to Scotland only*)

Amendments—Child Support, Pensions and Social Security Act 2000, s 1(2) – in force from a date to be appointed.

Child Support Act 1995, including prospective amendments by the Child Support, Pensions and Social Security Act 2000

1–9 (*amend Child Support Act 1991*)

10 (*repealed by Child Support, Pensions and Social Security Act 2000*, s 23)

11–17 (*amend Child Support Act 1991*)

Miscellaneous

18 Deferral of right to apply for maintenance assessment

(1)–(4) (*amend Child Support Act 1991*)

(5) ...

(6) Neither section 4(10) nor section 7(10) of the 1991 Act shall apply in relation to a maintenance order made in the circumstances mentioned in subsection (7) or (8) of section 8 of the 1991 Act.

(7) The Secretary of State may by regulations make provision for subsection 4(10), or section 7(10), of the 1991 Act not to apply in relation to such other cases as may be prescribed.

(8) Part I of the Schedule to the Child Support Act 1991 (Commencement No 3 and Transitional Provisions) Order 1992 (phased take-on of certain cases) is hereby revoked.

(9) At any time before 7th April 1997, neither section 8(3), nor section 9(5)(b), of the 1991 Act shall apply in relation to any case which fell within paragraph 5(2) of the Schedule to the 1992 Order (pending cases during the transitional period set by that Order).

Amendments—Child Support, Pensions and Social Security Act 2000, Sch 3, para 13(2) – in force from a date to be appointed.

19–23 (*amend Child Support Act 1991*)

24 ...

Amendments—Child Support, Pensions and Social Security Act 2000, Sch 3, para 13(3) – in force from a date to be appointed.

25 (*amends Social Security Administration Act 1992*)

Supplemental

26 Regulations and orders

(1) Any power under this Act to make regulations or orders shall be exercisable by statutory instrument.

(2) Any such power may be exercised to make different provision for different cases, including different provision for different areas.

(3) Any such power includes power –

(a) to make such incidental, supplemental, consequential or transitional provision as appears to the Secretary of State to be expedient; and
(b) to provide for a person to exercise a discretion in dealing with any matter.

(4) Subsection (5) applies to –

(a) the first regulations made under section 10;
(b) any order made under section 18(5).

(5) No regulations or order to which this subsection applies shall be made unless a draft of the statutory instrument containing the regulations or order has been laid before Parliament and approved by a resolution of each House.

(6) Any other statutory instrument made under this Act, other than one made under section 30(4), shall be subject to annulment in pursuance of a resolution of either House of Parliament.

27 Interpretation

(1) In this Act 'the 1991 Act' means the Child Support Act 1991.

(2) Expressions in this Act which are used in the 1991 Act have the same meaning in this Act as they have in that Act.

28 Financial provisions

There shall be paid out of money provided by Parliament –

(a) any expenditure incurred by the Secretary of State under or by virtue of this Act;
(b) any increase attributable to this Act in the sums payable out of money so provided under or by virtue of any other enactment.

29 (*applies to Northern Ireland only*)

30 Short title, commencement, extent etc

(1) This Act may be cited as the Child Support Act 1995.

(2) This Act and the 1991 Act may be cited together as the Child Support Acts 1991 and 1995.

(3) Section 29 and this section (apart from subsection (5)) come into force on the passing of this Act.

(4) The other provisions of this Act come into force on such day as the Secretary of State may by order appoint and different days may be appointed for different purposes.

(5) Schedule 3 makes minor and consequential amendments.

(6) This Act, except for –

(a) sections 17, 27 and 29,
(b) this section, and
(c) paragraphs 1, 18, 19 and 20 of Schedule 3,

does not extend to Northern Ireland.

[Schedules 1 and 2 amend Child Support Act 1991; Schedule 3 makes minor and consequential amendments.]

Child Support, Pensions and Social Security Act 2000

(Part I, Schs 1–3, 8 and 9)

PART I

CHILD SUPPORT

Maintenance calculations and interim and default maintenance decisions

1 Maintenance calculations and terminology

(1) In the Child Support Act 1991 ('the 1991 Act'), for section 11 (maintenance assessments) there shall be substituted –

'11 Maintenance calculations

(1) An application for a maintenance calculation made to the Secretary of State shall be dealt with by him in accordance with the provison made by or under this Act.

(2) The Secretary of State shall (unless he decides not to make a maintenance calculation in response to the application, or makes a decision under section 12) determine the application by making a decision under this section about whether any child support maintenance is payable and, if so, how much.

(3) Where –

(a) a parent is treated under section 6(3) as having applied for a maintenance calculation; but
(b) the Secretary of State becomes aware before determining the application that the parent has ceased to fall within section 6(1),

he shall, subject to subsection (4), cease to treat that parent as having applied for a maintenance calculation.

(4) If it appears to the Secretary of State that subsection (10) of section 4 would not have prevented the parent with care concerned from making an application for a maintenance calculation under that section he shall –

(a) notify her of the effect of this subsection; and
(b) if, before the end of the period of one month beginning with the day on which notice was sent to her, she asks him to do so, treat her as having applied not under section 6 but under section 4.

(5) Where subsection (3) applies but subsection (4) does not, the Secretary of State shall notify –

(a) the parent with care concerned; and
(b) the non-resident parent (or alleged non-resident parent), where it appears to him that that person is aware that the parent with care has been treated as having applied for a maintenance calculation.

(6) The amount of child support maintenance to be fixed by a maintenance calculation shall be determined in accordance with Part I of Schedule 1 unless an application for a variation has been made and agreed.

(7) If the Secretary of State has agreed to a variation, the amount of child support maintenance to be fixed shall be determined on the basis he determines under section 28F(4).

(8) Part II of Schedule 1 makes further provision with respect to maintenance calculations.'

(2) In the 1991 Act –

(a) for 'maintenance assessment', wherever it occurs, there shall be substituted 'maintenance calculation'; and
(b) for 'assessment' (or any variant of that term), wherever it occurs, there shall be substituted 'calculation' (or the corresponding variant) preceded, where appropriate, by 'a' instead of 'an'.

(3) For Part I of Schedule 1 to the 1991 Act, there shall be substituted the Part I set out in Schedule 1 to this Act.

2 Applications under section 4 of the Child Support Act 1991

(1) In section 4 of the 1991 Act (child support maintenance), subsection (10) shall be amended as follows.

(2) In paragraph (a), after 'maintenance order' there shall be inserted 'made before a prescribed date'.

(3) After paragraph (a), there shall be inserted –

'(aa) a maintenance order made on or after the date prescribed for the purposes of paragraph (a) is in force in respect of them, but has been so for less than the period of one year beginning with the date on which it was made; or'.

3 Applications by persons claiming or receiving benefit

For section 6 of the 1991 Act (applications by those receiving benefit) there shall be substituted –

'6 Applications by those claiming or receiving benefit

(1) This section applies where income support, an income-based jobseeker's allowance or any other benefit of a prescribed kind is claimed by or in respect of, or paid to or in respect of, the parent of a qualifying child who is also a person with care of the child.

(2) In this section, that person is referred to as "the parent".

(3) The Secretary of State may –

(a) treat the parent as having applied for a maintenance calculation with respect to the qualifying child and all other children of the non-resident parent in relation to whom the parent is also a person with care; and
(b) take action under this Act to recover from the non-resident parent, on the parent's behalf, the child support maintenance so determined.

(4) Before doing what is mentioned in subsection (3), the Secretary of State must notify the parent in writing of the effect of subsections (3) and (5) and section 46.

(5) The Secretary of State may not act under subsection (3) if the parent asks him not to (a request which need not be in writing).

(6) Subsection (1) has effect regardless of whether any of the benefits mentioned there is payable with respect to any qualifying child.

(7) Unless she has made a request under subsection (5), the parent shall, so far as she reasonably can, comply with such regulations as may be made by the Secretary of State with a view to the Secretary of State's being provided with the information which is required to enable –

(a) the non-resident parent to be identified or traced;
(b) the amount of child support maintenance payable by him to be calculated; and
(c) that amount to be recovered from him.

(8) The obligation to provide information which is imposed by subsection (7) –

(a) does not apply in such circumstances as may be prescribed; and
(b) may, in such circumstances as may be prescribed, be waived by the Secretary of State.

(9) If the parent ceases to fall within subsection (1), she may ask the Secretary of State to cease acting under this section, but until then he may continue to do so.

(10) The Secretary of State must comply with any request under subsection (9) (but subject to any regulations made under subsection (11)).

(11) The Secretary of State may by regulations make such incidental or transitional provisions as he thinks appropriate with respect to cases in which he is asked under subsection (9) to cease to act under this section.

(12) The fact that a maintenance calculation is in force with respect to a person with care does not prevent the making of a new maintenance calculation with respect to her as a result of the Secretary of State's acting under subsection (3).'

4 Default and interim maintenance decisions

For section 12 of the 1991 Act (interim maintenance assessments) there shall be substituted –

'12 Default and interim maintenance decisions

(1) Where the Secretary of State –

(a) is required to make a maintenance calculation; or
(b) is proposing to make a decision under section 16 or 17,

and it appears to him that he does not have sufficient information to enable him to do so, he may make a default maintenance decision.

(2) Where an application for a variation has been made under section 28A(1) in connection with an application for a maintenance calculation (or in connection with such an application which is treated as having been made), the Secretary of State may make an interim maintenance decision.

(3) The amount of child support maintenance fixed by an interim maintenance decision shall be determined in accordance with Part I of Schedule 1.

(4) The Secretary of State may by regulations make provision as to default and interim maintenance decisions.

(5) The regulations may, in particular, make provision as to –

(a) the procedure to be followed in making a default or an interim maintenance decision; and
(b) a default rate of child support maintenance to apply where a default maintenance decision is made.'

Applications for a variation

5 Departure from usual rules for calculating maintenance

(1) The 1991 Act shall be amended as follows.

(2) For sections 28A to 28C (which deal respectively with applications for departure directions, their preliminary consideration, and the imposition of a regular payments condition) there shall be substituted –

'Variations

28A Application for variation of usual rules for calculating maintenance

(1) Where an application for a maintenance calculation is made under section 4 or 7, or treated as made under section 6, the person with care or the non-resident parent or (in the case of an application under section 7) either of them or the child concerned may apply to the Secretary of State for the rules by which the calculation is made to be varied in accordance with this Act.

(2) Such an application is referred to in this Act as an "application for a variation".

(3) An application for a variation may be made at any time before the Secretary of State has reached a decision (under section 11 or 12(1)) on the application for a maintenance calculation (or the application treated as having been made under section 6).

(4) A person who applies for a variation –

- (a) need not make the application in writing unless the Secretary of State directs in any case that he must; and
- (b) must say upon what grounds the application is made.

(5) In other respects an application for a variation is to be made in such manner as may be prescribed.

(6) Schedule 4A has effect in relation to applications for a variation.

28B Preliminary consideration of applications

(1) Where an application for a variation has been duly made to the Secretary of State, he may give it a preliminary consideration.

(2) Where he does so he may, on completing the preliminary consideration, reject the application (and proceed to make his decision on the application for a maintenance calculation without any variation) if it appears to him –

- (a) that there are no grounds on which he could agree to a variation;
- (b) that he has insufficient information to make a decision on the application for the maintenance calculation under section 11 (apart from any information needed in relation to the application for a variation), and therefore that his decision would be made under section 12(1); or
- (c) that other prescribed circumstances apply.

28C Imposition of regular payments condition

(1) Where –

- (a) an application for a variation is made by the non-resident parent; and
- (b) the Secretary of State makes an interim maintenance decision,

the Secretary of State may also, if he has completed his preliminary consideration (under section 28B) of the application for a variation and has not rejected it under that section, impose on the non-resident parent one of the conditions mentioned in subsection (2) (a "regular payments condition").

(2) The conditions are that –

(a) the non-resident parent must make the payments of child support maintenance specified in the interim maintenance decision;
(b) the non-resident parent must make such lesser payments of child support maintenance as may be determined in accordance with regulations made by the Secretary of State.

(3) Where the Secretary of State imposes a regular payments condition, he shall give written notice of the imposition of the condition and of the effect of failure to comply with it to –

(a) the non-resident parent;
(b) all the persons with care concerned; and
(c) if the application for the maintenance calculation was made under section 7, the child who made the application.

(4) A regular payments condition shall cease to have effect –

(a) when the Secretary of State has made a decision on the application for a maintenance calculation under section 11 (whether he agrees to a variation or not);
(b) on the withdrawal of the application for a variation.

(5) Where a non-resident parent has failed to comply with a regular payments condition, the Secretary of State may in prescribed circumstances refuse to consider the application for a variation, and instead reach his decision under section 11 as if no such application had been made.

(6) The question whether a non-resident parent has failed to comply with a regular payments condition is to be determined by the Secretary of State.

(7) Where the Secretary of State determines that a non-resident parent has failed to comply with a regular payments condition he shall give written notice of his determination to –

(a) that parent;
(b) all the persons with care concerned; and
(c) if the application for the maintenance calculation was made under section 7, the child who made the application.'

(3) In section 28D (determination of applications) –

(a) for subsection (1) there shall be substituted –

'(1) Where an application for a variation has not failed, the Secretary of State shall, in accordance with the relevant provisions of, or made under, this Act –

(a) either agree or not to a variation, and make a decision under section 11 or 12(1); or
(b) refer the application to an appeal tribunal for the tribunal to determine what variation, if any, is to be made.';

(b) in each of subsections (2) and (3), for 'an application for a departure direction' there shall be substituted 'an application for a variation'; and
(c) in subsection (2), in paragraph (a) 'lapsed or' shall be omitted, at the end of paragraph (b) 'or' shall be inserted, and after that paragraph there shall be inserted –

'(c) the Secretary of State has refused to consider it under section 28C(5).'

(4) In section 28E (matters to be taken into account) –

(a) in subsections (1), (3) and (4), for 'any application for a departure direction' (wherever appearing) there shall be substituted 'whether to agree to a variation'; and
(b) in subsection (4)(a), for 'a departure direction were made' there shall be substituted 'the Secretary of State agreed to a variation'.

(5) For section 28F (departure directions) there shall be substituted –

'28F Agreement to a variation

(1) The Secretary of State may agree to a variation if –

(a) he is satisfied that the case is one which falls within one or more of the cases set out in Part I of Schedule 4B or in regulations made under that Part; and
(b) it is his opinion that, in all the circumstances of the case, it would be just and equitable to agree to a variation.

(2) In considering whether it would be just and equitable in any case to agree to a variation, the Secretary of State –

(a) must have regard, in particular, to the welfare of any child likely to be affected if he did agree to a variation; and
(b) must, or as the case may be must not, take any prescribed factors into account, or must take them into account (or not) in prescribed circumstances.

(3) The Secretary of State shall not agree to a variation (and shall proceed to make his decision on the application for a maintenance calculation without any variation) if he is satisfied that –

(a) he has insufficient information to make a decision on the application for the maintenance calculation under section 11, and therefore that his decision would be made under section 12(1); or
(b) other prescribed circumstances apply.

(4) Where the Secretary of State agrees to a variation, he shall –

(a) determine the basis on which the amount of child support maintenance is to be calculated in response to the application for a maintenance calculation (including an application treated as having been made); and
(b) make a decision under section 11 on that basis.

(5) If the Secretary of State has made an interim maintenance decision, it is to be treated as having been replaced by his decision under section 11, and except in prescribed circumstances any appeal connected with it (under section 20) shall lapse.

(6) In determining whether or not to agree to a variation, the Secretary of State shall comply with regulations made under Part II of Schedule 4B.'

6 Applications for a variation: further provisions

(1) For Schedule 4A to the 1991 Act there shall be substituted the Schedule 4A set out in Part I of Schedule 2.

(2) For Schedule 4B to that Act there shall be substituted the Schedule 4B set out in Part II of Schedule 2.

7 Variations: revision and supersession

For section 28G of the 1991 Act (effect and duration of departure directions) there shall be substituted –

> **'28G Variations: revision and supersession**
>
> (1) An application for a variation may also be made when a maintenance calculation is in force.
>
> (2) The Secretary of State may by regulations provide for –
>
> (a) sections 16, 17 and 20; and
> (b) sections 28A to 28F and Schedules 4A and 4B,
>
> to apply with prescribed modifications in relation to such applications.
>
> (3) The Secretary of State may by regulations provide that, in prescribed cases (or except in prescribed cases), a decision under section 17 made otherwise than pursuant to an application for a variation may be made on the basis of a variation agreed to for the purposes of an earlier decision without a new application for a variation having to be made.'

Revision and supersession of decisions

8 Revision of decisions

(1) Section 16 of the 1991 Act (revision of decisions) shall be amended as follows.

(2) In subsection (1), for 'of the Secretary of State under section 11, 12 or 17' there shall be substituted 'to which subsection (1A) applies'.

(3) After subsection (1), there shall be inserted –

> '(1A) This subsection applies to –
>
> (a) a decision of the Secretary of State under section 11, 12 or 17;
> (b) a reduced benefit decision under section 46;
> (c) a decision of an appeal tribunal on a referral under section 28D(1)(b).
>
> (1B) Where the Secretary of State revises a decision under section 12(1) –
>
> (a) he may (if appropriate) do so as if he were revising a decision under section 11; and
> (b) if he does that, his decision as revised is to be treated as one under section 11 instead of section 12(1) (and, in particular, is to be so treated for the purposes of an appeal against it under section 20).'

9 Decisions superseding earlier decisions

(1) Section 17 of the 1991 Act (decisions superseding earlier decisions) shall be amended as follows.

(2) In subsection (1), for paragraph (c) there shall be substituted –

> '(c) any reduced benefit decision under section 46;
> (d) any decision of an appeal tribunal on a referral under section 28D(1)(b);
> (e) any decision of a Child Support Commissioner on an appeal from such a decision as is mentioned in paragraph (b) or (d).'

(3) For subsection (4) there shall be substituted –

'(4) Subject to subsection (5) and section 28ZC, a decision under this section shall take effect as from the beginning of the maintenance period in which it is made or, where applicable, the beginning of the maintenance period in which the application was made.

(4A) In subsection (4), a "maintenance period" is (except where a different meaning is prescribed for prescribed cases) a period of seven days, the first one beginning on the effective date of the first decison made by the Secretary of State under section 11 or (if earlier) his first default or interim maintenance decision (under section 12) in relation to the non-resident parent in question, and each subsequent one beginning on the day after the last day of the previous one.'

Appeals

10 Appeals to appeal tribunals

For section 20 of the 1991 Act (appeals to appeal tribunals) there shall be substituted –

'20 Appeals to appeal tribunals

(1) A qualifying person has a right of appeal to an appeal tribunal against –

(a) a decision of the Secretary of State under section 11, 12 or 17 (whether as originally made or as revised under section 16);
(b) a decision of the Secretary of State not to make a maintenance calculation under section 11 or not to supersede a decision under section 17;
(c) a reduced benefit decision under section 46;
(d) the imposition (by virtue of section 41A) of a requirement to make penalty payments, or their amount;
(e) the imposition (by virtue of section 47) of a requirement to pay fees.

(2) In subsection (1), "qualifying person" means –

(a) in relation to paragraphs (a) and (b) –
  (i) the person with care, or non-resident parent, with respect to whom the Secretary of State made the decision, or
  (ii) in a case relating to a maintenance calculation which was applied for under section 7, either of those persons or the child concerned;
(b) in relation to paragraph (c), the person in respect of whom the benefits are payable;
(c) in relation to paragraph (d), the parent who has been required to make penalty payments; and
(d) in relation to paragraph (e), the person required to pay fees.

(3) A person with a right of appeal under this section shall be given such notice as may be prescribed of –

(a) that right; and
(b) the relevant decision, or the imposition of the requirement.

(4) Regulations may make –

(a) provision as to the manner in which, and the time within which, appeals are to be brought; and

(b) such provision with respect to proceedings before appeal tribunals as the Secretary of State considers appropriate.

(5) The regulations may in particular make any provision of a kind mentioned in Schedule 5 to the Social Security Act 1998.

(6) No appeal lies by virtue of subsection (1)(c) unless the amount of the person's benefit is reduced in accordance with the reduced benefit decision; and the time within which such an appeal may be brought runs from the date of notification of the reduction.

(7) In deciding an appeal under this section, an appeal tribunal –

(a) need not consider any issue that is not raised by the appeal; and
(b) shall not take into account any circumstances not obtaining at the time when the Secretary of State made the decision or imposed the requirement.

(8) If an appeal under this section is allowed, the appeal tribunal may –

(a) itself make such decision as it considers appropriate; or
(b) remit the case to the Secretary of State, together with such directions (if any) as it considers appropriate.'

11 Redetermination of appeals

'23A Redetermination of appeals

(1) This section applies where an application is made to a person under section 24(6)(a) for leave to appeal from a decision of an appeal tribunal.

(2) If the person who constituted, or was the chairman of, the appeal tribunal considers that the decision was erroneous in law, he may set aside the decision and refer the case either for redetermination by the tribunal or for determination by a differently constituted tribunal.

(3) If each of the principal parties to the case expresses the view that the decision was erroneous in point of law, the person shall set aside the decision and refer the case for determination by a differently constituted tribunal.

(4) The "principal parties" are –

(a) the Secretary of State; and
(b) those who are qualifying persons for the purposes of section 20(2) in relation to the decision in question.'

Information

12 Information required by Secretary of State

In section 14 of the 1991 Act (information required by the Secretary of State), in subsection (1), after 'such an application' there shall be inserted '(or application treated as made), or needed for the making of any decision or in connection with the imposition of any condition or requirement under this Act,'.

13 Information – offences

After section 14 of the 1991 Act there shall be inserted –

'14A Information – offences

(1) This section applies to –

(a) persons who are required to comply with regulations under section 4(4) or 7(5); and
(b) persons specified in regulations under section 14(1)(a).

(2) Such a person is guilty of an offence if, pursuant to a request for information under or by virtue of those regulations –

(a) he makes a statement or representation which he knows to be false; or
(b) he provides, or knowingly causes or knowingly allows to be provided, a document or other information which he knows to be false in a material particular.

(3) Such a person is guilty of an offence if, following such a request, he fails to comply with it.

(4) It is a defence for a person charged with an offence under subsection (3) to prove that he had a reasonable excuse for failing to comply.

(5) A person guilty of an offence under this section is liable on summary conviction to a fine not exceeding level 3 on the standard scale.'

14 Inspectors

(1) Section 15 of the 1991 Act (powers of inspectors) shall be amended as follows.

(2) For subsections (1) to (4) there shall be substituted –

'(1) The Secretary of State may appoint, on such terms as he thinks fit, persons to act as inspectors under this section.

(2) The function of inspectors is to acquire information which the Secretary of State needs for any of the purposes of this Act.

(3) Every inspector is to be given a certificate of his appointment.

(4) An inspector has power, at any reasonable time and either alone or accompanied by such other persons as he thinks fit, to enter any premises which –

(a) are liable to inspection under this section; and
(b) are premises to which it is reasonable for him to require entry in order that he may exercise his functions under this section,

and may there make such examination and inquiry as he considers appropriate.

(4A) Premises liable to inspection under this section are those which are not used wholly as a dwelling house and which the inspector has reasonable grounds for suspecting are –

(a) premises at which a non-resident parent is or has been employed;
(b) premises at which a non-resident parent carries out, or has carried out, a trade, profession, vocation or business;
(c) premises at which there is information held by a person ("A") whom the inspector has reasonable grounds for suspecting has information about a non-resident parent acquired in the course of A's own trade, profession, vocation or business.'

(3) In subsection (6), for the words from 'any person who' to the end of paragraph (d) there shall be substituted 'any such person'.

(4) After subsection (10) there shall be inserted –

'(11) In this section, "premises" includes –

(a) moveable structures and vehicles, vessels, aircraft and hovercraft;
(b) installations that are offshore installations for the purposes of the Mineral Workings (Offshore Installations) Act 1971; and
(c) places of all other descriptions whether or not occupied as land or otherwise,

and references in this section to the occupier of premises are to be construed, in relation to premises that are not occupied as land, as references to any person for the time being present at the place in question.'

Parentage

15 Presumption of parentage in child support cases

(1) In section 26(2) of the 1991 Act (cases in which the Secretary of State may assume a person to be the parent of a child for the purpose of making a maintenance calculation under that Act), before Case A there shall be inserted –

'CASE A1

Where –

(a) the child is habitually resident in England and Wales;
(b) the Secretary of State is satisfied that the alleged parent was married to the child's mother at some time in the period beginning with the conception and ending with the birth of the child; and
(c) the child has not been adopted.

CASE A2

Where –

(a) the child is habitually resident in England and Wales;
(b) the alleged parent has been registered as father of the child under section 10 or 10A of the Births and Deaths Registration Act 1953, or in any register kept under section 13 (register of births and still-births) or section 44 (Register of Corrections Etc) of the Registration of Births, Deaths and Marriages (Scotland) Act 1965, or under Article 14 or 18(1)(b)(ii) of the Births and Deaths Registration (Northern Ireland) Order 1976; and
(c) the child has not subsequently been adopted.

CASE A3

Where the result of a scientific test (within the meaning of section 27A) taken by the alleged parent would be relevant to determining the child's parentage, and the alleged parent –

(a) refuses to take such a test; or
(b) has submitted to such a test, and it shows that there is no reasonable doubt that the alleged parent is a parent of the child.'

(2) In that provision, after Case B there shall be inserted –

'CASE B1

Where the Secretary of State is satisfied that the alleged parent is a parent of the child in question by virtue of section 27 or 28 of that Act (meaning of "mother" and of "father" respectively.'

Disqualification from driving

16 Disqualification from driving

(1) After section 39 of the 1991 Act there shall be inserted –

'39A Commitment to prison and disqualification from driving

(1) Where the Secretary of State has sought –

(a) in England and Wales to levy an amount by distress under this Act; or
(b) to recover an amount by virtue of section 36 or 38,

and that amount, or any portion of it, remains unpaid he may apply to the court under this section.

(2) An application under this section is for whichever the court considers appropriate in all the circumstances of –

(a) the issue of a warrant committing the liable person to prison; or
(b) an order for him to be disqualified from holding or obtaining a driving licence.

(3) On any such application the court shall (in the presence of the liable person) inquire as to –

(a) whether he needs a driving licence to earn his living;
(b) his means; and
(c) whether there has been wilful refusal or culpable neglect on his part.

(4) The Secretary of State may make representations to the court as to whether he thinks it more appropriate to commit the liable person to prison or to disqualify him from holding or obtaining a driving licence; and the liable person may reply to those representations.

(5) In this section and section 40B, "driving licence" means a licence to drive a motor vehicle granted under Part III of the Road Traffic Act 1988.

(6) In this section "the court" means –

(a) in England and Wales, a magistrates' court;
(b) in Scotland, the sheriff.'

(2) In section 40 of the 1991 Act (commitment to prison), subsections (1) and (2) shall be omitted.

(3) Before section 41 of the 1991 Act there shall be inserted –

'40B Disqualification from driving: further provision

(1) If, but only if, the court is of the opinion that there has been wilful refusal or culpable neglect on the part of the liable person, it may –

(a) order him to be disqualified, for such period specified in the order but not exceeding two years as it thinks fit, from holding or obtaining a driving licence (a "disqualification order"); or
(b) make a disqualification order but suspend its operation until such time and on such conditions (if any) as it thinks just.

(2) The court may not take action under both section 40 and this section.

(3) A disqualification order must state the amount in respect of which it is made, which is to be the aggregate of –

(a) the amount mentioned in section 35(1), or so much of it as remains outstanding; and
(b) an amount (determined in accordance with regulations made by the Secretary of State) in respect of the costs of the application under section 39A.

(4) A court which makes a disqualification order shall require the person to whom it relates to produce any driving licence held by him, and its counterpart (within the meaning of section 108(1) of the Road Traffic Act 1988).

(5) On an application by the Secretary of State or the liable person, the court –

(a) may make an order substituting a shorter period of disqualification, or make an order revoking the disqualification order, if part of the amount referred to in subsection (3) (the "amount due") is paid to any person authorised to receive it; and
(b) must make an order revoking the disqualification order if all of the amount due is so paid.

(6) The Secretary of State may make representations to the court as to the amount which should be paid before it would be appropriate to make an order revoking the disqualification order under subsection (5)(a), and the person liable may reply to those representations.

(7) The Secretary of State may make a further application under section 39A if the amount due has not been paid in full when the period of disqualification specified in the disqualification order expires.

(8) Where a court –

(a) makes a disqualification order;
(b) makes an order under subsection (5); or
(c) allows an appeal against a disqualification order,

it shall send notice of that fact to the Secretary of State; and the notice shall contain such particulars and be sent in such manner and to such address as the Secretary of State may determine.

(9) Where a court makes a disqualification order, it shall also send the driving licence and its counterpart, on their being produced to the court, to the Secretary of State at such address as he may determine.

(10) Section 80 of the Magistrates' Courts Act 1980 (application of money found on defaulter) shall apply in relation to a disqualification order under this section in relation to a liable person as it applies in relation to the enforcement of a sum mentioned in subsection (1) of that section.

(11) The Secretary of State may by regulations make provision in relation to disqualification orders corresponding to the provision he may make under section 40(11).

(12) In the application to Scotland of this section –

(a) in subsection (2) for "section 40" substitute "section 40A";
(b) in subsection (3) for paragraph (a) substitute –

"(a) the appropriate amount under section 38;";

(c) subsection (10) is omitted; and
(d) for subsection (11) substitute –

"(11) The power of the Court of Session by Act of Sederunt to regulate the procedure and practice in civil proceedings in the sheriff court shall include power to make, in relation to disqualification orders, provision corresponding to that which may be made by virtue of section 40A(8).""

(4) In section 164(5) of the Road Traffic Act 1988 (power of constables to require production of driving licence etc.), after 'Road Traffic Offenders Act 1988' there shall be inserted ', section 40B of the Child Support Act 1991'.

(5) In section 27(3) of the Road Traffic Offenders Act 1988 (offence of failing to produce a licence), for the word 'then,' there shall be substituted ', or if the holder of the licence does not produce it and its counterpart as required by section 40B of the Child Support Act 1991, then,'.

17 Civil imprisonment: Scotland

(1) In section 40 of the 1991 Act (commitment to prison), for subsections (12) to (14) there shall be substituted –

'(12) This section does not apply to Scotland.'

(2) After section 40 there shall be inserted –

'40A Commitment to prison: Scotland

(1) If, but only if, the sheriff is satisfied that there has been wilful refusal or culpable neglect on the part of the liable person he may –

(a) issue a warrant for his committal to prison; or
(b) fix a term of imprisonment and postpone the issue of the warrant until such time and on such conditions (if any) as he thinks just.

(2) A warrant under this section –

(a) shall be made in respect of an amount equal to the aggregate of –

(i) the appropriate amount under section 38; and
(ii) an amount (determined in accordance with regulations made by the Secretary of State) in respect of the expenses of commitment; and

(b) shall state that amount.

(3) No warrant may be issued under this section against a person who is under the age of 18.

(4) A warrant issued under this section shall order the liable person –

(a) to be imprisoned for a specified period; but
(b) to be released (unless he is in custody for some other reason) on payment of the amount stated in the warrant.

(5) The maximum period of imprisonment which may be imposed by virtue of subsection (4) is six weeks.

(6) The Secretary of State may by regulations make provision for the period of imprisonment specified in any warrant issued under this section to be reduced where there is part payment of the amount in respect of which the warrant was issued.

(7) A warrant issued under this section may be directed to such person as the sheriff thinks fit.

(8) The power of the Court of Session by Act of Sederunt to regulate the procedure and practice in civil proceedings in the sheriff court shall include power to make provision –

(a) as to the form of any warrant issued under this section;
(b) allowing an application under this section to be renewed where no warrant is issued or term of imprisonment is fixed;
(c) that a statement in writing to the effect that wages of any amount have been paid to the liable person during any period, purporting to be signed by or on behalf of his employer, shall be sufficient evidence of the facts stated;
(d) that, for the purposes of enabling an inquiry to be made as to the liable person's conduct and means, the sheriff may issue a citation to him to appear before the sheriff and (if he does not obey) may issue a warrant for his arrest;
(e) that for the purpose of enabling such an inquiry, the sheriff may issue a warrant for the liable person's arrest without issuing a citation;
(f) as to the execution of a warrant of arrest.'

Financial penalties

18 Financial penalties

(1) In section 41 of the 1991 Act (arrears of child support maintenance), subsections (3) to (5) (which provide for the payment of interest on arrears) shall cease to have effect.

(2) For section 41A of the 1991 Act (arrears: alternative to interest payments) there shall be substituted –

'41A Penalty payments

(1) The Secretary of State may by regulations make provision for the payment to him by non-resident parents who are in arrears with payments of child support maintenance of penalty payments determined in accordance with the regulations.

(2) The amount of a penalty payment in respect of any week may not exceed 25% of the amount of child support maintenance payable for that week, but otherwise is to be determined by the Secretary of State.

(3) The liability of a non-resident parent to make a penalty payment does not affect his liability to pay the arrears of child support maintenance concerned.

(4) Regulations under subsection (1) may, in particular, make provision –

(a) as to the time at which a penalty payment is to be payable;
(b) for the Secretary of State to waive a penalty payment, or part of it.

(5) The provisions of this Act with respect to –

(a) the collection of child support maintenance;
(b) the enforcement of an obligation to pay child support maintenance,

apply equally (with any necessary modifications) to penalty payments payable by virtue of regulations under this section.

(6) The Secretary of State shall pay penalty payments received by him into the Consolidated Fund.'

19 Reduced benefit decisions

For section 46 of the 1991 Act (failure to comply with obligations imposed by section 6) there shall be substituted –

'46 Reduced benefit decisions

(1) This section applies where any person ("the parent") –

(a) has made a request under section 6(5);
(b) fails to comply with any regulation made under section 6(7); or
(c) having been treated as having applied for a maintenance calculation under section 6, refuses to take a scientific test (within the meaning of section 27A).

(2) The Secretary of State may serve written notice on the parent requiring her, before the end of a specified period –

(a) in a subsection (1)(a) case, to give him her reasons for making the request;
(b) in a subsection (1)(b) case, to give him her reasons for failing to do so; or
(c) in a subsection (1)(c) case, to give him her reasons for her refusal.

(3) When the specified period has expired, the Secretary of State shall consider whether, having regard to any reasons given by the parent, there are reasonable grounds for believing that –

(a) in a subsection (1)(a) case, if the Secretary of State were to do what is mentioned in section 6(3);
(b) in a subsection (1)(b) case, if she were to be required to comply; or
(c) in a subsection (1)(c) case, if she took the scientific test,

there would be a risk of her, or of any children living with her, suffering harm or undue distress as a result of his taking such action, or her complying or taking the test.

(4) If the Secretary of State considers that there are such reasonable grounds, he shall –

(a) take no further action under this section in relation to the request, the failure or the refusal in question; and
(b) notify the parent, in writing, accordingly.

(5) If the Secretary of State considers that there are no such reasonable grounds, he may, except in prescribed circumstances, make a reduced benefit decision with respect to the parent.

(6) In a subsection (1)(a) case, the Secretary of State may from time to time serve written notice on the parent requiring her, before the end of a specified period –

(a) to state whether her request under section 6(5) still stands; and
(b) if so, to give him her reasons for maintaining her request,

and subsections (3) to (5) have effect in relation to such a notice and any response to it as they have effect in relation to a notice under subsection (2)(a) and any response to it.

(7) Where the Secretary of State makes a reduced benefit decision he must send a copy of it to the parent.

(8) A reduced benefit decision is to take effect on such date as may be specified in the decision.

(9) Reasons given in response to a notice under subsection (2) or (6) need not be given in writing unless the Secretary of State directs in any case that they must.

(10) In this section –

(a) "comply" means to comply with the requirement or with the regulation in question; and "complied" and "complying" are to be construed accordingly;
(b) "reduced benefit decision" means a decision that the amount payable by way of any relevant benefit to, or in respect of, the parent concerned be reduced by such amount, and for such period, as may be prescribed;
(c) "relevant benefit" means income support or an income-based jobseeker's allowance or any other benefit of a kind prescribed for the purposes of section 6; and
(d) "specified", in relation to a notice served under this section, means specified in the notice; and the period to be specified is to be determined in accordance with regulations made by the Secretary of State.'

Miscellaneous

20 Voluntary payments

(1) After section 28I of the 1991 Act there shall be inserted –

'Voluntary payments

28J Voluntary payments

(1) This section applies where –

(a) a person has applied for a maintenance calculation under section 4(1) or 7(1), or is treated as having applied for one by virtue of section 6;
(b) the Secretary of State has neither made a decision under section 11 or 12 on the application, nor decided not to make a maintenance calculation; and
(c) the non-resident parent makes a voluntary payment.

(2) A "voluntary payment" is a payment –

(a) on account of child support maintenance which the non-resident parent expects to become liable to pay following the determination of the application (whether or not the amount of the payment is based on any estimate of his potential liability which the Secretary of State has agreed to give); and
(b) made before the maintenance calculation has been notified to the non-resident parent or (as the case may be) before the Secretary of State has notified the non-resident parent that he has decided not to make a maintenance calculation.

(3) In such circumstances and to such extent as may be prescribed –

(a) the voluntary payment may be set off against arrears of child support maintenance which accrued by virtue of the maintenance calculation taking effect on a date earlier than that on which it was notified to the non-resident parent;
(b) the amount payable under a maintenance calculation may be adjusted to take account of the voluntary payment.

(4) A voluntary payment shall be made to the Secretary of State unless he agrees, on such conditions as he may specify, that it may be made to the person with care, or to or through another person.

(5) The Secretary of State may by regulations make provision as to voluntary payments, and the regulations may in particular –

(a) prescribe what payments or descriptions of payment are, or are not, to count as "voluntary payments";
(b) prescribe the extent to which and circumstances in which a payment, or a payment of a prescribed description, counts.'

(2) Section 41B of the 1991 Act (repayment of overpaid child support maintenance) shall be amended as follows.

(3) After subsection (1) there shall be inserted –

'(1A) This section also applies where the non-resident parent has made a voluntary payment and it appears to the Secretary of State –

(a) that he is not liable to pay child support maintenance; or
(b) that he is liable, but some or all of the payment amounts to an overpayment,

and, in a case falling within paragraph (b), it also appears to him that subsection (1)(a) or (b) applies.'

(4) For subsection (7) there shall be substituted –

'(7) For the purposes of this section –

(a) a payment made by a person under a maintenance calculation which was not validly made; and
(b) a voluntary payment made in the circumstances set out in subsection (1A)(a),

shall be treated as an overpayment of child support maintenance made by a non-resident parent.'

21 Recovery of child support maintenance by deduction from benefit

For section 43 of the 1991 Act (contribution to maintenance by deduction from benefit) there shall be substituted –

'43 Recovery of child support maintenance by deduction from benefit

(1) This section applies where –

(a) a non-resident parent is liable to pay a flat rate of child support maintenance (or would be so liable but for a variation having been agreed to), and that rate applies (or would have applied) because he falls within paragraph 4(1)(b) or (c) or 4(2) of Schedule 1; and
(b) such conditions as may be prescribed for the purposes of this section are satisfied.

(2) The power of the Secretary of State to make regulations under section 5 of the Social Security Administration Act 1992 by virtue of subsection (1)(p) (deductions from benefits) may be exercised in relation to cases to which this section applies with a view to securing that payments in respect of child support maintenance are made or that arrears of child support maintenance are recovered.

(3) For the purposes of this section, the benefits to which section 5 of the 1992 Act applies are to be taken as including war disablement pensions and war widows' pensions (within the meaning of section 150 of the Social Security Contributions and Benefits Act 1992 (interpretation)).'

22 Jurisdiction

(1) Section 44 of the 1991 Act (jurisdiction) shall be amended as follows.

(2) In subsection (1), after 'United Kingdom' there shall be inserted ', except in the case of a non-resident parent who falls within subsection (2A)'.

(3) After subsection (2) there shall be inserted –

'(2A) A non-resident parent falls within this subsection if he is not habitually resident in the United Kingdom, but is –

(a) employed in the civil service of the Crown, including Her Majesty's Diplomatic Service and Her Majesty's Overseas Civil Service;
(b) a member of the naval, military or air forces of the Crown, including any person employed by an association established for the purposes of Part XI of the Reserve Forces Act 1996;
(c) employed by a company of a prescribed description registered under the Companies Act 1985 in England and Wales or in Scotland, or under the Companies (Northern Ireland) Order 1986; or
(d) employed by a body of a prescribed description.'

(4) Subsection (3) shall cease to have effect.

23 Abolition of the child maintenance bonus

Section 10 of the Child Support Act 1995 (which provides for the child maintenance bonus) shall cease to have effect.

24 Periodical reviews

Article 3(4) of the Social Security Act 1998 (Commencement No. 2) Order 1998 (which saved section 16 of the 1991 Act for certain purposes) is revoked; and accordingly that section shall cease to have effect for all purposes.

25 Regulations

In section 52 of the 1991 Act (regulations and orders), for subsection (2) there shall be substituted –

'(2) No statutory instrument containing (whether alone or with other provisions) regulations made under –

(a) section 6(1), 12(4) (so far as the regulations make provision for the default rate of child support maintenance mentioned in section 12(5)(b)), 28C(2)(b), 28F(2)(b), 30(5A), 41(2), 41A, 41B(6), 43(1), 44(2A)(d), 46 or 47;
(b) paragraph 3(2) or 10A(1) of Part I of Schedule 1; or
(c) Schedule 4B,

or an order made under section 45(1) or (6), shall be made unless a draft of the instrument has been laid before Parliament and approved by a resolution of each House of Parliament.

(2A) No statutory instrument containing (whether alone or with other provisions) the first set of regulations made under paragraph 10(1) of Part I of Schedule 1 as substituted by section 1(3) of the Child Support, Pensions and Social Security Act 2000 shall be made unless a draft of the instrument has been laid before Parliament and approved by a resolution of each House of Parliament.'

26 Amendments

Schedule 3 (amendment of enactments) shall have effect.

27 Temporary compensation payment scheme

(1) This section applies where –

(a) a maintenance assessment is made before a prescribed date following an application for one under section 4, 6 or 7 of the 1991 Act; or
(b) a fresh maintenance assessment has been made following either a periodic review under section 16 of the 1991 Act or a review under section 17 of that Act (as they had effect before their substitution by section 40 or 41 respectively of the Social Security Act 1998),

and the effective date of the assessment is earlier than the date on which the assessment was made, with the result that arrears of child support maintenance have become due under the assessment.

(2) The Secretary of State may in regulations provide that this section has effect as if it were modified so as –

(a) to apply to cases of arrears of child support maintenance having become due additional to those referred to in subsection (1);
(b) not to apply to any such case as is referred to in subsection (1).

(3) If this section applies, the Secretary of State may in prescribed circumstances agree with the absent parent, on terms specified in the agreement, that –

(a) the absent parent will not be required to pay the whole of the arrears, but only some lesser amount; and
(b) the Secretary of State will not, while the agreement is complied with, take action to recover any of the arrears.

(4) The terms which may be specified are to be prescribed in or determined in accordance with regulations made by the Secretary of State.

(5) An agreement may be entered into only if it is made before 1st April 2002 and expires before 1st April 2003.

(6) If the absent parent enters into such an agreement, the Secretary of State may, while the absent parent complies with it, refrain from taking action under the 1991 Act to recover the arrears.

(7) Upon the expiry of the agreement, if the absent parent has complied with it –

(a) he ceases to be liable to pay the arrears; and
(b) the Secretary of State may make payments of such amounts and at such times as he may determine to the person with care.

(8) If the absent parent fails to comply with the agreement he becomes liable to pay the full amount of any outstanding arrears (as well as any other amount payable in accordance with the assessment).

(9) The Secretary of State may by regulations provide for this section to have effect as if there were substituted for the dates in subsection (5) such later dates as are prescribed.

(10) In this section, 'prescribed' means prescribed in regulations made by the Secretary of State.

(11) Regulations under this section shall be made by statutory instrument.

(12) No statutory instrument containing regulations under subsection (9) is to be made unless a draft of the instrument has been laid before Parliament and approved by a resolution of each House of Parliament; but otherwise a statutory instrument containing regulations under this section shall be subject to annulment in pursuance of a resolution of either House of Parliament.

28 Pilot schemes

(1) Any regulations made under –

- (a) provisions inserted or substituted in the 1991 Act by this Part of this Act (or Schedule 1, 2 or 3); and
- (b) in so far as they are consequential on or supplementary to any such regulations, regulations made under any other provisons in the 1991 Act,

may be made so as to have effect for a specified period not exceeding 12 months.

(2) Any regulations which, by virtue of subsection (1), are to have effect for a limited period are referred to in this section as 'a pilot scheme'.

(3) A pilot scheme may provide that its provisions are to apply only in relation to –

- (a) one or more specified areas or localities;
- (b) one or more specified classes of person;
- (c) persons selected by reference to prescribed criteria, or on a sampling basis.

(4) A pilot scheme may make consequential or transitional provision with respect to the cessation of the scheme on the expiry of the specified period.

(5) A pilot scheme ('the previous scheme') may be replaced by a further pilot scheme making the same provision as that made by the previous scheme (apart from the specified period), or similar provision.

(6) A statutory instrument containing (whether alone or with other provisions) a pilot scheme shall not be made unless a draft of the instrument has been laid before Parliament and approved by resolution of each House of Parliament.

29 Interpretation, transitional provisions, savings, etc.

(1) In this Part, 'the 1991 Act' means the Child Support Act 1991.

(2) The Secretary of State may in regulations make such transitional and transitory provisions, and such incidental, supplementary, savings and consequential provisions, as he considers necessary or expedient in connection with the coming into force of this Part or any provision in it.

(3) The regulations may, in particular –

- (a) provide for the amount of child support maintenance payable by or to any person to be at a transitional rate (or more than one such rate successively) resulting from the phasing-in by way of prescribed steps of any increase or decrease in the amount payable following the coming into force of this Part or any provision in it;
- (b) provide for a departure direction or any finding in relation to a previous determination of child support maintenance to be taken into account in a decision as to the amount of child support maintenance payable by or to any person.

(4) Section 175(3) and (5) of the Social Security Contributions and Benefits Act 1992 (supplemental power in relation to regulations) applies to regulations made under this section as it applies to regulations made under that Act.

(5) The power to make regulations under this section is exercisable by statutory instrument.

(6) A statutory instrument containing regulations under this section shall be subject to annulment in pursuance of a resolution of either House of Parliament.

[...]

SCHEDULES

SCHEDULE 1

SUBSTITUTED PART I OF SCHEDULE 1 TO THE CHILD SUPPORT ACT 1991

'PART I

CALCULATION OF WEEKLY AMOUNT OF CHILD SUPPORT MAINTENANCE

1 General rule

(1) The weekly rate of child support maintenance is the basic rate unless a reduced rate, a flat rate or the nil rate applies.

(2) Unless the nil rate applies, the amount payable weekly to a person with care is –

- (a) the applicable rate, if paragraph 6 does not apply; or
- (b) if paragraph 6 does apply, that rate as apportioned between the persons with care in accordance with paragraph 6,

as adjusted, in either case, by applying the rules about shared care in paragraph 7 or 8.

2 Basic rate

(1) The basic rate is the following percentage of the non-resident parent's net weekly income –

15% where he has one qualifying child;
20% where he has two qualifying children;
25% where he has three or more qualifying children.

(2) If the non-resident parent also has one or more relevant other children, the appropriate percentage referred to in sub-paragraph (1) is to be applied instead to his net weekly income less –

15% where he has one relevant other child;
20% where he has two relevant other children;
25% where he has three or more relevant other children.

3 Reduced rate

(1) A reduced rate is payable if –

- (a) neither a flat rate nor the nil rate applies; and
- (b) the non-resident parent's net weekly income is less than £200 but more than £100.

(2) The reduced rate payable shall be prescribed in, or determined in accordance with, regulations.

(3) The regulations may not prescribe, or result in, a rate of less than £5.

4 Flat rate

(1) Except in a case falling within sub-paragraph (2), a flat rate of £5 is payable if the nil rate does not apply and –

(a) the non-resident parent's net weekly income is £100 or less; or
(b) he receives any benefit, pension or allowance prescribed for the purposes of this paragraph of this sub-paragraph; or
(c) he or his partner (if any) receives any benefit prescribed for the purposes of this paragraph of this sub-paragraph.

(2) A flat rate of a prescribed amount is payable if the nil rate does not apply and –

(a) the non-resident parent has a partner who is also a non-resident parent;
(b) the partner is a person with respect to whom a maintenance calculation is in force; and
(c) the non-resident parent or his partner receives any benefit prescribed under sub-paragraph (1)(c).

(3) The benefits, pensions and allowances which may be prescribed for the purposes of sub-paragraph (1)(b) include ones paid to the non-resident parent under the law of a place outside the United Kingdom.

5 Nil rate

The rate payable is nil if the non-resident parent –

(a) is of a prescribed description; or
(b) has a net weekly income of below £5.

6 Apportionment

(1) If the non-resident parent has more than one qualifying child and in relation to them there is more than one person with care, the amount of child support maintenance payable is (subject to paragraph 7 or 8) to be determined by apportioning the rate between the persons with care.

(2) The rate of maintenance liability is to be divided by the number of qualifying children, and shared among the persons with care according to the number of qualifying children in relation to whom each is a person with care.

7 Shared care – basic and reduced rate

(1) This paragraph applies only if the rate of child support maintenance payable is the basic rate or a reduced rate.

(2) If the care of a qualifying child is shared between the non-resident parent and the person with care, so that the non-resident parent from time to time has care of the child overnight, the amount of child support maintenance which he would otherwise have been liable to pay the person with care, as calculated in accordance with the preceding paragraphs of this Part of this Schedule, is to be decreased in accordance with this paragraph.

(3) First, there is to be a decrease according to the number of such nights which the Secretary of State determines there to have been, or expects there to be, or both during a prescribed twelve-month period.

(4) The amount of that decrease for one child is set out in the following Table –

Number of nights	Fraction to subtract
52 to 103	One-seventh
104 to 155	Two-sevenths
156 to 174	Three-sevenths
175 or more	One-half

(5) If the person with care is caring for more than one qualifying child of the non-resident parent, the applicable decrease is the sum of the appropriate fractions in the Table divided by the number of such qualifying children.

(6) If the applicable fraction is one-half in relation to any qualifying child in the care of the person with care, the total amount payable to the person with care is then to be further decreased by £7 for each such child.

(7) If the application of the preceding provisons of this paragraph would decrease the weekly amount of child support maintenance (or the aggregate of all such amounts) payable by the non-resident parent to the person with care (or all of them) to less than £5, he is instead liable to pay child support maintenance at the rate of £5 a week, apportioned (if appropriate) in accordance with paragraph 6.

8 Shared care – flat rate

(1) This paragraph applies only if –

(a) the rate of child support maintenance payable is a flat rate; and
(b) that rate applies because the non-resident parent falls within paragraph 4(1)(b) or (c) or 4(2).

(2) If the care of a qualifying child is shared as mentioned in paragraph 7(2) for at least 52 nights during a prescribed 12-month period, the amount of child support maintenance payable by the non-resident parent to the person with care of that child is nil.

9 Regulations about shared care

The Secretary of State may by regulations provide –

(a) for which nights are to count for the purposes of shared care under paragraphs 7 and 8, or for how it is to be determined whether a night counts;
(b) for what counts, or does not count, as "care" for those purposes; and
(c) for paragraph 7(3) or 8(2) to have effect, in prescribed circumstances, as if the period mentioned there were other than 12 months, and in such circumstances for the Table in paragraph 7(4) (or that Table as modified pursuant to regulations made under paragraph 10A(2)(a)), or the period mentioned in paragraph 8(2), to have effect with prescribed adjustments.

10 Net weekly income

(1) For the purposes of this Schedule, net weekly income is to be determined in such manner as is provided for in regulations.

(2) The regulations may, in particular, provide for the Secretary of State to estimate any income or make an assumption as to any fact where, in his view, the information at his disposal is unreliable, insufficient, or relates to an atypical period in the life of the non-resident parent.

(3) Any amount of net weekly income (calculated as above) over £2,000 is to be ignored for the purposes of this Schedule.

10A Regulations about rates, figures, etc.

(1) The Secretary of State may by regulations provide that –

(a) paragraph 2 is to have effect as if different percentages were substituted for those set out there;
(b) paragraph 3(1) or (3), 4(1), 5, 7(7) or 10(3) is to have effect as if different amounts were substituted for those set out there.

(2) The Secretary of State may by regulations provide that –

(a) the Table in paragraph 7(4) is to have effect as if different numbers of nights were set out in the first column and different fractions were substituted for those set out in the second column;
(b) paragraph 7(6) is to have effect as if a different amount were substituted for that mentioned there, or as if the amount were an aggregate amount and not an amount for each qualifying child, or both.

10B Regulations about income

The Secretary of State may by regulations provide that, in such circumstances and to such extent as may be prescribed –

(a) where the Secretary of State is satisfied that a person has intentionally deprived himself of a source of income with a view to reducing the amount of his net weekly income, his net weekly income shall be taken to include income from that source of an amount estimated by the Secretary of State;
(b) a person is to be treated as possessing income which he does not possess;
(c) income which a person does possess is to be disregarded.

10C References to various terms

(1) References in this Part of this Schedule to "qualifying children" are to those qualifying children with respect to whom the maintenance calculation falls to be made.

(2) References in this Part of this Schedule to "relevant other children" are to –

(a) children other than qualifying children in respect of whom the non-resident parent or his partner receives child benefit under Part IX of the Social Security Contributions and Benefits Act 1992; and
(b) such other description of children as may be prescribed.

(3) In this Part of this Schedule, a person "receives" a benefit, pension, or allowance for any week if it is paid or due to be paid to him in respect of that week.

(4) In this Part of this Schedule, a person's "partner" is –

(a) if they are a couple, the other member of that couple;
(b) if the person is a husband or wife by virtue of a marriage entered into under a law which permits polygamy, another party to the marriage who is of the opposite sex and is a member of the same household.

(5) In sub-paragraph (4)(a), "couple" means a man and a woman who are –

(a) married to each other and are members of the same household; or
(b) not married to each other but are living together as husband and wife.'

SCHEDULE 2

SUBSTITUTED SCHEDULES 4A AND 4B TO THE 1991 ACT

PART I

SUBSTITUTED SCHEDULE 4A

'SCHEDULE 4A

APPLICATIONS FOR A VARIATION

1 Interpretation

In this Schedule, "regulations" means regulations made by the Secretary of State.

2 Applications for a variation

Regulations may make provision –

(a) as to the procedure to be followed in considering an application for a variation;
(b) as to the procedure to be followed when an application for a variation is referred to an appeal tribunal under section 28D(1)(b).

3 Completion of preliminary consideration

Regulations may provide for determining when the preliminary consideration of an application for a variation is to be taken to have been completed.

4 Information

If any information which is required (by regulations under this Act) to be furnished to the Secretary of State in connection with an application for a variation has not been furnished within such period as may be prescribed, the Secretary of State may nevertheless proceed to consider the application.

5 Joint consideration of applications for a variation and appeals

(1) Regulations may provide for two or more applications for a variation with respect to the same application for a maintenance calculation to be considered together.

(2) In sub-paragraph (1), the reference to an application for a maintenance calculation includes an application treated as having been made under section 6.

(3) An appeal tribunal considering an application for a variation under section 28D(1)(b) may consider it at the same time as an appeal under section 20 in connection with an interim maintenance decision, if it considers that to be appropriate.'

PART II

SUBSTITUTED SCHEDULE 4B

'SCHEDULE 4B

APPLICATIONS FOR A VARIATION: THE CASES AND CONTROLS

PART I

THE CASES

1 General

(1) The cases in which a variation may be agreed are those set out in this Part of this Schedule or in regulations made under this Part.

(2) In this Schedule "applicant" means the person whose application for a variation is beng considered.

2 Special expenses

(1) A variation applied for by a non-resident parent may be agreed with respect to his special expenses.

(2) In this paragraph "special expenses" means the whole, or any amount above a prescribed amount, or any prescribed part, of expenses which fall within a prescribed description of expenses.

(3) In prescribing descriptions of expenses for the purposes of this paragraph, the Secretary of State may, in particular, make provision with respect to –

(a) costs incurred by a non-resident parent in maintaining contact with the child, or with any of the children, with respect to whom the application for a maintenance calculation has been made (or treated as made);
(b) costs attributable to a long-term illness or disability of a relevant other child (within the meaning of paragraph 10C(2) of Schedule 1);
(c) debts of a prescribed description incurred, before the non-resident parent became a non-resident parent in relation to a child with respect to whom the maintenance calculation has been applied for (or treated as having been applied for) –

(i) for the joint benefit of both parents;
(ii) for the benefit of any such child; or
(iii) for the benefit of any other child falling within a prescribed category;

(d) boarding school fees for a child in relation to whom the application for a maintenance calculation has been made (or treated as made);
(e) the cost to the non-resident parent of making payments in relation to a mortgage on the home he and the person with care shared, if he no longer has an interest in it, and she and a child in relation to whom the application for a maintenance calculation has been made (or treated as made) still live there.

(4) For the purposes of sub-paragraph (3)(b) –

(a) "disability" and "illness" have such meaning as may be prescribed; and
(b) the question whether an illness or disability is long-term shall be determined in accordance with regulations made by the Secretary of State.

(5) For the purposes of sub-paragraph (3)(d), the Secretary of State may prescribe –

(a) the meaning of "boarding school fees"; and
(b) components of such fees (whether or not itemised as such) which are, or are not, to be taken into account,

and may provide for estimating any such component.

3 Property or capital transfers

(1) A variation may be agreed in the circumstances set out in sub-paragraph (2) if before 5th April 1993 –

(a) a court order of a prescribed kind was in force with respect to the non-resident parent and either the person with care with respect to the application for the maintenance calculation or the child, or any of the children, with respect to whom that application was made; or
(b) an agreement of a prescribed kind between the non-resident parent and any of those persons was in force.

(2) The circumstances are that in consequence of one or more transfers of property of a prescribed kind and exceeding (singly or in aggregate) a prescribed minimum value –

(a) the amount payable by the non-resident parent by way of maintenance was less than would have been the case had that transfer or those transfers not been made; or
(b) no amount was payable by the non-resident parent by way of maintenance.

(3) For the purposes of sub-paragraph (2), "maintenance" means periodical payments of maintenance made (otherwise than under this Act) with respect to the child, or any of the children, with respect to whom the application for a maintenance calculation has been made.

4 Additional cases

(1) The Secretary of State may by regulations prescribe other cases in which a variation may be agreed.

(2) Regulations under this paragraph may, for example, make provision with respect to cases where –

(a) the non-resident parent has assets which exceed a prescribed value;
(b) a person's lifestyle is inconsistent with his income for the purposes of a calculation made under Part I of Schedule 1;
(c) a person has income which is not taken into account in such a calculation;
(d) a person has unreasonably reduced the income which is taken into account in such a calculation.

PART II

REGULATORY CONTROLS

5—(1) The Secretary of State may by regulations make provision with respect to the variations from the usual rules for calculating maintenance which may be allowed when a variation is agreed.

(2) No variations may be made other than those which are permitted by the regulations.

(3) Regulations under this paragraph may, in particular, make provision for a variation to result in –

(a) a person's being treated as having more, or less, income than would be taken into account witout the variation in a calculation under Part I of Schedule 1;
(b) a person's being treated as liable to pay a higher, or a lower, amount of child support maintenance than would result without the variation from a calculation under that Part.

(4) Regulations may provide for the amount of any special expenses to be taken into account in a case falling within paragraph 2, for the purposes of a variation, not to exceed such amounts as may be prescribed or as may be determined in accordance with the regulations.

(5) Any regulations under this paragraph may in particular make different provision with respect to different levels of income.

6—The Secretary of State may by regulations provide for the application, in connection with child support maintenance payable following a variation, of paragraph 7(2) to (7) of Schedule 1 (subject to any prescribed modifications).'

SCHEDULE 3

AMENDMENT OF ENACTMENTS RELATING TO CHILD SUPPORT

1 The Army Act 1955 (3 & 4 Eliz. 2 c. 18)

(1) Section 150A of the Army Act 1955 (enforcement of maintenance assessment by deductions from pay) shall be amended as follows.

(2) In subsections (1), (2)(a), (3)(a) (twice) and (4), for 'maintenance assessment' there shall be substituted 'maintenance calculation'.

(3) In subsection (3) (twice), for 'the assessment' there shall be substituted 'the calculation'.

2 The Air Force Act 1955 (3 & 4 Eliz. 2 c. 19)

(1) Section 150A of the Air Force Act 1955 (enforcement of maintenance assessment by deductions from pay) shall be amended as follows.

(2) In subsections (1), (2)(a), (3)(a) (twice) and (4), for 'maintenance assessment' there shall be substituted 'maintenance calculation'.

(3) In subsection (3) (twice), for 'the assessment' there shall be substituted 'the calculation'.

3 The Matrimonial Causes Act 1973 (c. 18)

(1) The Matrimonial Causes Act 1973 shall be amended as follows.

(2) In section 29 (duration of continuing financial provision orders in favour of children, and age limit on making certain orders in their favour) –

(a) in subsections (5)(a), (7) (three times) and (8)(a), for 'maintenance assessment' there shall be substituted 'maintenance calculation';
(b) in subsections (5)(a) and (b)(ii) and (6)(b), for 'current assessment' there shall be substituted 'current calculation';
(c) in subsection (6)(b), for 'maintenance assessments' there shall be substituted 'maintenance calculations'; and
(d) in subsection (6)(b), for 'those assessments' there shall be substituted 'those calculations'.

(3) In section 31 (variation, discharge, etc., of certain orders for financial relief) –

(a) in subsections (11)(c) and (12)(a) and (c), for 'maintenance assessment' there shall be substituted 'maintenance calculation'; and
(b) in subsection (11)(twice), for 'the assessment' there shall be substituted 'the calculation'.

(4) In section 52 (interpretation), in subsection (1), for 'maintenance assessment' there shall be substituted 'maintenance calculation'.

4 The Domestic Proceedings and Magistrates Courts Act 1978 (c. 22)

(1) The Domestic Proceedings and Magistrates Courts Act 1978 shall be amended as follows.

(2) In section 5 (age limit on making orders for financial provision for children and duration of such orders) –

(a) in subsections (5)(a), (7) (three times) and (8)(a), for 'maintenance assessment' there shall be substituted 'maintenance calculation';
(b) in subsections (5)(a) and (b)(ii) and (6)(b), for 'current assessment' there shall be substituted 'current calculation'; and
(c) in subsection (6)(b), for 'those assessments' there shall be substituted 'those calculations'.

(3) In section 20 (variation, revival and revocation of orders for periodical payments) –

(a) in subsections (9A)(c) and (9B)(a) and (c), for 'maintenance assessment' there shall be substituted 'maintenance calculation'; and
(b) in subsection (9A) (three times), for 'the assessment' there shall be substituted 'the calculation'.

(4) In section 88 (interpretation), in subsection (1), for 'maintenance assessment' there shall be substituted 'maintenance calculation'.

5 The Family Law (Scotland) Act 1985 (c. 37)

(1) The Family Law (Scotland) Act 1985 shall be amended as follows.

(2) In section 5 (variation and recall of decrees of aliment), in subsection (1A), for 'maintenance assessment' there shall be substituted 'maintenance calculation'.

(3) In section 7 (agreements about aliment), in subsection (2A), for 'maintenance assessment' there shall be substituted 'maintenance calculation'.

(4) In section 13 (orders for periodical allowance), in subsection (4A), for 'maintenance assessment' there shall be substituted 'maintenance calculation'.

(5) In section 16 (agreements about financial provision), in subsection (3)(d), for 'maintenance assessment' there shall be substituted 'maintenance calculation'.

(6) In section 27 (interpretation), in subsection (1), for 'maintenance assessment' there shall be substituted 'maintenance calculation'.

6 The Insolvency Act 1986 (c. 45)

In section 281 of the Insolvency Act 1986 (effect of discharge on a bankrupt), in subsection (5)(b), for 'maintenance assessment' there shall be substituted 'maintenance calculation'.

7 The Debtors (Scotland) Act 1987 (c. 18)

(1) The Debtors (Scotland) Act 1987 shall be amended as follows.

(2) In section 72 (effect of sequestration on diligence against earnings), in subsection (4A), for 'maintenance assessment' there shall be substituted 'maintenance calculation'.

(3) In section 106 (interpretation), in the definition of 'maintenance order'; in paragraph (j), for 'maintenance assessment' there shall be substituted 'maintenance calculation'.

8 The Income and Corporation Taxes Act 1998 (c. 1)

(1) The Income and Corporation Taxes Act 1988 shall be amended as follows.

(2) In section 347B (qualifying maintenance payments) –

(a) in subsections (8) and (9)(a) and (c), for 'maintenance assessment' there shall be substituted 'maintenance calculation';
(b) in subsection (9)(b) and (c), for 'the assessment' there shall be substituted 'the calculation'; and
(c) for subsection (11) there shall be substituted –

'(11) In this section "maintenance calculation" means a maintenance calculation made under the Child Support Act 1991 or a maintenance assessment made under the Child Support (Northern Ireland) Order 1991.'

(3) In section 617 (social security benefits and contributions), in subsection (2)(ae), for 'section 24 of the Child Support Act 1995 or under any corresponding enactment' there shall be substituted 'any enactment corresponding to section 24 of the Child Support Act 1995'.

9 The Finance Act 1988 (c. 39)

In the Finance Act 1988, in each of subsection (5A) of section 36 (annual payments) and subsection (8A) of section 38 (maintenance payments under existing obligations: 1989–90 onwards), for 'maintenance assessment made' there shall be substituted 'maintenance calculation or maintenance assessment made respectively'.

10 The Children Act 1989 (c. 41)

(1) Schedule 1 to the Children Act 1989 (financial provision for children) shall be amended as follows.

(2) In paragraph 3 –

(a) in sub-paragraph (5)(a), (7) (three times) and (8)(a), for 'maintenance assessment' there shall be substituted 'maintenance calculation';
(b) in sub-paragraph (5)(a) and (b)(ii) and (6)(b), for 'current assessment' there shall be substituted 'current calculation';
(c) in sub-paragraph (6)(b), for 'maintenance assessments' there shall be substituted 'maintenance calculations'; and
(d) in sub-paragraph (6)(b), for 'those assessments' there shall be substituted 'those calculations'.

(3) In paragraph 6 –

(a) in sub-paragraph (9) (three times), for 'the assessment' there shall be substituted 'the calculation'; and
(b) in sub-paragraph (9)(c), for 'maintenance assessment' there shall be substituted 'maintenance calculation'.

(4) In paragraph 16(3), for 'maintenance assessment' there shall be substituted 'maintenance calculation'.

11 The Child Support Act 1991 (c. 48)

(1) The 1991 Act shall be amended as follows.

(2) For 'absent parent' (or any variant of that expression), wherever it occurs, there shall be substituted 'non-resident parent' (or the corresponding variant) preceded, where appropriate, by 'a' instead of 'an'.

(3) In section 4 (child support maintenance) –

(a) in subsection (4)(a), after 'be' there shall be inserted 'identified or'; and
(b) in subsection (9), after 'an application' there shall be inserted 'treated as made'.

(4) In section 7 (right of a child in Scotland to apply for assessment) –

(a) in subsection (1), for paragraph (b) there shall be substituted –

'(b) no parent has been treated under section 6(3) as having applied for a maintenance calculation with respect to the child.'; and

(b) in subsection (1) –

(i) after 'qualifying child if' there shall be inserted '(a)';
(ii) after 'maintenance order' there shall be inserted 'made before a prescribed date'; and
(iii) at the end there shall be inserted 'or

(b) a maintenance order made on or after the date prescribed for the purposes of paragraph (a) is in force in respect of them, but has been so for less than the period of one year beginning with the date on which it was made.'.

(5) In section 8 (role of the courts with respect to maintenance for children) –

(a) in subsection (1), after 'duly made' there shall be inserted '(or treated as made)';
(b) in subsection (3), at the beginning insert 'Except as provided in subsection (3A),';
(c) for subsection (3A) there shall be substituted –

'(3A) Unless a maintenance calculation has been made with respect to the child concerned, subsection (3) does not prevent a court from varying a maintenance order in relation to that child and the non-resident parent concerned –

(a) if the maintenance order was made on or after the date prescribed for the purposes of section 4(1)(a) or 7(1)(a); or
(b) where the order was made before then, in any case in which section 4(10) or 7(10) prevents the making of an application for a maintenance calculation with respect to or by that child.'; and

(d) in subsection (6), for paragraph (b) there shall be substituted –

'(b) the non-resident parent's net weekly income exceeds the figure referred to in paragraph 10(3) of Schedule 1 (as it has effect from time to time pursuant to regulations made under paragraph 10A(1)(b)); and'.

(6) In section 9 (agreements about maintenance), in subsection (6), for paragraphs (a) and (b) there shall be substituted –

'(a) no parent has been treated under section 6(3) as having applied for a maintenance calculation with respect to the child; or

(b) a parent has been so treated but no maintenance calculation has been made,'.

(7) In section 14 (information required by Secretary of State), in subsection (1), after 'any application' there shall be inserted 'made or treated as made'.

(8) In section 26 (disputes about parentage), in subsection (1), after 'made' there shall be inserted 'or treated as made'.

(9) In section 27A (recovery of fees for scientific tests) –

(a) in subsection (1)(a), after 'made' there shall be inserted 'or treated as made'; and

(b) in subsection (1)(b), after 'made' there shall be inserted 'or, as the case may be, treated as made'.

(10) In section 28 (power of the Secretary of State to bring or defend actions of declarator), in subsection (1)(a) –

(a) after 'made', where it first occurs, there shall be inserted 'or treated as made'; and

(b) for 'or assessment was made' there shall be substituted 'was made or treated as made or the calculation was made'.

(11) In section 28ZA (decisions involving issues that arise on appeal in other cases), in subsection (1) –

(a) in paragraph (a), for the wrods 'in relation to a maintenance assessment' there shall be substituted 'or with respect to a reduced benefit decision under section 46'; and

(b) for paragraph (b) there shall be substituted –

'(b) an appeal is pending against a decision given in relation to a different matter by a Child Support Commissioner or a court.'

(12) In section 28ZB (appeals involving issues that arise on appeal in other cases) –

(a) in subsection (1), for paragraph (a) there shall be substituted –

'(a) an appeal ("appeal A") in relation to a decision or the imposition of a requirement falling within section 20(1) is made to an appeal tribunal, or from an appeal tribunal to a Child Support Comissioner;'; and

(b) in subsection (4), for the words 'or assessment' there shall be substituted 'or the imposition of the requirement'.

(13) In section 28ZC (restrictions on liability in certain cases of error) –

(a) in subsection (1)(b)(i), at the end there shall be inserted 'or one treated as having been so made, or under section 46 as to the reduction of benefit';

(b) in subsection (1)(b)(ii), for the words from 'a decision' to the end there shall be substituted 'any decision (made after the commencement date) referred to in section 16(1A)';

(c) in subsection (1)(B)(iii), for the words from 'a decision' to the end there shall be substituted 'any decision (made after the commencement date) referred to in section 17(1)';

(d) in subsection (3), after 'liability' there shall be inserted 'or the reduction of a person's benefit'; and

(e) in subsection (6), in the definition of 'adjudicating authority', at the end there shall be inserted 'or, in the case of a decision made on a referral under section 28D(1)(b), an appeal tribunal'.

(14) Sections 28H (departure directions: decisions and appeals) and 28I (transitional provisions relating to departure directions) shall cease to have effect.

(15) In section 30 (collection and enforcement of certain forms of maintenance), for subsection (2) there shall be substituted –

> '(2) The Secretary of State may, except in prescribed cases, arrange for the collection of any periodical payments, or secured periodical payments, of a prescribed kind which are payable for the benefit of a child even though he is not arranging for the collection of child support maintenance with respect to that child.'.

(16) In section 32 (regulations about deduction from earnings orders), in subsection (2), after paragraph (b) there shall be inserted –

> '(bb) for the amount or amounts which are to be deducted from the liable person's earnings not to exceed a prescribed proportion of his earnings (as determined by the employer);'.

(17) In section 33 (liability orders), after subsection (5) there shall be inserted –

> '(6) Where regulations have been made under section 29(3)(a) –
>
> (a) the liable person fails to make a payment (for the purposes of subsection (1)(a) of this section); and
> (b) a payment is not paid (for the purposes of subsection (3)),
>
> unless the payment is made to, or through, the person specified in or by virtue of those regulations for the case of the liable person in question.'

(18) In section 47 (fees), after subsection (3) there shall be inserted –

> '(4) The provisions of this Act with respect to –
>
> (a) the collection of child support maintenance;
> (b) the enforcement of any obligation to pay child support maintenance,
>
> shall apply equally (with any necessary modifications) to fees payable by virtue of regulations made under this section.'

(19) In section 51 (supplementary power to make regulations), in subsection (2) –

(a) for paragraph (a)(ii) and (iii) there shall be substituted –

> '(ii) the making of decisions under section 11;
> (iii) the making of decisions under section 16 or 17;'; and

(b) for paragraph (b) there shall be substituted –

> '(b) extending the categories of case to which section 16, 17 or 20 applies;'.

(20) In section 54 (interpretation) –

(a) in the definition of 'application for a departure direction', for 'departure direction' there shall be substituted 'variation', and after '28A' there shall be inserted 'or 28G';
(b) after the definition of 'deduction from earnings order' there shall be inserted –

> '"default maintenance decision" has the meaning given in section 12;';

(c) in the definition of 'interim maintenance assessment', for the word 'assessment' there shall be substituted the word 'decision';

(d) for the definition of 'maintenance assessment' there shall be substituted –

' "maintenance calculation" means a calculation of maintenance made under this Act and, except in prescribed circumstances, includes a default maintenance decision and an interim maintenance decision;';

(e) the definitions of 'assessable income', 'current assessment', 'departure direction' and 'maintenance requirement' shall be omitted; and

(f) after the definition of 'qualifying child' there shall be inserted –

' "voluntary payment" has the meaning given in section 28J.'.

(21) In section 58 (short title, commencement and extent) –

(a) in subsection (9), after '35' there shall be inserted ', 40'; and

(b) in subsection (10), after '28' there shall be inserted ', 40A'.

(22) In Schedule 1 (maintenance assessments) –

(a) paragraph 13 (which relates to assessments under which the amount payable is nil) shall cease to have effect;

(b) in paragraph 14 (which provides for consolidated applications and assessments), the existing text shall be sub-paragraph (1) of that paragraph, and after that sub-paragraph there shall be inserted –

'(2) In sub-paragraph (1), the references (however expressed) to applications for maintenance calculations include references to applications treated as made.'; and

(c) in paragraph 16 (which is about the termination of assessments) –

(i) in sub-paragraph (1), paragraphs (d) and (e) shall cease to have effect,

(ii) sub-paragraphs (2) to (9) shall cease to have effect; and

(iii) in sub-paragraph (10), the words ', or should be cancelled' shall cease to have effect.

12 The Social Security Administration Act 1992 (c. 5)

In section 7A of the Social Security Administration Act 1992 (sharing of functions as regards certain claims and information), in subsection (6)(a) –

(a) after 'application' there shall be inserted '(or an application treated as having been made)'; and

(b) for 'maintenance assessment' there shall be substituted 'maintenance calculation'.

13 The Child Support Act 1995 (c. 34)

(1) The Child Support Act 1995 shall be amended as follows.

(2) In section 18 (deferral of right to apply for maintenance assessment), subsection (5) (which enables the Secretary of State by order to repeal any of the provisions of section 18) shall cease to have effect.

(3) Section 24 (which provides for the making of regulations under which compensation could be paid for a reduction in child support maintenance attributable to changes in child support legislation, and which is now spent) shall cease to have effect.

14 Prisoners' Earnings Act 1996 (c. 33)

In section 1 of the Prisoners' Earnings Act 1996 (power to make deductions and impose levies), in subsection (4), in paragraph (d) of the definition of 'net weekly earnings', for 'maintenance assessment' there shall be substituted 'maintenance calculation'.

15 The Social Security Act 1998 (c. 14)

(1) The Social Security Act 1998 shall be amended as follows.

(2) In Schedule 2 (decisions against which no appeal lies), for paragraph 8 and the heading preceding it there shall be substituted –

> **8 'Reduction in accordance with reduced benefit decision**
>
> A decision to reduce the amount of a person's benefit in accordance with a reduced benefit decision (within the meaning of section 46 of the Child Support Act.'.

[Schedules 4–7 relate to pensions and social security.]

SCHEDULE 8

DECLARATIONS OF STATUS: CONSEQUENTIAL AMENDMENTS

...

11 The Child Support Act 1991 (c. 48)

The Child Support Act 1991 shall be amended as follows.

12—In section 26(2) (cases where Secretary of State may make maintenance calculation despite denial of parentage), in Case C (where there has been a declaration under section 56 of the Family Law Act 1986), after 'section' there shall be inserted '55A or'.

13—For section 27 (declarations of parentage) there shall be substituted—

> **'27 Applications for declaration of parentage under Family Law Act 1986**
>
> (1) This section applies where—
>
> (a) an application for a maintenance calculation has been made (or is treated as having been made), or a maintenance calculation is in force, with respect to a person ('the alleged parent') who denies that he is a parent of a child with respect to whom the application or calculation was made or treated as made;
> (b) the Secretary of State is not satisfied that the case falls within one of those set out in section 26(2); and
> (c) the Secretary of State or the person with care makes an application for a declaration under section 55A of the Family Law Act 1986 as to whether or not the alleged parent is one of the child's parents.
>
> (2) Where this section applies—
>
> (a) if it is the person with care who makes the application, she shall be treated as having a sufficient personal interest for the purposes of subsection (3) of that section; and

(b) if it is the Secretary of State who makes the application, that subsection shall not apply.

(3) This section does not apply to Scotland.'

14—In section 27A(2)(b) (Secretary of State to recover fees for scientific tests if a court has made a declaration of parentage under section 27), for 'section 27' there shall be substituted 'section 55A of the Family Law Act 1986'.

SCHEDULE 9

REPEALS AND REVOCATIONS

PART I

CHILD SUPPORT

Chapter or number	Citation	Extent of repeal or revocation
10 & 11 Geo 6 c 24	The Naval Forces (Enforcement of Maintenance Liabilities) Act 1947	In section 1(1) paragraph (aaa)
3 & 4 Eliz 2 c 18	The Army Act 1955	In section 150A, in subsection (2), paragraph (b) and the word 'or' preceding it, and in subsection (3), the words 'or cancels' and 'or (as the case may be) that it has been cancelled'
3 & 4 Eliz 2 c 19	The Air Force Act 1955	In section 150A, in subsection (2), paragraph (b) and the word 'or' preceding it, and in subsection (3), the words 'or cancels' and 'or (as the case may be) that it has been cancelled'
1973 c 18	The Matrimonial Causes Act 1973	In section 29, in subsection (7), the words 'or is cancelled', 'or was cancelled' and 'or, as the case may be, the date with effect from which it was cancelled'; and in subsection (8), paragraph (b) and the word 'and' preceding it
1978 c 22	The Domestic Proceedings and Magistrates' Courts Act 1978	In section 5, in subsection (7), the words 'or is cancelled', 'or was cancelled' and 'or, as the case may be, the date with effect from which it was cancelled'; and in subsection (8), paragraph (b) and the word 'and' preceding it

Chapter or number	Citation	Extent of repeal or revocation
1989 c 41	The Children Act 1989	In Schedule 1, in paragraph 3(7), the words 'or is cancelled', 'or was cancelled' and 'or, as the case may be, the date with effect from which it was cancelled; and in paragraph 3(8), paragraph (b) and the word 'and' preceding it
1991 c 48	The Child Support Act 1991	In section 15(10), the definition of 'specified' and the preceding word 'and' In section 17(1), the word 'and' after paragraph (b) In section 28D(2)(a), 'lapsed or' Sections 28H and 28I Section 40(1) and (2) Section 41(3) to (5) Section 44(3) Section 46B(3) In section 54, the definitions of 'assessable income', 'current assessment', 'departure direction' and 'maintenance requirement'. In Schedule 1, paragraph 13, and in paragraph 16, sub-paragraph (1)(d) and (e), sub-paragraphs (2) to (9), and in sub-paragraph (10) the words ', or should be cancelled' Schedule 4C
1992 c 5	The Social Security Administration Act 1992	In section 170(5), in the definition of 'the relevant enactments', paragraph (ab)
1992 c 6	The Social Security (Consequential Provisions) Act 1992	In Schedule 2, paragraph 113
1995 c 18	The Jobseekers Act 1995	In Schedule 2, paragraph 20(2), (4) and (7)
1995 c 34	The Child Support Act 1995	Sections 1, 2 and 3 Sections 6, 7, 8, 9, 10 and 11 Section 14(2) and (3) Section 18(3) and (5) Section 19 Section 22 Section 24 Section 26(4)(c) Schedules 1 and 2 In Schedule 3, paragraphs 12, 15 and 20(a)

Chapter or number	Citation	Extent of repeal or revocation
1998 c 14	The Social Security Act 1998	Section 42 In Schedule 7, paragraphs 20, 24, 25, 28, 34, and 35; in paragraph 36, the words '(1) and'; and paragraphs 37, 38, 39, 40, 43, 46, 48(1), (2), (3) and (5)(a), (b) and (c), 53 and 54
SI 1998/2780 (C 66)	The Social Security Act 1998 (Commencement No 2) Order 1998	Article 3(4)
1999 c 10	The Tax Credits Act 1999	In Schedule 1, paragraph 6(i) In Schedule 2, paragraph 17(a)

INDEX

References are to paragraph numbers.